ALPHA BOOKS

Published by the Penguin Group

Penguin Group (USA) Inc., 375 Hudson Street, New York, New York 10014, USA

Penguin Group (Canada), 90 Eglinton Avenue East, Suite 700, Toronto, Ontario M4P 2Y3, Canada (a division of Pearson Penguin Canada Inc.)

Penguin Books Ltd., 80 Strand, London WC2R 0RL, England

Penguin Ireland, 25 St. Stephen's Green, Dublin 2, Ireland (a division of Penguin Books Ltd.)

Penguin Group (Australia), 250 Camberwell Road, Camberwell, Victoria 3124, Australia (a division of Pearson Australia Group Pty. Ltd.)

Penguin Books India Pvt. Ltd., 11 Community Centre, Panchsheel Park, New Delhi—110 017, India

Penguin Group (NZ), 67 Apollo Drive, Rosedale, North Shore, Auckland 1311, New Zealand (a division of Pearson New Zealand Ltd.)

Penguin Books (South Africa) (Pty.) Ltd., 24 Sturdee Avenue, Rosebank, Johannesburg 2196, South Africa

Penguin Books Ltd., Registered Offices: 80 Strand, London WC2R 0RL, England

Publisher: *Marie Butler-Knight*
Product Manager: *Phil Kitchel*
Senior Managing Editor: *Jennifer Chisholm*
Senior Acquisitions Editor: *Randy Ladenheim-Gil*
Book Producer: *Lee Ann Chearney/Amaranth*
Development/Senior Production Editor: *Christy Wagner*
Copy Editor: *Michael Brumitt*
Illustrator: *Chris Eliopoulos*
Cover/Book Designer: *Trina Wurst*
Indexer: *Aamir Burki*
Layout/Proofreading: *Angela Calvert, Mary Hunt*

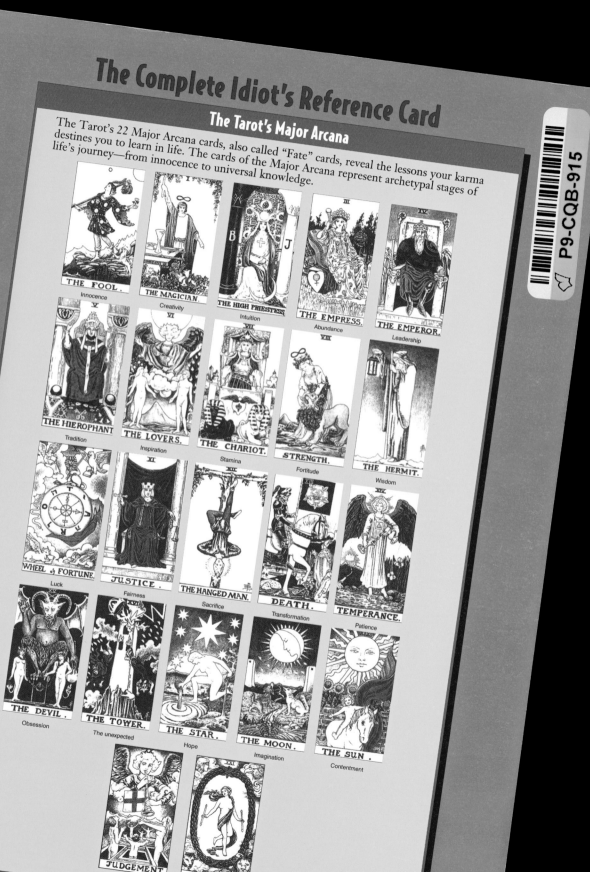

The Complete Idiot's Reference Card

The Tarot's Major Arcana

The Tarot's 22 Major Arcana cards, also called "Fate" cards, reveal the lessons your karma destines you to learn in life. The cards of the Major Arcana represent archetypal stages of life's journey—from innocence to universal knowledge.

THE FOOL. — Innocence
THE MAGICIAN. — Creativity
THE HIGH PRIESTESS. — Intuition
THE EMPRESS. — Abundance
THE EMPEROR. — Leadership
THE HIEROPHANT. — Tradition
THE LOVERS. — Inspiration
THE CHARIOT. — Stamina
STRENGTH. — Fortitude
THE HERMIT. — Wisdom
WHEEL of FORTUNE. — Luck
JUSTICE. — Fairness
THE HANGED MAN. — Sacrifice
DEATH. — Transformation
TEMPERANCE. — Patience
THE DEVIL. — Obsession
THE TOWER. — The unexpected
THE STAR. — Hope
THE MOON. — Imagination
THE SUN. — Contentment
JUDGEMENT.

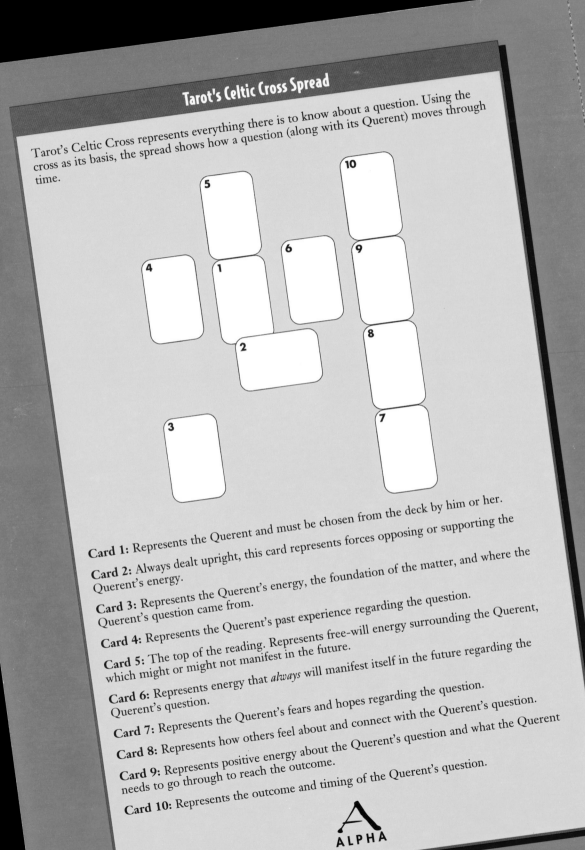

Tarot's Celtic Cross Spread

Tarot's Celtic Cross represents everything there is to know about a question. Using the cross as its basis, the spread shows how a question (along with its Querent) moves through time.

Card 1: Represents the Querent and must be chosen from the deck by him or her.

Card 2: Always dealt upright, this card represents forces opposing or supporting the Querent's energy.

Card 3: Represents the Querent's energy, the foundation of the matter, and where the Querent's question came from.

Card 4: Represents the Querent's past experience regarding the question.

Card 5: The top of the reading. Represents free-will energy surrounding the Querent, which might or might not manifest in the future.

Card 6: Represents energy that *always* will manifest itself in the future regarding the Querent's question.

Card 7: Represents the Querent's fears and hopes regarding the question.

Card 8: Represents how others feel about and connect with the Querent's question.

Card 9: Represents positive energy about the Querent's question and what the Querent needs to go through to reach the outcome.

Card 10: Represents the outcome and timing of the Querent's question.

THE

COMPLETE IDIOT'S GUIDE® TO

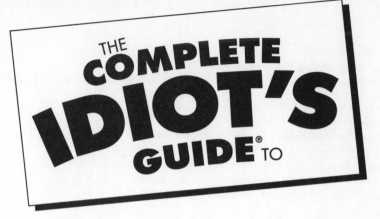

Tarot

Second Edition

by Arlene Tognetti and Lisa Lenard

ALPHA

A member of Penguin Group (USA) Inc.

Contents at a Glance

Contents

Foreword

The old adage "a picture is worth a thousand words" very aptly describes the power of the Tarot cards, for they have the power to invoke images beyond our wildest dreams. As we all know, pictures describe life in a way words alone can never express.

Whether you're an idiot or a genius, *The Complete Idiot's Guide to Tarot, Second Edition*, will show you how the images of fortune-telling cards can express your past, present, and future destiny. And you don't have to be a great Eastern yogi to read the future. In fact, the great Western yogi, Yogi Berra, expressed it this way: "You can observe a lot by watching." This is the premise behind the Tarot and fortune revelation—observation!

The images of the Tarot cards date back to antiquity, and some sources say to more than several thousand years ago. The collection of symbols and archetypal images found in the cards is like a history of human consciousness in visual form—a picture show of the complete human drama.

When you begin to work with the cards, you'll find that you are responsive to certain images but not to others. This is quite normal. Pictures, after all, are subjective, and the truth they reveal to each of us is a very personal truth. Two people can watch a film and come away with entirely different feelings about it. They both saw the same images, but each picked up different messages from them. Reactions to the Tarot cards are equally as personal because our unconscious mind selects the "movies" in the cards that we are about to see. And these "movies" are really our previews of the coming attractions in our life!

Work with the images in the cards, as explained in these pages, and you will come to master the pictures to such an extent that they will instantly speak to you and invoke strong responses, just like your favorite movies do. Once you have developed a personal history with the cards, you can use this book to introduce yourself to other forms of divination (fortune-telling) such as working with numerology, psychic readings, dreamwork, and astrology.

The Complete Idiot's Guide to Tarot, Second Edition, will teach you to use your mind as a high-definition video camera capable of recording the most subtle images. It will show you how to heighten your imagination—the image machine engine of human potential. Not if, but when, you become steeped in the knowledge this book has to offer, you will truly be able to see the past, present, and future with the power of vivid imagery.

The phrase "Know thyself" is one of the oldest of adages. The sages of ancient India believed that if you are able to know your own truth, you are worthy to know the truths of others. The ancient language of these sages is Sanskrit, and the Sanskrit word for knowledge is *Vidya*. It is the ancient root of our modern word *video*. The sages say "to see is to know," so one who sees vividly becomes a seer.

Fortune-telling is merely the ability of being able to see vividly for the benefit of oneself and others. The future is right around the corner, and with *The Complete Idiot's Guide to Tarot, Second Edition*, it will be within your sight.

Dennis Flaherty

Dennis Flaherty is a practicing astrologer and Tarot reader with more than 25 years of experience. He has served four times as the president of the Washington State Astrological Association, is certified in both Western and Vedic astrology, and has won many awards within the New Age community. He writes regularly for publications such as *The Mountain Astrologer* and lectures at seminars and conferences. He is the founder and director of the respected Northwest Institute of Vedic Sciences in Seattle where he teaches, consults, and tutors on astrology and the Tarot.

Introduction

Sometimes what you're looking for might not be so much a glimpse of the future, as a glimpse of your own true self. We think that the better we know ourselves, the more likely we are to have the confidence and self-esteem to work through our life decisions fully and with the care essential to produce splendid outcomes.

The Tarot can be a wonderful tool to help you get in touch with yourself. Instead of waiting passively for life to happen to you—reacting to events and emotions without fully understanding or appreciating what's going on around you—you can use the Tarot to enhance your active participation in the events and emotions of your life.

Nothing but a pack of cards, you say? Think again. The Tarot can lead you on a marvelous journey of self-discovery. And you hold the key!

How to Use This Book

Having a Tarot deck to work with as you read this book will certainly enhance your Tarot journey, but it's not a requirement. In addition to the Universal Waite Deck that we use in the book, literally hundreds of Tarot decks are available to choose from, and you can learn a little bit about the subject before you decide which deck is right for you.

This book is divided into six parts:

Part 1, "All About Tarot," introduces you to the Tarot and its history. You'll look at both the ancient and more modern symbolism that make up the Tarot and learn how to use that symbolism to hold a mirror up to yourself.

Part 2, "Getting to Know the Cards," gives you a closer look at the cards. You'll explore some of the Tarot decks available and then do a few exercises to help you train yourself to become a better Tarot observer. Last, you'll start the Tarot journal you'll be keeping as you become a master of the art.

Part 3, "The Major Arcana: A Fool for the World," is where you'll start meeting each card on an individual basis. Here you'll take an archetypal journey through the Major Arcana and learn each card's upright and reversed meanings, from the Fool (key 0) to the World (key 21).

Part 4, "The Minor Arcana: Wands, Cups, Swords, and Pentacles," continues the journey through the cards of the Minor Arcana. You'll meet each Minor Arcana suit—Wands, Cups, Swords, and Pentacles—and find out why each suit has its own particular energy. You'll learn about both the Royal Court and the everyday cards for each suit and discover that free will is an important part of the Tarot and its lessons.

Part 5, "Tarot Readings Any Fool Can Do," is where you'll find a variety of Tarot spreads to get you started doing your own work with the Tarot. After you read about each spread, you will go step by step through an actual sample spread and learn how we interpreted the cards. Space is provided after each spread for you to try one of your own, too!

Part 6, "More Ways to Interpret the Tarot," introduces you to some other metaphysical tools. Learn more about the hundreds of Tarot decks you can choose from, explore the spiritual aspects of the Tarot, and discover the connections between the Tarot and numerology.

Extras

In addition to helping you understand and learn about the Tarot, we've provided additional information to make your journey even more enlightening and enjoyable in boxes like these:

In the Cards

This is where you'll find fascinating extra tidbits of information that you will be interested to learn about the Tarot.

Card Catalog

These boxes introduce you to the language of the Tarot so you understand the terminology as well as the cards.

Fools Rush In

These boxes warn you against throwing caution to the wind and help you avoid making Tarot mistakes.

Wheel of Fortune

Everyone could use an extra tip here and there, and you'll find them in these boxes that help you find success in spinning the Tarot's Wheel of Fortune.

Acknowledgments

Lisa thanks Arlene, Arlene, Arlene, and Arlene, the Wonder Woman of the Tarot. Fast, witty, clever, and—despite Temperance's projections—patient, she made this book a joy and a breeze.

Arlene wishes to thank Lisa for being fast, quick, sharp, humorous, and keeping me to task. Lisa has been a great inspiration when I needed the knowledge and skills of a real writer pro. Our voice became one in this book. Also, I'd like to thank one of my greatest mentors, Dorothy B. Hughes (who passed on in 1987), a famous astrologer and metaphysical teacher. She called me, and I quote, "ugly accurate" when it came to my Tarot reading skill. I thank her for her deep belief in me. And to my friends, students, and family, who understood they could not get hold of me anytime they wanted because I was online writing with Lisa, a *big* thank you for being patient! And last but not least, thanks to Daniel Bernstein and Brad Reppen for training and educating me about the computer world and cyberspace!

And we both thank Lee Ann Chearney at Amaranth, book producer par excellence, for all the magic she makes behind the scenes—our Magician. You wouldn't be reading this book without Lee Ann!

Much gratitude as well goes to Kay Lagerquist, for her way with numbers. Also thanks to Bobbie Bensaid at U.S. Games Systems, Inc.

Thanks also to the great team at Alpha for their wonderful synergy and enthusiasm. Thanks to publisher Marie Butler-Knight, senior acquisitions editor Randy Ladenheim-Gil, product manager Phil Kitchel, senior managing editor Jen Chisholm, and developmental and senior production editor Christy Wagner.

Special Thanks to the Technical Reviewer

The Complete Idiot's Guide to Tarot, Second Edition, was reviewed by an expert who double-checked the accuracy of what you'll learn here to help us ensure that this book gives you everything you need to know about the Tarot. Special thanks are extended to David Pond.

David Pond holds a Master of Science degree in experimental metaphysics from Central Washington University. He is co-author of *The Metaphysical Handbook,* which covers Tarot, astrology, *I Ching*, numerology, and palmistry. He has published chapters in two of Llewellyn's *New World Astrology* series and many articles in *The Mountain Astrologer* and *The International Astrologer* magazines. David has been a professional Tarot reader and astrologer for more than 20 years.

Trademarks

All terms mentioned in this book that are known to be or are suspected of being trademarks or service marks have been appropriately capitalized. Alpha Books and Penguin Group (USA) Inc. cannot attest to the accuracy of this information. Use of a term in this book should not be regarded as affecting the validity of any trademark or service mark.

Part 1

All About Tarot

So you think a Tarot deck is nothing but a pack of cards? Think again. The pictures on the 78 Tarot cards are worth more than a thousand words—they paint a picture of you. Tarot symbolism encompasses everything from ancient cave paintings to Jungian archetypes and in the process creates a unique metaphor for the story of your life and where you're going.

Chapter 1

What Is Tarot?

In This Chapter

◆ Your future in a pack of cards?

◆ The reader and the Querent

◆ How Tarot works

◆ Are you a Fool?

Admit it—you're curious. Who isn't? Everyone wants to know about the future!

Hindsight might give you 20/20 vision for understanding what's happened in the past, but what (or who) helps you figure out what's coming up in the future? When you think of fortune-tellers, do you picture Whoopi Goldberg in the movie *Ghost*, channeling spirits with a crystal ball? How about the Wizard of Oz (the mighty Oz sees all, knows all!), dispensing magical powers to eager applicants who've proven themselves worthy? Is it even *possible* to "predict" or "tell" someone what his or her future will be? Remember a little thing called Free Will? We do. (We know some skeptics are among us.)

So right now you're curious about the Tarot. What, exactly, *do* Tarot cards have to say about the future—most particularly, about *yours?* Let's take a closer look at the cards.

Just a Pack of Cards?

We've seen you lingering in the New Age section of your local bookstore, eyeing the *Tarot decks*. Maybe you've heard about the Tarot from friends or co-workers who've gotten readings. Their enthusiasm has you wondering. Flipping through the deck, the medieval-looking drawings on the cards seem so exotic. What could these mystical talismans possibly mean for you? Is it all just a bunch of hooey in a fancy-looking deck of cards? *If nothing else*, you think to yourself, *it's some fun for a Saturday afternoon.* Yet you have that nagging question of how that situation at work is going to turn out. What would the cards have to say?

Card Catalog

The **Tarot** is an ancient method of fortune-telling that uses the 78 cards of the **Tarot deck** to create a story of you—past, present, and future.

From time to time, we all look for guidance. It could be on a grand scale, something that will affect the very course of our lives, such as deciding whom to marry or where to live. Or it could be something of smaller consequence but important in the moment. We look to a lot of sources to help us make our decisions. Here's a list of some of the sources most of us don't think twice about consulting every day:

- We look to the five-day weather forecast to get a handle on whether we'll need to carry an umbrella, break out the sun block, or put the snow tires on the SUV.

- How about listening to the radio for the daily traffic reports? It's essential to know the most efficient and beneficial route for getting to the office on time.

- Hey, admit it. Do you check your daily horoscope?

- Status meetings at work or guidance counseling at school help give us a good perspective on what we've already accomplished, what needs to be done today, and how to tackle future challenges.

- Medical doctors and other health-care professionals tell us how to develop good life habits to keep our bodies healthy, while psychologists and therapists offer good counsel to help improve our mental well-being and promote healthy relationships with others.

- Many of us turn to our faith in a higher power to draw inspiration and guidance through prayer and the study of sacred texts.

We have so many choices to make every day! We're just like the guy in the 7 of Cups card: bewildered with choices. Which choice is the best one? Who can help us make our choices? And how will things turn out?

Tarot is one of many metaphysical tools that enable us to look into our lives and find some extra information we hadn't really understood or known about before. Working with the Tarot brings to light a confirmation of things you've always known (your own inner wisdom) or it adds a new perspective to a perplexing question or problem. Tarot gives the guy in the 7 of Cups a context for understanding not only what his choices are, but how he feels about them.

Are you like the guy in the 7 of Cups—faced with too many choices and not enough perspective to decide which is the right choice to make?

Meet Your Magician!

To help you understand how to use the Tarot, just consider us your Magician. Throughout this book, we'll be your teacher and guide, unlocking the creative power of the cards and showing you how to interpret their many meanings.

Study the Magician card shown in the following figure. The Magician invokes the Cup, Wand, Sword, and Pentacle on the table as the instruments of his creativity. What a wonderful garden blossoms from the fruits of his efforts!

We'll let you in right now on the great secret of the Tarot: The power to make the Tarot more than just a deck of cards lies within you! That's right. With practice, you can learn to become your own Magician, your own wizard, your own *oracle*. As Glinda the Good Witch told Dorothy at the end of the Yellow Brick Road, she'd always possessed within herself the power to make her own wishes and dreams come true. And so do you. The Tarot is an instrument of insight into your own Free Will. *You* are the one who possesses the magic. Let's find out more.

We'll be your Magician: a teacher and guide to the Tarot.

THE MAGICIAN.

Card Catalog

Oracles are sacred objects or altars used by many cultures throughout history for the reception of divine guiding messages and holy truths. The site of the oracle is considered a holy place, and often only priests or shamans can visit it. Shamans or high priestesses were believed to have had divine connections. Therefore, they became the "speakers" of the messages. Many ancient sites, such as the ruins at Monte Alban in Oaxaca, Mexico, contain structures archaeologists believe were used by priest-astronomers to interpret divine meanings for everyday events.

A Tarot Primer

The Tarot reveals what's *really happening* below the surface of events around us. The Tarot is a visual medium; those of you who love pictures, art, music, design—anything picture-related—can appreciate all the rich colors, symbols, numbers, and archetypes present in the Tarot cards. It doesn't take a degree in math or science to work with this wonderful medium of enlightenment and personal awareness. It's easy! The 78 Tarot cards represent every element of life, every emotion we will experience, every lesson that needs to be learned, and every condition possible to know. The story the Tarot tells every time you receive a *reading* allows you to know more and gives you the decision-making edge extra knowledge can provide.

You're in the Cards

The Tarot opens your intuitive sense. Its pictures stimulate your gut feelings. Do you already have a Tarot deck? Start shuffling. The Tarot cards absorb the thoughts, ideas, and curiosity of the person who shuffles the deck. By shuffling and concentrating on the question at hand, it's your energy that's being reflected through the deck of the Tarot. Your subconscious wisdom is shuffled into the cards. When the cards are thrown into different patterns, or *spreads*, the relationships between the cards reveal your personal wisdom as you infused it into the deck.

The 78 cards of the Tarot deck are divided into 22 *Major Arcana* cards, which lead us through the archetypal passages in life's journey, and 56 *Minor Arcana* cards, which illustrate the various things that happen to each of us from day to day. We'll look at the Major Arcana in Part 3 and the Minor Arcana in Part 4, but you can sneak a peek at them now.

> **Card Catalog**
>
> **Tarot spreads** are different methods of laying out the cards during a Tarot reading. **Tarot readings** occur when the cards are laid out to reveal a particular story.

The Sun, a Major Arcana card, and the 10 of Cups, a Minor Arcana card, represent two ways we move into the light of contentment, joy, and strength in awareness. The Sun depicts a mythological motif, while the 10 of Cups shows one way we deal with everyday challenges and opportunities.

The first difference you'll notice is that the Major Arcana seem to represent mythological motifs, while the Minor Arcana show more everyday events. That's exactly the case: The Major Arcana cover the big stuff, while the Minor Arcana are the everyday cards. The Minor Arcana are further divided into four suits:

- Wands
- Cups
- Swords
- Pentacles

Card Catalog

The Tarot deck contains 22 **Major Arcana** and 56 **Minor Arcana** cards. The Major Arcana cards depict an archetypal journey through life, while the Minor Arcana cards show everyday events.

These correspond to clubs, hearts, spades, and diamonds in a regular deck of cards. Each of the 4 suits has 14 cards: 10 numbered cards (the Ace through 10) and 4 royal cards (a Page, Knight, Queen, and King).

The four suits of the Tarot deck—Wands, Cups, Swords, and Pentacles—correlate to the four elements of the astrological signs of the zodiac, and for good reason: They're the four energies of life. You'll find out more about the fascinating relationship between the Tarot and astrology when we look at each card in detail in Parts 3 and 4.

Life Energies: The Tarot Suits and Their Astrological Elements

Suit	Element	Meaning	Corresponding Astrological Signs
Wands	Fire	Action, initiate	Aries, Leo, Sagittarius
Cups	Water	Emotion, intuition	Cancer, Scorpio, Pisces
Swords	Air	Communication, mental activities	Gemini, Libra, Aquarius
Pentacles	Earth	Possessions, the physical	Taurus, Virgo, Capricorn

You can think about the Tarot in a number of ways: as a tool for connecting with the universal unconscious, as a way to get in touch with your sixth sense of what's true, or as an unfolding story revealed in pictures. Any way you look at it, interpreting the Tarot is fun!

The Reader and the Querent

People like Arlene, the expert co-author of this book, who have studied the Tarot for many years, are called Tarot *readers*. As with any method of fortune-telling, reading the Tarot is much more than merely memorizing what each card or symbol means. In addition to understanding Tarot cards, Tarot readers have strong backgrounds in disciplines ranging from psychology to mythology and recognize that a reading opens life's possibilities rather than narrows them to an inevitable course of action.

Just as certain people are natural painters while others can't draw a stick figure, some people are naturally good at reading the Tarot. The best Tarot readers understand that no card has any one meaning, but rather is a *metaphor* for a variety of interpretations.

The person asking the reader a question is called the *Querent*. Querents might ask specific questions: "When will I meet my soul mate?" or "Will I win the lottery?" They might ask about the world: "What's going to happen in the year 2005?" or "Will any film ever top *Lord of the Rings?*" Specific Tarot spreads can address different types of questions, such as how to set a goal, make a decision, or find a solution to a problem. Readings can span a time frame ("What's going to happen in my life this year?") or reveal a message ("What's my purpose or mission in life?"). You'll learn all about different Tarot spreads you can do in Part 5.

Card Catalog

A Tarot **reader** makes interpretations of cards for a **Querent,** a person who asks a question of the Tarot. *Querent* comes from the Latin word *quaero,* meaning "to inquire or seek, or to embark on a quest." Readers consider Tarot cards **metaphors,** rich images that hold meanings that can be transferred or carried over to the Querent's particular situation or question.

Many Tarot practitioners do a daily reading where no question is asked at all. Often, they don't even interpret the cards when they select them, but merely make a note of what they are. Then, at the end of the day, they come back to them and note the connections between the cards selected and the day's events.

The reader and the Querent don't necessarily have to be in the same place. Readings today take place online or with the absent Querent thinking about the question as the reader deals the cards.

What if the Querent wants to know about a family member, a spouse or life partner, or another person? The Tarot will answer the question through the energy of the Querent him- or herself. Whatever information is revealed through the Tarot will have to do with the Querent's own relationship to the person the Querent wants to know about. Remember, it's the *Querent's* energy that infuses the cards for a reading, and theirs is the energy that will come through.

Tarot Q&A

We know you've still got a lot of questions, so we'll get a jump-start on answering the five questions we get asked the most:

- Does Tarot really work?

- *How* does Tarot work?

- Can you read your own cards?

- Does Tarot seal your fate?

- When can you start reading the cards?

We'll answer these questions in the following five sections. Keep in mind, though, first and foremost, that Tarot is not a magic trick. We'll say it again: The magic in Tarot comes from *you!*

Does Tarot Really Work?

Okay, if the cards indicate wealth and financial reward, should you run out and buy that new Armani suit or dress? Maybe, maybe not. The reader's skill of interpreting the Tarot involves the ability to remain objective, to accurately describe the message of the cards, and, with the Querent's help, to put that message in the right perspective.

The cards are a great tool, but they're not so great at giving orders or pronouncing ultimatums. The message of the cards, properly understood, gently (or not so gently, depending on the situation) guides you to arrive at the correct decision that already waits in your heart. That doesn't mean the Tarot does this by providing an easy excuse to let you get your own way and buy that convertible!

Now, wait a second. If the cards are showing what you already know in your heart to be true, why bother? The answer is that the cards are in touch with a universal intelligence—our human collective unconscious—something we westerners are not always good at tapping into. Like the dream world that opens your mind as you sleep (Sigmund Freud called dreams the "royal road to the unconscious"), the Tarot cards awaken that place deep within you that is in touch with your human nature.

Tarot works when you look closely enough to get the real message, to both receive and understand it for what it really is. This means coming to the reading with an open and unprejudiced mind. Don't assume anything—either as reader or Querent—and be ready for anything. The true message of the Tarot might surprise you!

How Does Tarot Work?

We'd like to call on a really smart guy, psychoanalysis pioneer Carl Gustav Jung (1875–1961), to answer this question for us. Jung was fascinated by the patterns of life and the way seemingly unconnected events were in fact connected. He noted that every day of human experience is filled with what could only be called meaningful coincidences, or *synchronicity*.

Jung's study of synchronistic events led him to examine ancient occult practices from astrology to the *I Ching*, and the Tarot was no exception. He found that the mysteries revealed by these practices were in fact not mysteries at all, but events common to each of us on our paths of life.

Card Catalog _____

Synchronicity is the principle of meaningful coincidence, studied in depth by psychoanalysis pioneer Carl Jung. Jung also postulated that human experience could be categorized into common **archetypes**: typical patterns, situations, images, or metaphors that recur among all humankind.

Jung called our common situations (and common recurrent characters) *archetypes* and believed that ancient fortune-telling methods revealed these archetypes to us symbolically. He noted that although modern science "is based on the principle of causality," occult methods look to a "picture of the moment." Jung concluded the pictures on Tarot cards are "descended from the archetypes of transformation."

We agree with Jung that Tarot cards are a way for us to connect to the archetypal wisdom of the human collective unconscious. The Tarot deck in its entirety is a portrait of the human condition, its potential, and its possibilities. Shuffle the deck and deal the cards: Your Tarot reading is a reflection of those possibilities inherent in *your* life and present situation.

In the Cards _____

What have dreams got to do with the Tarot? A whole lot, it turns out. The metaphors in our dreams and in Tarot cards have a lot in common. Jung asserted that all humans share common archetypes, but that most of us can get in touch with them only through our unconscious. Dreams are one way of tapping into our unconscious thoughts, feelings, and awareness—and the Tarot is another.

Can You Read Your Own Cards?

Most Tarot readers read their own cards every day. Yes, they're pros, but how do you think they got to be pros? A serious student of the Tarot devotes a lot of time to reading her or his own cards—and coming to understand intuitively what those cards are saying.

Likewise, the best way for you to begin to study the Tarot is to pick a deck that appeals to you (more on Tarot decks is covered in Chapter 22) and then live with those cards for a while. Spread them out. Pick them up and look at them. Lose yourself in the pictures. Work through the exercises in Part 2 that are designed to help you become familiar with the Tarot and to explore your own emotions and reactions to the deck.

Don't read ahead to the "meanings" of the cards we give in Parts 3 and 4. Those meanings are only launching points for your study of the Tarot, and you shouldn't let yourself be limited by them—not now at the beginning of your journey, and not later on either, when you know the cards well. Ultimately, Tarot cards are a tool to unlock your imagination, and how you read the cards—alone or with someone else— is up to you.

Does Tarot Seal Your Fate?

No. Nothing "seals" your fate. Your life path is a series of possibilities, branching off in one direction or another with each decision you make. A Tarot reading might sug- gest to you what could happen if you continue along a certain path, but it's up to you to take the responsibility of choosing your own direction, if you dare.

Much of the fear and superstition associated with the Tarot—and with all the occult sciences—is that they somehow *do* foretell the future and seal your fate. *Nothing* about the Tarot is inexorable or inevitable. *What you do with what the cards show is up to you!* The Tarot reveals possibilities and probabilities, not certainties. In fact, the only thing that's certain about life is that nothing's certain. Fate is what you make it.

When Can You Start Reading the Cards?

When can you begin giving readings? Today!

One of Arlene's most memorable first readings was about a former boyfriend. The question: "Why did the relationship end?" (Arlene felt unhappy about the ending, of course.)

The cards came up to tell her that everything about the relationship provided lessons for Arlene to get her ready for the next relationship. *Whoa*, Arlene said to herself.

Then, one year later, sure enough, a more compatible relationship came. Practice makes perfect—not only with the Tarot cards, but with relationships, too!

Do You *Really* Want to Know the Future?

Sometimes what we're looking for might be not so much a glimpse of the future, but a glimpse of our true selves. The better we know ourselves, the more likely we are to have the confidence and self-esteem to work through our life decisions fully and with the care essential to produce splendid outcomes.

The Tarot can be a wonderful tool to help you get in touch with yourself. Instead of waiting passively for life to happen *to* you—reacting to events and emotions without fully understanding or appreciating what's going on around you—you can use the Tarot to enhance your experience and active participation in the events and emotions of your life.

How proactive are you? Let's imagine your apartment lease is up in six months. You're not happy where you are but can't decide where to move. You …

♦ Wallow in indecision for months and end up extending your lease to put off the move for another year.

♦ Muse about moving to a city or town you've always loved, like Las Vegas, Nevada, or St. Michael's, Maryland. You've been talking about it for years, actually. But you wait until the last minute to take it seriously and lose the opportunity to plan a move to that dream location.

♦ Embark on a diligent search for a new apartment without addressing your feelings about where you'd really want to live or why you'd want to live there. Just moving anywhere is progress enough. And forget about *buying* a house … that's too much to contemplate, much less *do!*

♦ Pack up your belongings and move back in with your parents or another family member. It's really just temporary.

Fools Rush In

Are you secretly looking for an oracle to divine your true path and tell you what to do? Avoid that temptation and listen to your own inner voice. When you take responsibility for your decisions into your own hands, heart, and mind, Tarot can become a wonderful tool for personal exploration and growth. But it's not a substitute for your Free Will. Don't be a slave to the cards!

The Tarot is only one tool you can use to make your life decisions resonate closer to your heart's true desire. It's not about surrendering to fate or being handed a one-way ticket to the future. It's about making choices that are honest and that feel right for you. It's about getting in touch with your own life energy and using that energy to live up to your fullest potential as a human being.

What road should you take? What future lies in store for you? How will you grow and learn? Come on the journey through the Tarot with us, and you'll find yourself a Fool for the world!

The Fool embarks on the journey of life.

The Least You Need to Know

- Tarot cards are a tool for understanding ourselves and connecting to a great universal wisdom: the human collective unconscious.

- A Tarot deck consists of 78 cards. The 22 Major Arcana cards describe the passages of life's journey. The 56 Minor Arcana cards describe everyday issues and events.

- The Minor Arcana cards are divided into four suits: Wands, Cups, Swords, and Pentacles.

- The Tarot reveals the possibilities and presents a forum for self-exploration but does not predict or tell your future. *You* choose your own fate.

Chapter 2

Back to the Future

In This Chapter

- The images of the Tarot are ancient history
- Gypsies really *are* fortune-tellers
- Tarot and psychology

Arlene's grandmother always said, "Many things are around us, if only we look," and when we look at the history of the Tarot, we find that not only does every picture tell a story, every picture tells *many* stories. Although no one can say for certain, the Tarot seems to have appeared in similar guises in different parts of the world at different times throughout history. What *is* clear, though, is that humans have been using pictures to tell their stories—past, present, *and* future—for a very, very long time. In this chapter, we'll learn some of the ways we've told stories with pictures—and what Tarot's got to do with it.

From Cave Painters to Tarot Card Artists

From the ancient cave paintings discovered at Lascaux, France, to the *petroglyphs* found throughout the American Southwest, artists have been using rocks as their canvasses for thousands of years. Pictures, in fact, are quite probably the earliest form of symbolic communication and were used by neighboring tribes who had no other language in common. After all, a stick boar eating a stick man could explain far more than mere grunts and frantic gestures, and people who understood the pictures lived to pass them on another day.

Card Catalog

Petroglyphs are a form of ancient carving on stone that use representative pictures to tell their stories.

Think for a moment how it would be if you had to communicate with someone who didn't speak *your* language. What would *you* do? Use hand signals? Charades? Twenty questions? Or would you draw a picture?

Even if you're not an artist, you can draw simple symbols: stars, crosses, or the moon, for example. Then you could add a little color to help get a feeling across. White, red, black, and yellow are some of the colors used in early Tarot. (We'll discuss some of that color symbolism in Chapter 4.)

Pictures tell a thousand stories, and for those who came before us, even a temporary drawing on the sand could be the best way to get the message across. Although symbols such as arrows, fertile seeds, the sun, the moon, a child, a king, a priest or priestess, a shaman, a bird, a rose, or a wild animal each meant something unique to different tribes, they also had a universal meaning that often transcended particular nuances and interpretations. This general quality was often the only way tribes with different languages *could* understand each other.

Like their cave-dwelling ancestors, Tarot artists use pictures to communicate the symbolic meanings of Tarot cards. As you'll learn in Chapter 22, Tarot decks cater to every taste, from the traditional Marseilles deck to the Mother Peace deck, a modern feminist deck with its perfectly round cards (edges, after all, are masculine).

A Picture's Worth a Thousand Words

Card Catalog

Like petroglyphs, **hieroglyphs** are another form of ancient stone carving. Hieroglyphs are a more symbolic system, using ancient alphabets (rather than the pictures of petroglyphs) to tell the stories.

The documented roots of Tarot date back to China, the Middle East, and Egypt by as many as 15,000 years ago in seemingly unconnected occurrences. Even today we can understand the collective meaning of a cross, a star, or the color red or black used in ancient drawings and pictorial *hieroglyphs*.

To see exactly how a picture's worth a thousand words, though, let's take a closer look at the Major Arcana card, the Magician. First, look at the figure itself: The Magician holds his hands in an attitude of power and command, creating from his table of elements the gifts of life and the potentials of creation. He's the artist who will draw on an empty canvas.

His physical presence, or his attitude, reveals one hand pointing toward heaven and the other hand pointing to earth, while a Wand conducting energy from above reaches for divine guidance and inspiration to create what he desires.

The Magician (key 1).

Heaven has always been looked upon as a somehow magical place from which all energy comes. Even in early times, the sun was an obvious light- and heat-generating globe in the sky. From this, a further assumption was made: Something else must be out there that keeps other energies flowing.

The fact that the Magician is pointing toward heaven sends a message, as if he were searching for something higher, brighter, or more insightful—as if he were reaching, maybe, for a Divine Understanding, *just like you are.*

When you look at a Tarot spread, you add all the pictures together to create a story. If the Magician is the first card in your spread, your story might begin with the magic of creation or a divine message. Most spreads are arranged chronologically, telling stories that begin in the past and progress to the future, but you shouldn't limit yourself to this linear way of storytelling any more than a good book does.

In a way, Tarot readers were the original storytellers, and today's Tarot readers continue that storytelling tradition. The Tarot deck's pictures can relate images, feelings, conditions, worldly issues, or a sense of destiny, or they can describe conditions yet to be. And you thought it was just a deck of cards!

Reaching for a Divine Understanding

Perhaps because of its roots in the Hebrew Kabbalah, Tarot was often seen as a way of talking to God, and thus was a right reserved for kings and queens—never serfs. Indeed, until the nineteenth century, nonroyals caught using Tarot were often put to death. Historical Tarot decks can be found dating back to the fourteenth century, but it wasn't until the invention of the printing press that they became widely accessible. With the advent of modern science, Tarot was relegated to the *esoteric* or "unexplainable," and its use became another pawn in power struggles. Some believe that Roman Catholic priests, aware of the power of the Tarot, were very careful to keep it away from the common people.

The art of divining became popular throughout history precisely because it was a great way to "see" if there would be a wedding or a new king or queen coming. Tarot could predict droughts and wars, too, so people could take steps to avoid the worst of those threats.

In the Cards

Where does the word *Tarot* come from? Here are a few possibilities:

♦ Egyptian: *tar*, "a path" + *ro*, *ros*, or *rog*, "royal"
♦ Hungarian Gypsy: *tar*, "a pack of cards"
♦ Hindustani: *taru*, "a pack of cards"

It's easy to see why Tarot was considered a way of talking to God; it *does* get us in touch with things we can't seem to see without "divine" intervention. Tarot cards seem to have a magical way of picking up our unconscious and conscious minds at once and, in so doing, reflect how we feel about a given situation. In other words, Tarot cards confirm the conditions and events around us—*even if we're not aware of them ourselves!*

Seeing It in a Dream: Prophecies and Portents

It should come as no surprise that the Tarot has close connections to dream theory. Both, after all, are symbolic systems, and both are subject to a variety of interpretations.

In ancient Greece, the Oracle at Delphi was the most popular of all the oracles because her predictions always came true—even when people took extraordinary steps to avoid them. In Greek mythology, the hero Perseus's grandfather, Acrisius, for example, went so far as to set his daughter and Perseus adrift at sea after the Oracle predicted Perseus would bring about Acrisius's death. Although Perseus never knew his grandfather, this prophesy came true: Acrisius was killed many years later by a wayward discus thrown by the grandson he never knew.

Tarot imagery is like dream imagery; we can't always immediately figure out just what it's trying to show us. But also like dream imagery, Tarot reveals itself when we stop "thinking" about it and let the images reveal themselves to us.

Scientists, philosophers, and psychologists continue to debate the true nature and function of dreams. Some modern researchers believe dreams are no more than a way to purge the brain of excess information and prepare for a new day of input, while others on the opposite end of the spectrum are busy exploring the connection between dreams and psychic intuition.

Throughout history, though, powerful, evocative dream images have captivated and consumed us. Dreams are the seeming bridge between conscious and unconscious understanding, between the known and the unknown that lives together in each of us. At the very least, dreams prod us toward something internal and allow us to become familiar with a particular fear, joy, truth, or enlightenment.

Some people say they dream in color, while others claim they dream in black and white. Some don't remember their dreams, while others remember every detail. Some people claim they don't dream at all. The long and short of it is that everyone is unique in the way they dream, and there's no right or wrong way. Dreams are as individual as we are and reflect the particular things we're working on, musing on, or worrying about at any particular moment. (Read more about Tarot and dreams in Chapter 23.)

East vs. West

The Chinese *I Ching* and Tarot are both ways of looking at a particular moment in time from its past, present, and future angles. Unlike Tarot, though, the *I Ching* is rooted in Eastern philosophies, where collective understanding is taken for granted. The *I Ching* originated in the idea that a pattern encircles all knowledge. We westerners (and not just those of us west of the Mississippi) take a far more individual approach to our lives. The symbols of the Tarot deck reflect this.

Card Catalog

The *I Ching* is a method of fortune-telling that uses 64 sections, each of which is a 6-lined hexagram. Depending on how you choose to consult the *I Ching*, you can cast sticks or even coins to arrive at patterns within the hexagrams. These patterns in turn lead to numbers, and each number has an assigned meaning.

Humankind's Insatiable Curiosity About the Future

It's important to remember that the *I Ching* is not a "wrong" way of divining the future any more than Tarot is a "right" way. What *is* important is that they're both tools we can use to get in touch with ourselves. We humans have always been curious about our futures. We, your authors, think it has something to do with our knowledge of our own mortality.

On the other hand, we might just want to know if a tall, dark stranger is going to enter our lives. And as one of Arlene's students requested recently, "Can I get his phone number and e-mail address, too?"

The Mystery of the Mystical

By the nineteenth century, Tarot, along with other esoteric arts like astrology, the study of the relationship between the heavens and earth; palmistry, the study of the hand; and numerology, the study of the meaning of numbers; began enjoying a renaissance. Science, after all, hadn't provided all the answers people had been seeking, particularly about foretelling the future, and it had become clear that it probably never would.

It was during this time that members of the Hermetic Order of the Golden Dawn began to research the Tarot in depth. The deck we're using in this book, in fact, is the one commissioned by a leading member of that society, A. E. Waite. *The Pictorial Key to the Tarot*, written by Waite and published in 1910, is still used to interpret the cards, although his meanings are often too limited in scope.

In the Cards

A. E. Waite commissioned artist Pamela Colman Smith to draw the deck you see illustrated in this book (called the Universal Waite Deck) around 1900. Not only did Smith have the unique honor of drawing the deck of Tarot cards, she also was the only female member of the Hermetic Order of the Golden Dawn. Waite insisted she do the drawing, despite the prevalent idea that "a woman couldn't do it." Well, you see the results; they speak for themselves. The Universal Waite Deck, published by U.S. Games Systems, Inc., features the beautiful coloring of artist Mary Hanson-Roberts, adding yet another dimension to a classic Tarot deck.

What the Gypsy Said

Many believe the Gypsies were entrusted with various forms of ancient knowledge when the peoples who had that knowledge, such as the Hebrews, Moors, and Egyptians, began to be persecuted during the Crusades and the Spanish Inquisition. The Tarot and fortune-telling cards were among these methods and the Gypsies considered them ways to prove their psychic powers to possible doubters.

Transient in nature, Gypsies were considered very mysterious people, and they were often outcasts in whatever society they migrated into. Their token, "Cross my palm with silver, and I will tell you your fortune," has become emblematic of the way most people view them. Gypsies, in fact, continue to be stereotyped in ways that other ethnic groups have long overcome.

Actually, though, the Gypsies did have psychic gifts, handed down through their families, generation after generation. They were so good at "reading people well," in fact, that they were often blamed for "creating" the very situations that they foretold.

If a Gypsy said, "The king looks to be in bad health and might not live the year out," when the king did die, guess who got blamed? Because they were both so different and so psychic, the Gypsies were terribly feared: People actually believed that *they* created the king's death by their powers or rituals. In reality, of course, the Gypsies only knew it was the king's time, but their knowledge got them into trouble time and time again.

Wheel of Fortune
Any true fan of rocker Bruce Springsteen can tell you the story Bruce tells of, as a young man, standing frightened and paralyzed on the edge of a dark grove (how Dante!) that he needed to pass through to reach the river of life when a Gypsy woman called him onward and gave him a vital message: *you can't do it alone—you need help.* And so we go together to the river with the E Street Band: *It's alright to have a good time.*

What's in the Cards?

The desire to know one's fortune is as old as time and will always be of interest to the curious, which is just about all of us. Humankind is always seeking more information, more knowledge, more power—more, at any rate, of something.

In today's Tarot lexicon, the phrase *getting a reading* is used more often than *fortune-telling.* Having your cards read can mean finding out more information or empowering yourself with the extra knowledge a reading can give you.

The following are some of the questions people want readings to answer:

- How can I handle this situation?

- How can I help my children?

- How can I get a new job?

- How can I improve my financial situation?

- Should I go back to school?

- Will we be okay in an uncertain world?

- What is my spiritual path?

- How can I improve my life?

- When will I get married?

You get the idea. We're sure you have somewhat similar questions of your own as well.

Fools Rush In _____

Don't ask the cards questions you don't want to know the answers to, and don't ask the cards to tell you things when your mind is already made up about the answer. You won't read the cards the way they advise, but instead will see what you want to see! You have to watch your personal biases and be objective to read the cards correctly. Ask the Tarot for help or advice, but always do so with an open mind.

Tarot and Psychology

A lot of modern Tarot readers have also studied the humanities, psychology, hypnotherapy, or other areas of human relations, making them talented observers of human nature. Tarot has long been a remarkable tool for helping the Querent, or questioner of the cards, understand events and how to handle them, but this additional training adds another dimension to a reading. Tarot readers can determine a person's attitude or state of mind at the time of a reading, psychoanalyze a situation, or help the Querent see the spiritual reason behind a not-so-obvious spiritual situation.

We humans learn lessons in everything we do and with everyone we come into contact with. One of Arlene's teachers used to tell her, "Everything happens for a reason." "But what's the reason?" Arlene always asked. Now that Arlene's been studying the Tarot for a long time, she's got some possible answers. For example, if you were in a relationship that didn't end well, the purpose of your being in that relationship might have been to let you know about disharmony or challenges that you needed to work with. When we have disharmony around us, the counterbalance is to find harmony for ourselves.

Think about it: When you feel uncomfortable about anything, your natural desire is to get back to feeling comfortable again. We call that "learning about the dark side of an issue," and it can make us look for or seek the light or a more peaceful side.

More than anything, it's important to know both sides of a story, and that includes the pros and cons of a relationship. You can ask yourself some questions:

- What is the root cause of this difficult condition?

- Is it the other person, or is it me? Or is it something in our past conditioning?

- Did we learn some difficult patterns and now we have to work them out with each other in order to grow?

Sounds like a lot of work, doesn't it? We assure you that your growth and development come from challenging your *shadow side*. Looking at a weakness and working with it will turn it, in the end, into a strength.

Card Catalog _____
Your **shadow side** is your archetypal hidden self, your secret nature.

The Shadow Knows: Archetype and Myth

Carl Jung's detailed analysis of the relationship of archetype and *myth* to human understanding was surely one of the major revelations of the twentieth century. Remember Jung's archetypes from Chapter 1? Jung explained that certain types, or what he called archetypes, are common to us all.

Here are some fun modern examples to connect you with the archetypal characters.

Card Catalog _____
Myths are the stories we tell ourselves to explain the unexplainable. Archetypes are the various types common to all our stories. Jung called archetypes "mythological motifs."

Archetypes (According to L. Frank Baum, George Lucas, and J.R.R. Tolkien)

Archetype	*Wizard of Oz* Example	*Star Wars* Example	*Lord of the Rings* Example
The Wise Old Man	The Professor	Obi-Wan Kenobi	Gandalf
The Trickster	The Wizard (Yes, we know it's the same guy.)	Han Solo	Sauraman
The *Persona* (or the Hero)	Dorothy	Luke Skywalker	Frodo
The Darkness	The Wicked Witch (Can't you just hear that music?)	Darth Vader	Sauron (represented by the Black Riders)
The Divine Child	Toto	R2D2 and C3PO	Sam and Gollum
The *Animus* and the *Anima* (or the male and female spirits, respectively)	The Scarecrow, the Tin Man, and the Lion	Luke and Princess Leia	Aragorn/Arwen
The Great Mother	Glinda the Good Witch	Yoda	Galadriel

You're probably wondering what all this has to do with the Tarot, and the answer is everything! The archetypes we've listed here in fun are engaging to all of us precisely because they're familiar mythological motifs most of us can relate to. Dorothy's, Luke's, and Frodo's journeys concern us because we recognize that they're *our* archetypal journeys, too. The Wicked Witch, Darth Vader, and the Black Riders frighten us because they're our shadows as well. Our shadow side, according to Jung, consists of the archetypes we hold in our unconscious self, along with thoughts and feelings we'd rather not acknowledge in the light of day.

Card Catalog

In Jungian psychology, the **anima** and **animus** represent the female and male soul of a human being, respectively, while the **persona** represents the way a person presents him- or herself to the world.

But more important for our purposes, the archetypes Jung committed to paper are the same archetypes that can be found in every Tarot deck. The Fool is the child in all of us, the High Priestess our anima, and the Devil our secret terrors. If archetypes are about the journey of life, Tarot cards are a vehicle to help us on our way.

Symbol and Metaphor

Although we'll be using the term *symbol* in this book, we'd like to take a minute now to clarify what we mean by this. Arlene insists her students use the word *metaphor* instead of *symbol*, in fact, and here's why: If you've taken any English class, you probably know that symbols tend to get clichéd and predictable. But when we talk about symbols, we don't want you to think this way. Symbols are as diverse and individual as we are, and if one thing must always "stand for" another, then the real meaning of symbols gets lost in the process.

So let's think of symbols as metaphors. The rich images of metaphors open meaning rather than close it. Instead of standing for just one thing, a metaphor invites you to think and feel the connection. A train can be a train or it can be something else entirely, from the one you took with your Grandma when you were a child to the "lonesome whistle blowing all those miles down the track." Your symbols, in other words, are *yours*.

> ### Wheel of Fortune
>
> "A thing is a phallic symbol if it's longer than it's wide," singer-songwriter Melanie sang years ago. We'd like to remind you that just because something's longer than it is wide, it's not necessarily a phallic symbol. It might be simply the Washington Monument, a pencil, a sword, or a wand! As Freud himself once said, "Sometimes a cigar is just a cigar."

Tarot for a New World

In the Steven Spielberg film *AI: Artificial Intelligence*, the young robot hero wants nothing more than to be a real boy and make some real human connections. In fact, as more and more of us work at home, real human connections occur far less frequently. Yet at the time this book is published, we live in a world of six billion people and growing.

It's probably not likely that people will ever rely solely on computer connections instead of human ones, but we do know that we're in greater need of connecting to and grounding ourselves in human compassion than ever before. We crave the spiritual insight and growth that will lead us to enlightened personal and, we hope, global awareness.

For this reason, it's important to remember that all worship is a form of spiritual development, and there's a constant need to maintain a balance in our lives between the material world and the spiritual world. Sometimes that's not so easy with saving for college for the kids or the higher stress levels that come with trying to get things done for every member of the family—not to mention the fact that we live in uncertain and challenging times, full of both risk and opportunity.

In short, most of us feel as if the world is moving along more quickly than it used to. Fortunately for all of us though, Tarot has its place in this new world, because it can help us maintain a positive approach to the many changes and transitions our new world demands. Tarot helps us keep our spiritual center and gives us the faith that everything *does* happen for a reason. Life *is* a continuum.

The Least You Need to Know

- Tarot can be traced to Egyptian hieroglyphics and the Hebrew Kabbalah.

- The need to know the future is as natural as being human.

- Tarot cards' pictures use symbols, archetypes, dreams, and myths to tell their stories.

- Tarot can get us in touch with our neglected spiritual selves.

Chapter 3

What Tarot Reveals About You

In This Chapter

◆ How Tarot can help you answer the big questions

◆ Let the pictures do the talking

◆ Tarot and why you are the way you are

◆ Tarot and your relationships

The Tarot is more than a tool for answering your questions—it's also a tool for becoming more aware of why you behave the way you do. You can also use the Tarot to learn how another person feels about you, how your boss feels about your work, if now is the time to buy that dream house, or if the person you met Saturday night is your next big romance.

In other words, you can use Tarot's symbols on every step of your journey of self-discovery, just as a therapist can help you use your dreams for the same purpose. You gotta admit, though, Tarot's cheaper, and it's a lot more fun, too. In this chapter, we'll show you how you can use the Tarot on your own journey of self-discovery.

Who Am I? Where Do I Come From? Where Am I Going?

You're not the only person who has asked these questions. The journey represented by the Tarot's Major Arcana illustrates these questions in a unique way.

The Fool, the Hanged Man, and the World represent the beginning, middle, and culmination of life's journey.

The Tarot reminds us that everything *is* interconnected and that a synchronicity to events exists that is more than mere coincidence. With this in mind, we can use the symbols of the Tarot to begin to find some personal answers to those big questions.

Arlene believes life has its up and downs, which she prefers to call ebbs and flows. The wheel of life is constantly turning to bring us luck or a challenge. It's all about serendipity, yet at the same time, everything happens for a reason and everything is interwoven.

The great thing about Tarot is that you can figure out the reason something has occurred. Whatever your spiritual system, though, Tarot can help you stay in touch with yourself.

Signposts on Life's Journey

For an answer to the question "Who am I?" you need look no further than the Fool card that begins the journey of the Tarot's Major Arcana. Cavalier and carefree, the young man in this picture is so caught up in his daydreams (which include questions like "Who am I?") that watching where he's going is the last thing on his mind.

The Fool represents beginnings, whether in the journey of life, a new job, or simply a new day. When this card comes up in a reading, you can be assured of a fresh start.

If you've ever looked back to see where you came from to discover where to go next, you'll feel a strong connection with the Hanged Man. Representing the middle of the Major Arcana's journey, the Hanged Man is literally stuck in the middle, hanging by his ankle while he considers what's next.

The Hanged Man can also be viewed as an *allegory* for the midpoint in life, when we step back to look at where we've been. This card also encourages a spiritual approach, something many people seek at this point in their lives.

The World represents the culmination of life's journey and answers the question "Where am I going?" This card symbolizes completion, a life well lived, a project well done, even a song well sung, or a dinner well served. The important thing to remember when the World comes up in a reading is that as soon as one journey ends, another is sure to begin. That's what the circularity represented in this card is all about.

Card Catalog

An **allegory** is a story with a hidden meaning. The allegory of the prodigal son, for example, is really about a parent's love for his child.

Sister Wendy Finds Herself in Art (and Tells Bill Moyers)

Maybe you've heard of Sister Wendy, the popular Roman Catholic nun who delights in celebrating and contemplating great works of art as well as sharing her thoughts with us. *Sister Wendy's Odyssey* is an oft-repeated PBS interview with Bill Moyers in which she talks about using art as a forum for people to discover their "true" selves. Sister Wendy Beckett hosted *The Story of Painting*, the wonderful PBS series on the history of art and published a book based on the shows. She's also the author of several other art books and books on spiritual subjects, such as *Meditations on Silence*.

In the Cards

When a Tarot artist paints a picture for a particular Tarot card, she is representing what core issues are going on within that card's meaning. If you allow the picture to speak to you in the way that Sister Wendy suggests, each card's own particular story will be personalized for you in your own unique way.

According to Sister Wendy, your true self emerges when you have the courage and concentration to look at a great work of art and react to it on a pure and personal level. She urges you not to fake a response by saying what you think you should say, but to truly consider the difficult and often perplexing emotional reactions that a great masterpiece can elicit if you're honest and open to its message. In other words, you can't come to an image with preconceived notions or ideas about how to respond. If you do, you're not allowing the image to reveal itself, to challenge, and, perhaps, to change you.

Just as you can come to know a work of art in this way, you can learn about yourself on a "higher" emotional level. Sister Wendy suggests taking postcards or reproductions of paintings and meditating on the image from time to time until you feel you've really understood the painting—and also understood your own position and emotional reaction to it.

Just as you can develop this personal connection to a painting, you can learn to find personal meanings in each Tarot card. Let's find out how.

Using Tarot Cards to Learn About Yourself

Tarot cards are reflections of you and your feelings or ideas at a particular time. One of the things that comes out of getting a reading is self-awareness, and in addition to reminding you of what you already know about yourself, Tarot can help you awaken some new concepts or ideas about yourself that you might never have thought of before.

> **Wheel of Fortune**
>
> How do the cards know what you haven't told them? The Tarot deck hears more than your words; it's in tune with your feelings and energies, even the ones you haven't acknowledged to yourself yet! Be honest with the Tarot, and the cards will be honest with you.

With the Tarot, you can see your psychological profile, emotional condition, and what you're feeling at the time of the reading. The insights you get from a reading—perhaps just a little change of consciousness or some added information—can lead you to change how you feel about things. And when your feelings change, so, too, do the meanings of the cards for you. Because the Tarot cards are a *reflective* tool, *they* change each time *you* change, perhaps initiating a progression of changes.

Here's an exercise for using the Tarot's Major Arcana cards to learn about yourself:

Begin by taking all 22 Major Arcana cards out of the deck. The Major Arcana cards tell you about questions and issues of destiny and karma in your life. Put the rest of the deck aside and then, as you're shuffling the 22 cards, ask, "Tarot, show me my present lessons I am learning right now."

You should shuffle several times, concentrating on allowing the Tarot to reflect where and what you're learning now.

When you're finished shuffling (and that's whenever you *feel* you have finished), divide the 22 cards into 3 stacks, and either pick 1 card from each stack *or* 3 from 1 of the stacks. You, the seeker, are in control here. The three Major Arcana cards you select will reflect you and your present lessons. Try it and see for yourself! Write down in the space provided what each picture looks like. Don't worry about identifying each of the cards in any other way except than by describing their images.

Card 1 : _____

Card 2 : _____

Card 3 : _____

What did you see? People? Trees or flowers? Images you can't yet define? What's important about this exercise is *your* initial reactions to the cards. We want you to learn to trust your instincts.

Holding Up a Mirror

Looking at Tarot cards really *is* like holding up a mirror. How you feel about a subject or person at the time you ask the cards is always shown exactly by the cards. In other words, even if *you* don't know how you're feeling, the cards will reflect aspects of yourself you might be unaware of.

Counting Your Blessings

Here's a "quickie," a positive affirmation exercise for you to use to count your blessings. Take your Tarot deck and start shuffling. When you're finished shuffling, divide the deck into three stacks and as you do, ask, "What good things are around me?"

After you've divided the deck into three stacks, pick one card from each stack or three from one stack (as always in Tarot, the choice is yours). The key cards are any of the Aces (four are in the deck) or the 9 of Cups (the wish card). (See later in the chapter for more on the keys.) All these cards are a resounding "*Yes!*" to any condition around you or an affirmation of a good condition developing. These five cards will show you that things are happening for the better soon.

If you don't get these key cards, don't worry. What messages do the cards you *did* get seem to be giving you? The cards will reveal what's up and coming around you.

The four Aces and the 9 of Cups are all positive, affirming cards that show good things are happening.

Your Relationships with Other People

The Tarot can show the reason why someone is upset with you or why your boyfriend or girlfriend doesn't want to get too close to you. Maybe the reading will show he or she had trouble with past relationships and is leery of getting that close to another person again.

At the very least, through the Tarot we can see some of the reasons why people act the way they do. Then, instead of judging them, we can begin to understand why they behave that way because the Tarot can reflect a person's behavior or perception at the time of the reading and why they are feeling a certain way *now*. One of Arlene's clients hadn't had a relationship in a long time. Her reading showed that she would not only be involved in a relationship within the next six months, but would be married within a year and a half! The client found it hard to believe, but it turned out to be true.

Do you have a relationship question? If so, the Tarot can help you discover the best way to answer it.

When Everything Blows Up

When Arlene worked in the restaurant business at the Los Angeles Airport, every morning she would throw a spread of cards to see how the day was going to go. One morning, the cards that came up were Swords and the Tower, forecasting arguments and confusion for the day. Naturally, Arlene thought to herself, *What the heck is this all about?*

Still, she decided she'd best listen to these cards and just be herself, do her job, not argue with anyone at work—and pay attention to what was going on around her.

Soon enough, everything started going wrong with food orders, and the boss started to accuse other employees of creating the problems. When Arlene says "everything," she means *everything* got out of control (just as the Tower card suggests can happen). Because of her reading, though, she just watched and kept silent and negotiated through the day's events by being calm and unharried.

As much as the cards "predicted" what happened, it didn't happen *to* Arlene, but *around* Arlene. As people were later let go or quit because of the problems at work, Arlene was delighted she hadn't gotten into the quarrels. The cards were right, and by listening to their "advice," Arlene avoided a situation that could have gone very differently. As in-tune with the cards as she is, it still amazes Arlene how they can give you a warning of conditions to come, even though you had no previous clue. So when that "negative" or "counseling" card appears, take heed.

The 4 of Swords, the Hermit, and the High Priestess are counseling cards: "Take a break!" they say.

Letting the Tarot Help You

How much would *you* like to know through the Tarot? Some people are a little fearful, shy, or unsure about what they want to know. It's possible, too, that when you learn about something, it will be very different than you thought it would be.

Here are some questions to help you decide if you're ready for the Tarot to help you:

- Do you want to dive into the mystery of a relationship—or of life?

- Do you want to find out more about what you're really learning—or not learning—from your career?

- Are you unhappy about a situation around you or worried that your happiness might come to an end?

- Are you worried about your health or someone else's?

- Do you want some help with a difficult decision or need some input from another source?

- Are you concerned about the global situation and how it may affect you and those you care about?

The Tarot can help you know more about these things so you can get your life moving in the direction you want. Sure, it can be a little scary to think that you have a new job or a big move coming up. And these days, with the world seeming less benign than it once did, the old saying, "Crisis is the best counselor," seems particularly apt.

Sometimes clients come to Arlene and say they really want something new. But when the Tarot cards reveal they *will* soon have a new job or house, they freak out and say, "Wow! I don't know if I'm ready for that yet." How we handle a crisis can only make us stronger. We all truly desire a peaceful transition when it comes to making a change from one career to another or from one relationship to another. But as we know, it doesn't always work that way.

Arlene has found that a good and calming way to phrase a Tarot question about change is to ask *how* to make the transition. In our confusing world, the ability to navigate rough waters in life and come to a peaceful shore is the goal.

For example, you could ask the Tarot to give you advice on how you should go about attaining a new job or new career. The cards will reflect how to manage your energies to the highest level you can at the time of the reading.

Arlene was once asked by a teacher if she had ever been through any changes before. Of course, Arlene replied. "Was it easy?" the teacher asked. When Arlene said no, he thought a bit and then asked, "But you overcame the fear or the difficulty, and you are now settled, right?"

When Arlene said yes, he said, "Good! Then you are familiar with the process of the ebbs and flows of change. You will do that again and again in your life."

Arlene's reaction was "Great!" on one hand and "Oh, dang it!" on the other. But think about it—isn't life's progress worth the trouble it takes to get there? When you use the Tarot to help you navigate the rocky parts, it can keep you centered and grounded.

Even when we think we want something to happen, sometimes we're afraid of it, or sometimes it seems too good to be true and we just *can't* believe it. But remember, life has its cycles, its ebbs and flows, and Tarot seems to pick up on them, good cycles as well as the more difficult ones. Do you dare venture in a particular direction? Why not? After all, life is a journey of many avenues. You've had new jobs, new relationships, and changes of residence before. Why couldn't they happen again, but this time with the added help of a Tarot reading?

Fools Rush In _____

Never use the Tarot to spy on someone or to ask for information that could harm someone else! We always ask for the highest good to come through in a reading, and we as readers want to assist the Querent on his or her journey of life by allowing the free will of the individual to play out. The reader informs, enlightens, and empowers *you* to your highest good and potential.

Understanding Your Mission and Purpose in Life

As with so many areas the Tarot can help you with, this is another where a Tarot exercise is the key. This exercise can help you understand your mission and purpose in life.

Take the 22 Major Arcana cards from the deck, and set aside the rest of the deck. Mix these 22 cards without looking at their faces. Keep them moving in your hands and concentrate on this question: "What is my mission or purpose in life?"

Numerologically, the number 22 is considered one of two Master Numbers (the other is 11), a number imbued with divine power and possibility. Each Major Arcana card

In the Cards

The number of the Major Arcana cards is no accident. Twenty-two is a significant number in symbolic systems ranging from the Hebrew Kaballah to numerology. According to the Kaballah, for example, the Tree of Life has 22 paths, and the Hebrew alphabet has 22 letters.

Card Catalog

The **key** numbers of the Major Arcana cards represent the card's position in the archetypal life journey represented by the cards and can be thought of literally as keys to opening up a card's meanings and possibilities.

has a number, called a *key*, which represents its position on the archetypal life journey represented by the cards. In the Universal Waite Deck, this number is top and center on the card, in Roman numerals, and the name of the card appears on the bottom. Of course, numbered Minor Arcana cards have numbers, too, which also appear at the top, but no title appears on the cards.

When you're ready, fan the 22 Major Arcana cards face down and then pick 3 of them, 1 at a time, and place them face down in front of you. Then put the rest of the Major Arcana away.

Now take the rest of the deck you had put aside (the 56 Minor Arcana cards) and start mixing or shuffling these, asking the question, "How will I fulfill my purpose?"

When you're ready, fan these cards out in front of you as you did the Major Arcana cards. Then pick four cards, one at a time, keeping these cards face down as well. The idea is that you will pick or gravitate toward cards whose pictures you don't yet see. We want the subconscious to pick the images for you.

Now you have three Major Arcana cards, your mission or purpose in life, and four Minor Arcana cards, how you will fulfill your purpose. Remember, the cards you pick today are for present and near-future events you will soon learn about and hopefully accomplish. Now turn all seven cards over and place them in their upright positions. What do you have? Write down the cards here:

Major Arcana cards: "What is my mission or purpose in life?"

Card 1: _____

Card 2: _____

Card 3: _____

Minor Arcana cards: "How will I fulfill my purpose?"

Card 4: _____

Card 5: _____

Card 6: _____

Card 7: _____

Now, using the images of the cards, tell a story about yourself. You can be anything or anyone in each of the cards; the important thing is that this is *your* story.

When you've read more about the cards themselves in Parts 3 and 4, you'll want to come back to this exercise and look at the cards again. For now, though, you should just note the cards and your initial impressions of them.

The Therapeutic Relationship

If you're a fan of *The Sopranos*, chances are you're familiar with Tony's relationship with Dr. Melfi, which is hardly a typical—or even desirable—therapist-client relationship. Your relationship with your Tarot reader—or with your Querent—is the same kind of therapeutic relationship that occurs between a therapist and client, but it should *never* be the kind of dysfunctional relationship *The Sopranos* depicts so well.

Who's Reading Your Cards?

Who's reading your cards can be the single most important decision you make about a Tarot reading. Just as Dr. Melfi might do Tony Soprano more harm than good, the wrong Tarot reader can leave you with the wrong impression of Tarot.

Your personal reaction to a particular Tarot reader might have nothing to do with his or her skills as a reader. What's important in a reader-Querent relationship is chemistry, and, as with any relationship, you click with some people and don't click with others.

But how do you go about finding the reader who's right for you? Here are a few suggestions:

◆ Ask your friends if they have a reader they like.

◆ Check your local continuing education programs for Tarot classes and get to know your teacher if you take a class.

◆ Talk to people at your local metaphysical bookstore and get to know the owner and the salespeople. Ask them about Tarot readers they know and like.

◆ Take advantage of any local metaphysical publications and read the stories they print on local Tarot readers and read the ads for ones that "connect" to you.

How Much Should You Tell the Reader About Yourself?

In the same way you talk to your therapist or doctor, we think that the more a reader knows about you, the better she or he can interpret your cards. Those of the Skeptical School will immediately say, "Well, there, you see? You tell them what you want to hear and then they tell it back to you." But that's not how the Tarot works at all. You might tell your reader your heart's desire, but the cards reveal the what, when, and if of how it might or might not unfold. Is this "telling" the future? Or counseling hearts?

We'd like to ask you a few questions, and we'd like you to look into your heart of hearts to answer them.

- ◆ Do you believe your future is in your hands?

- ◆ Do you believe the rest of your life begins today?

- ◆ Do you believe that "telling" the future is really the same as counseling hearts?

You already know the answers to these questions. But let's go over them again to make sure we're all playing with the same deck:

- ◆ Your future *is* in your hands.

- ◆ The rest of your life begins *today*.

- ◆ Tarot, like all esoteric methods that get you in touch with your heart of hearts, can both "tell" your future and counsel your heart.

The rest is up to you—with the cards' able assistance, of course.

The Least You Need to Know

- ◆ The pictures of Tarot are works of art meant to open your imagination.

- ◆ Tarot cards can reveal things about yourself that you haven't known or realized.

- ◆ The Tarot can help you better deal with your relationships and life changes.

- ◆ The more your Tarot reader knows about you, the more she can help you understand your needs and desires.

- ◆ The Tarot cards are all about the journey of life—*your* journey of life.

Part 2

Getting to Know the Cards

It's time to take a closer look at Tarot cards. Tarot decks come in a variety of shapes and sizes, and there's one to suit every taste (and budget). How you respond to different decks is a highly individual affair, and which deck you feel most comfortable with is a matter of intuition as well. As you get to know your Tarot deck, you'll want to start recording its messages in a Tarot journal of your own.

Chapter 4

Contemplating Tarot Cards

In This Chapter

◆ Tarot decks and cards

◆ Tarot colors and imagery

◆ Tarot mythology

If you've never gone to the Tarot section of your bookstore and looked at decks, do so soon. You'll be amazed at how many different decks there are, and in Chapter 22, we'll be looking at them in more detail. The best bookstores will let you examine each of the decks before you buy one so you can find the one that's right for you. But before you make that deck-shopping trip, we'd like to talk a little bit about just what it is you're seeing.

Different Strokes for Different Folks

People like different decks for different reasons. People love to browse through the many decks available in stores and online. An audience exists for every deck, because each Tarot deck has its own unique, rich symbolism.

We believe it is important to learn the basics with one deck. Once you become comfortable working with Tarot's images, you can move on to other decks that are attractive to you. When Lisa or Arlene do readings, they have a deck for others to shuffle and a separate deck(s) of their favorites for personal use.

In the Cards

Arlene is particularly fond of her Aquarian deck. She's an Aquarius, after all, and this deck is named after her sign. She loves the beautiful pastels; they're more romantic, she feels, nice and flowing, softer. Arlene found this deck when her first Tarot teacher was discussing the different zodiac sign decks. Arlene picked the deck for her sign, and it's been her favorite ever since.

In the Cards

A. E. Waite, who supervised the design of the Universal Waite Deck, is primarily responsible for the Fool beginning the Tarot deck today. He felt that its "unnumbered" key 0 naturally belonged before the Magician, at the beginning of life's journey. It's hard to believe the Fool could be anywhere else.

The Deck You See in This Book

We're using the Universal Waite Deck in this book for a number of reasons, the main one being that it depicts the most common Tarot deck in the country today and, therefore, the one you're most likely to find and see illustrated in other books.

A. E. Waite's Tarot decks were the first to use symbolic design rather than stylized drawings to depict each card. This is especially evident in earlier versions of the Minor Arcana cards, which look much more like the common playing cards we see today. The early 3 of Cups, for example, literally had three cups on it. In the Universal Waite Deck, though, this card has the three dancing women who, in most modern decks, appear in various guises on the card.

The 3 of Cups has a symbolic design in the Universal Waite Deck.

So What Do All These Cards Mean?

Have we told you often enough that what the cards "mean" is ultimately up to you? Although it's true that each card has a number of divinatory meanings and that many Tarot authors, including us, will try to "explain" those meanings, at heart, Tarot is an instinctual art and is at its best when its meanings are found intuitively.

The High Priestess, for example, has a different meaning according to each expert you consult, as shown in the following table.

What Does the High Priestess "Mean"?

Meaning	Authority/Book
"Subconscious knowledge"	Leo Louis Martello in *Reading the Tarot*
"Intuitive awareness"	Anthony Louis in *Tarot: Plain and Simple*
"A card of waiting and gestation"	Nancy Garen in *Tarot Made Easy*
"Hidden influences"	Eden Gray in *The Complete Guide to the Tarot*
"Secrets, mysteries, the truth not yet revealed"	A. E. Waite in *The Pictorial Guide to the Tarot*

What all these differences of opinion confirm is that you shouldn't think of a card's meaning as cast in stone, but rather as a door that opens to a variety of possibilities. To us, the High Priestess is a card about those very possibilities, about listening to your intuition, and following its lead. But what this card means to *you*, well, that's up to you.

Sharpening Your Powers of Observation

Are you wondering how the experts "see" all the meanings in the High Priestess card? Did you have to go back to the Universal Waite card to examine the High Priestess's face and dress, her pomegranates, the moon, or the Torah scroll?

If so, you're not alone. We're all inundated with so much information that everyone uses some sort of selective filtering to get through their days. If you read the license plate number of every car that passed you on the freeway, for example, you wouldn't be able to pay much attention to traffic. So you selectively filter out the extraneous information, like license plate numbers, to get on with the job of driving.

The High Priestess in the
Universal Waite deck.

The problem is that we've become *too good* at selective filtering, so when we first encounter the rich imagery of Tarot cards, we look at them the way we're used to looking at everything: We just read the headline. When we look at the High Priestess this way, we see a lady in a blue cloak with a funny pointed hat.

One of the first things you'll want to do in your encounter with Tarot cards is to turn off your selective filtering system and let all that imagery in. To help you do this, we've designed an exercise to get you started.

The Moon: A Tarot Exercise

For this exercise, you should select the Moon card from your Tarot deck. (If you don't have a deck yet, you can use the following picture, but remember that the colors are missing.) Place the card comfortably before you, and let it tell you its story.

The Moon (key 18).

As you study the details of the card's design, write down what you see, using the following questions to guide you.

Are there animals? If so, what are they?

_____

_____

Are there shapes? If so, what are they? Are they large or small? Realistic or stylized?

_____

_____

Are there elements (fire, earth, air, water) present? If so, how are they depicted?

_____

_____

Are there human figures? If so, how are they depicted?

_____

_____

What about vegetation? Are there trees or flowers? If so, what are they?

_____

_____

What colors are in the card? What do these colors mean to you?

_____

_____

What other symbols do you see in the card? What do they mean to you?

_____

_____

Rather than tell you what _we_ see in this card, we suggest that you have someone else do the exercise, too. After you've both finished, compare your notes. Did she see things you didn't or vice versa? Did you see things she's certain aren't even there? Are there images that you absolutely disagree about?

For now, just note all your and your friend's thoughts about this card. Save them for Chapter 11, where we discuss the Moon card in more detail.

> **Wheel of Fortune**
>
> The key to studying any Tarot card is to *relax*. Don't demand that the card show you everything at once. Don't worry that you're missing something someone else might have seen. What you see in the card is what's there for you—and that's what is important.

Tarot Cards and Color Theory 101

Just as we might not consciously be aware of archetypal symbolism, we confront color symbolism on a daily basis without giving it a thought. But think about it: What color is the cape that is tossed before a bull? Red, the color of anger. And what color are those ubiquitous happy faces? Yellow, the color of optimism.

At the same time, remember that to think each color can only represent the meanings we suggest here is to limit the color's potential. With that in mind, let's look at some traditional color symbolism.

Color Symbolism

Color	Possible Meanings
White	The soul (white light), innocence, purity, naïveté, faith
Yellow	The sunny yellow kitchen, vitality, good energy, healing, enthusiasm
Orange	Healing powers, playful, fun, flirtatious (red + yellow)
Red	Passion for life, aggression, danger, power, desire, lust, stop sign
Green	Prosperity, growth, money, springtime, the Emerald City
Blue	Tranquility, thoughtfulness, peace, calmness, deep as the ocean, high as the sky
Purple	Problem-solving, intuition, the psychic realm, resurrection, royalty, red + blue = passionate problem-solving
Brown	Earthy connection, grounded, serious, thoughtful, subtlety, quietness, solid commitment, the brown bear, perseverance
Black	The beginning and the end, the abyss, the culmination of things, the completion of a cycle, the void, termination, the unknown; all colors are included in black, the universal color, which used to be considered bad luck, evil, darkness

Certain colors might mean other things to you. If so, you can record them here.

Personal Color	Symbolism	Color	Personal Meanings

A Matter of Mythology (Greek, That Is)

We don't expect you to be steeped in mythology like someone with a classics background. We know that the most you might know about Ulysses is that James Joyce wrote a famous and controversial book with that title or that George Clooney updated the mythic journey home in the Coen brothers' classic film *O Brother, Where Art Thou?*

But the mythology Tarot symbolism uses comes from more than just those old Greek and Roman stories. It also is drawn from, for example, Christian-era angels such as Raphael, Michael, and Gabriel; Egyptian gods like Ankh and Anubis; Wiccan symbols like black cats and roses; and Hebrew letters such as the "YHVH" that stand for the Hebrew God, Yahweh.

You don't have to be a classics scholar to recognize the inherent meaning in any of these symbols. But just in case you want a little background, the following table lists some of the most common mythological symbols used in Tarot.

Fools Rush In

When is a bull just a plain bull? Tarot artists rely on many different mythological systems when illustrating the cards. If you're not familiar with something on a card, will you miss its meaning? We don't think so. The most important meaning of a card is *what it means to you*. So if a bull is just a plain bull to you, then that's what it is.

Symbol	Meaning
From Christian Mythology	
Angels:	
Raphael	Angel of the air (superconscious)
Michael	Angel of fire (consciousness)
Gabriel	Angel of water (subconscious)
Cross	Union of God and earth
Crown	The will vs. cosmic purpose
Devil	Spiritual blindness, temptation

continues

continued

Symbol	Meaning
From the Hebrew Kaballah	
Lightning	The life power from the Tree of Life
Scroll (Torah)	Divine law; hidden mysteries
Stone	Unity of father and son, spirit and body
From Egyptian Mythology	
Ankh	Life; male + female
Anubis	Jackal-headed god representing the mind
Sphinx	The mystery of life
From Greek Mythology	
Bull	The element earth
Moon	Emotions and intuition
Ram's head	Mars, the planet of action

These four mythological systems are just a few of the many that Tarot artists have used. The Universal Waite Deck alone also includes numerological, mathematical, and astrological symbolism, for example. Other popular Tarot decks use Native American, Goddess, and African myths, to name but three. If a particular mythological imagery appeals to you, learn more about it. Your local library will have a wealth of information on any mythology you want to study in depth.

Common Images in the Cards

Because we're using the Universal Waite Deck in this book, we'd like to explore some of the common images these cards use before we move on to more exercises where you get to know the cards better yourself. But remember, the "meanings" we list here are just suggestions. The cards will have unique meanings for you.

Common Images in the Universal Waite Deck

Image	Possible Meaning
Banner	Freedom from material possessions
Birds	Messengers from the sky who give us warning or enlightenment
Butterfly	The immortality of the soul
Cat	The psychic mysteries of life

Image	Possible Meaning
Chain	Self-imposed restriction
Circle	Wholeness, continuity
Crown	Mastery
Dog	Friend of humans
Eagle	Power
Flame	Spirit
Grapes	Abundance and fertility
Horse	Creating action and powerful movement in your life
Leaves	Vitality
Lily	Purity
Mountains	Abstract thought
Olive branch	Peace
Palm	Victory over death
Scales	Balanced judgment
Serpent	Wisdom
Star	Luck, good fortune, hope
Stream	The flow of life
Veil	Hidden things
Wheel	The whole of cosmic expression
Yod	The tenth letter of the Hebrew alphabet, hand of God, blessings from heaven

Now that you've got a basic understanding of some of the Tarot's symbolic systems, you're ready to take a good long look at the cards themselves. That's what the next chapter is all about.

The Least You Need to Know

- Different Tarot decks are available to suit every taste.

- The colors used on Tarot cards have a variety of meanings.

- The myths of many societies—from Greek to Native American—can be found in Tarot cards.

- Certain images are common to all Tarot decks—male and female, for example.

- What you see in a Tarot card is up to you.

What Do *You* See in the Cards?

In This Chapter

- How the Tarot can help you make big decisions
- Finding personal meaning in the cards
- Getting rid of preconceived notions

So far, we've talked mostly about symbolic systems and the fact that the Tarot is one of them. It's obvious we think this concept is very important to an understanding of the Tarot, and now that you've got it firmly in hand, we'd like to take that lesson and apply it to the cards. In this chapter, we'll take a good long look at the cards and at what *you* see when you look at them.

Walking the Fool's Path

Through the Tarot's Major Arcana cards, you can see the cycles that are repeated throughout your life. Each of the Major Arcana cards has a number (or key), and that number tells what you're learning and how that lesson might express itself.

The first six cards, the Fool (key 0) through the Hierophant (key 5), show us as "begin-ners" who have not yet been shaped by more mature societal forces.

The next six cards, the Lovers (key 6) through Justice (key 11), represent our interme-diate steps, where we learn to apply our knowledge to new challenges.

The next five cards, the Hanged Man (key 12) through the Tower (key 16), show our process of wrestling with our inner demons and of beginning a process of regeneration and deeper learning.

The final five Major Arcana cards, the Star (key 17) through the World (key 21), mean that we've achieved group consciousness and that we're pretty advanced life journeyers.

Along our journey in life, we all wonder what's ahead of us. Your questions might include some or all of the following:

- What is my future?
- Whom will I meet?
- What is my calling?
- Is there someone out there for me?

Fools Rush In

The Tarot can warn you of possible events that might not be so pleasant and foretell new hope of things to come that will change your life for the better. How you walk the Fool's path, though, is up to you.

You can think of the Tarot as a wonderful journey during which you're seeking the opportunities and possibilities we've all longed for. The Tarot can reveal a new start in life after a difficult phase or tell you of new relationships on the horizon. It can direct you toward a new career opportunity you hadn't thought of or reflect new skills, new people, and new conditions up ahead. Just follow the Yellow Brick Road of the Fool's journey through the Major Arcana: Your dreams are at the end of the rainbow!

Tarot and Life's Cycles

It's interesting to watch how the Tarot exactly reflects the *life lessons* you might be going through at any given time. People who have had regular readings throughout their lives, for example, note that in their 20s Temperance (key 14) and the Hierophant (key 5) came up over and over again to represent their life's lessons.

Card Catalog

Your **life lessons** reflect both the lessons that all of us learn as we go through our lives (the Major Arcana) and the lessons you must learn yourself in your own life (the Minor Arcana).

Why do certain cards show up at certain times in people's lives? Well, in answer to the question, "What do I need to learn now?" Temperance answers, "Great patience with life and a tempering of energies. Adaptation to current conditions." The Hierophant's response to this same question is, "Learn to deal with the institutions or conventions of society."

For people in their 20s, these cards show up again and again, making it clear that people this age need to learn these particular lessons. The funny thing is, most of them don't want to hear it! Although these cards reflect the lessons 20-somethings usually need to develop and integrate into their lives, like all of us, they'd rather see the Sun (key 19), the Lovers (key 6), and other cards showing great personal success and good relationships.

Later, when these same people are in their 30s, they will receive the cards of marriage, prosperity, and good relations. Temperance and the Hierophant no longer appear in their readings, but the Sun and the Lovers do. By this time, they are ready for these lessons and no longer wonder why these specific cards appear.

Tarot cards such as Temperance (key 14) and the Hierophant (key 5) are common in Tarot readings for people in their 20s. Cards such as the Sun (key 19) and the Lovers (key 6) begin to appear for people in their 30s.

What does this mean? It means that *certain cards will come up at certain times in your life to reflect the lessons you're able to handle at that time*. So when you're 60 or 70, the cards that appear won't have shown themselves before. The cards you receive at any given time represent what you need to grow into—and even at 60 and 70, we're still growing.

Tarot and Life's Big Decisions

Once you understand the reflective nature of the cards, you can begin to see how they can help you with the big decisions in your life. Here, it's the Minor Arcana, or daily, cards that come into play, showing you how current events have, are, or will be played out.

Arlene cannot give financial advice because she is not a broker or CPA, but clients nonetheless ask her money-related questions. During a more prosperous time for the stock market, for example, one client asked if her profits in a particular stock would increase more than the previous year. When the answering spread revealed that she should be cautious about expecting more and that there would likely be a decrease in her investment in the next three to six months, Arlene asked the woman if she could take out some of her original investment in this stock and put that into a CD or something else to keep it safe. The client said, no, she would rather keep it all in the stock market for at least another year.

That reading took place in January 2002. Turn on any TV or read any newspaper, and you can see that the client should have paid more attention to what the cards told her. As a reader, however, Arlene only makes suggestions, and never tells the client what to do. The cards can give us advice or alert us to trends and cycles, but they (and their reader) cannot control free will. What you do with what the cards reveal is always up to you.

What Brings You to the Tarot?

Most people who take a Tarot class or get a reading want help with making a major decision in their life—and they need to know *now!* We know you can go for months or years and not really feel the need or urge to get a reading, but then all of a sudden—especially when a negative situation happens or something crashes and burns in your life—you'll want to turn to someone else to help guide you out of the "bad" cycle.

Some people seek out their ministers, rabbis, counselors, mentors, or grandmas—or a darn good Tarot reader or psychic. It usually takes a desperate or uncomfortable situation to motivate someone to get a reading, but then it's in just such circumstances that we usually look for some kind of help.

Help! The desperate phone calls come in, begging for readings.

Help! I need to take a class *now* to understand my life better.

Help! I need guidance *now!*

Arlene hears anxiety in every voice, so she tries to help everybody. She can't, of course, replace other forms of counsel or therapy that may be needed for certain situations. If you need a lawyer, you should see a lawyer. If you need a doctor, see a doctor. If you need a therapist, see a therapist. But if you need a spiritual advisor or insight of a higher nature, that's when you should seek out a Tarot reader.

Looking for Personal Meaning

Each of us sees what's happening from our own particular point of view, and because of this, no two versions of any story are exactly the same. Think about it—even if you and your brother are sitting across from each other at the same table eating dinner, he's looking at you, and you're looking at him, so your points of view are different!

This is what personal meaning is all about: your own particular perspective in your own particular story. Tarot can help you understand just what your story is, but how you live your story is up to you. We all want to develop a sense of individualism and follow our own drummer instead of the rest of the band. The key to this is inside you; it's your story and no one else's. No one else can—or should—tell you how to live your life, because it's *your* life and no one else's. Here's an example.

The middle-age son of a wealthy family recently came to see Arlene. He'd rather be driving an old Ford pickup than his Mercedes, wearing jeans than his suit and tie. But this 47-year-old doesn't want to make his 70-something-year-old mom angry, so when he visits his family, he puts on the suit and tie he keeps in the trunk of his Mercedes.

When Arlene did a reading for him, she told him he needed to be what and who he wanted to be. Nobody *really* cares but him, she told him. But somewhere along the line, this guy developed a pattern that told him he had to please others first, that his needs were secondary to those of his family, and that the things he needed weren't important. But that's not true for *anyone*. We all need to learn to be true to ourselves before we can be true to others.

Finding personal meaning is about learning to have the self-confidence to be true to ourselves. And getting in tune with that personal meaning can be found through the Tarot cards.

Reading for Other People

Objectivity is important in any reading, and the closer you are to the individual emotionally, the less likely you are to be intuitive. Arlene can't read for her mom, for example, because when she tries, she focuses on her view of her mom, rather than on what the cards are really showing. If we know someone well, we'll try to make the cards fit the picture we have of that person rather than what the cards are actually saying.

So don't read for people you can't be objective about, such as your best friend or a loved one. If you know too much about one's situation, have a preconceived notion about what the person is asking, or have a stake in the question, you just can't be objective and you shouldn't even try.

Follow these tips for giving an ethical reading:

◆ Be objective. If you can't, find someone else to do the reading.

◆ Provide constructive counsel. If anything looks "negative," work with the Querent to turn the negativity around.

◆ Use the cards to empower the Querent to make his or her own personal judgments and decisions without you.

◆ Be aware when you're doing a reading that you're helping a person find his or her past more clearly and that you have to be gentle with that process.

◆ As much as some people say they don't believe it, they're all ears when you give them a reading. Your responsibility is to give them something to go on after they walk out your door and don't have you sitting across the table to answer questions.

Your Personal Response to the Cards: A Tarot Exercise

What cards you're most and least drawn to can reveal a lot about you. For this exercise, you should place all 22 Major Arcana cards facing you so you can look at them all, individually and together. Let the cards speak to you, and listen to what they have to say.

It's possible you already know which card you love the most. For example, a student of Arlene's was always attracted to the Sun card, no matter what deck it came out of. She said she identified with the picture of the child on the horse, the sunflowers, and the light colors because it was "her." When Arlene asked her which card out of the entire deck most repelled her or made her feel most uncomfortable, she said, "Oh my, of course, the Devil card." She couldn't stand to look at it or work with it, she added.

Arlene told her she should take some time now to handle the Devil card. Otherwise, it will be harder to relate to that card correctly later because she will have a prejudice against it. "That's true," the client agreed. "Let me try to make friends with the Devil." And she did.

Like Arlene's client, you, too, might know which card really turns you off, gives you the creeps, or you just hate to see. A businessman Arlene knows, for example, hates the Tower card and the chaos it seems to represent. As you learn more about which cards attract and repel you, at the same time you allow each card to "speak" to you equally, ultimately leading to clearer and more insightful readings.

This exercise is about your *personal* response, though, so what *we* think of particular cards has nothing to do with it. The Tower might be the card you like best, and the Moon the one you like the least. Remember, *there are no right or wrong answers.*

What Cards Are You Most Drawn To?

One Major Arcana card probably leaps out at you. Is it the Star, pouring her dual pitchers of water into stream and lake? Is it the happy Lovers couple or the cheerful, innocent Fool? Maybe you're drawn to the power of the Emperor, the Empress, or the Hierophant. Whatever card just *gets* you, though, record it here.

Favorite card: _____

Chances are, you like other cards as well. Pick out two other cards that appeal to you, and list them here.

Card: _____

Card: _____

Now place these three cards next to each other in front of you. Look at the cards, together and individually. What colors are they? Do they have images in common? Use the following space to note what you like about these cards.

What colors are in the cards? What do these colors mean to you?

_____

_____

Are there human figures on the cards? If so, how are they depicted? Why do you like them?

_____

_____

Are there shapes? If so, what are they? Are they large or small? Realistic or stylized? What is it about these shapes that you like?

_____

_____

Are there elements (fire, earth, air, water) present? If so, how are they depicted? What do these elements mean to you?

_____

_____

Are there animals? If so, what are they? Why do you like these particular animals?

_____

_____

What about vegetation? Are there trees or flowers? If so, what are they? What do they remind you of?

_____

_____

What other symbols do you see in these cards? What do they mean to you?

_____

_____

What have you found? Are you drawn to certain colors? Certain people? Certain animals or shapes? What are they? Why are you drawn to them? Think about your answers to these questions and then move on to the next part of this exercise.

What Cards Are You Least Drawn To?

Just as you're drawn to a certain card or cards, there's probably one card that just gets your goat. It could be that old goat, the Devil, in all his horned splendor, or Death peering out from beneath his visor. Maybe something about the Hermit or the Hierophant disturbs you. Whatever card bothers you the most, though, record it here.

Least favorite card: _____

You probably don't like some other cards either. Pick out two of them, and list them here.

Card: _____

Card: _____

Now place these three cards next to each other in front of you and look at them. Once again note their colors, their imagery, and their symbols. Use the following space to note what you dislike about these particular cards.

What colors are in the cards? What do these colors mean to you? Why don't you like them?

_____

_____

Are there human figures? If so, how are they depicted? What is it about them that you don't like?

_____

_____

Are there shapes? If so, what are they? Are they large or small? Realistic or stylized? What do you dislike about these particular shapes?

_____

_____

Are there elements (fire, earth, air, water) present? If so, how are they depicted? Why don't you like them?

_____

_____

Are there animals? If so, what are they? Do you know why you dislike these animals?

_____

_____

What about vegetation? Are there trees or flowers? If so, what are they? Why don't you like them?

_____

_____

What other symbols do you see in these cards? What do they mean to you? Are there reasons they turn you off?

_____

_____

What have you found? Do you dislike certain colors? Certain people? Certain animals or shapes? What are they? Why don't you like them? Think about your answers to these questions. After you have, we think you'll find that some of the answers to why you don't like certain cards can be found in the next section.

Life in the Tower

Bad experiences seem to color our perceptions for a long time after the fact, no matter how hard we may try to focus on the positive. It often seems as if we humans tend to remember negative events far better than we remember the pleasant ones. What's wrong with us, for goodness sake? Are we complete idiots—or just Fools?

Much about the mind remains a mystery, even with the enormous leaps and bounds knowledge is making in this new century. For whatever reason, we're very good at hiding behind the fears or traumas *we know* rather than taking steps that might introduce us to new ones. Without even realizing it, we become so overly cautious or fearful about the same thing happening again that if something comes up that looks anything like a former trauma, we jump back and say, "Oh no! I don't want to go through *that* again!"

Right? If a situation looks even remotely familiar, we might run in the opposite direction. "Not another guy named Ken!" or "Not another boss who tells long-winded jokes!" These things might have nothing to do with what was really traumatic about the old event, but the mind has associated the trauma with all sorts of unrelated baggage.

We call this "life in the Tower." Take out the Tower Major Arcana card and look at it. What's happening in this card, and why is it so scary?

This card kind of looks like a bad year in California—everything from rain to lightning, from mud slides to fires. What else could possibly go wrong? Maybe it would be better to just crawl off somewhere and hide—that way, nothing can find us.

But what about the *good things* that happen unexpectedly? What about that tall, dark stranger or that chance encounter?

No growth exists without risk. You've got to break through the old destructive patterns before you can develop more constructive ones. You've got to get rid of your excess baggage and learn that life in the Tower isn't always a bad thing.

Breaking Through Preconceived Notions

So how do we stop these destructive patterns? First of all, we learn to use our intuition about every new event in our lives, rather than assume, because of our bad experiences, that it will come out the same as it did the last time. No matter what went wrong in the past, it is just that: *in the past.*

The Tower (key 16).

THE TOWER.

It's years later now. You have a new opportunity to try again. Let's say you went through a messy divorce and now you've met someone new. "Oh wonderful, I finally found the right person. This is so great. I can't wait to get started in this new direction." And then, *boom!* Fear and anxiety creep over you. "Oh no. It could happen again. I don't want to go through another loss." So halfway through this promising relationship, you cut it off. Because of your experience and the associated bad memories, instead of looking at the possibility that this relationship could be good for you and help you heal from the old one, you run.

But you know, "You got to get up on the horse that kicked you." Fear and trauma can—and will—get in the way of you finding happiness whenever they can. But if you listen to what the cards have to say, Tarot can help you separate your *real* fears from your *imagined* ones.

In the Cards

We all get into patterns in our lives; they make things easier and keep the unexpected from throwing us for a loop. But sometimes the very patterns we think are protecting us can be keeping us from living our lives to their greatest potential. The Tarot can help you separate the good patterns from the destructive ones so you can get your life moving in a direction that's right for you.

There's No Such Thing as Good Cards and Bad Cards

So here comes the Devil—the Devil card, that is. This is one seriously ugly dude. Just look at him—he's all hair and horns, and he's got those people in chains at his feet. The Devil is a bad card, right?

The Devil (key 15).

THE DEVIL .

Repeat after us: "There is no such thing as good cards or bad cards. There is no such thing as good cards or bad cards." Now close your eyes and click your heels three times, and before you know it, you're back in Kansas. Oops, wrong story!

Or is it? Just as Dorothy's power to get back to Kansas was inside her all along, the Tarot's power resides inside you. Yes, these are graphic pictures; the Tarot's a very graphic tool. It uses pictures to relay messages, and some of those pictures are pretty ugly.

When the cards look difficult, they can indeed be reflecting the shadow side of a situation, but they're also sending important information you must pay attention to. Would Dorothy have believed the Ruby Slippers could get her home if she hadn't followed the Yellow Brick Road all the way to the witch's tower?

If a card like the Devil or the Tower appears in a reading, you should think of it as a wake-up call, not an all-points bulletin. Ask yourself, "What is this card trying to tell me? Is there someone in my life who is not good for me? Or is there a situation I should think twice about before I leap into it?"

It's always better to be prepared or forewarned so that we might be able to change our course of action. And no matter what cards come up for you, all the Tarot cards in the deck should be welcomed as having some information that can help you avoid unnecessary difficulties. So if a card looks scary, it's there to warn you rather than predict what's coming. Taking heed is using your head!

Take Nothing for Granted

Sometimes you'll put out a spread of cards and decide, "This is not answering my question. I don't like what I see." Okay, reshuffle the cards and see what comes up. See if you can get a "better answer." Guess what? The same cards come up, or if not, you'll get something with a similar meaning! What's going on here?

Even when the cards don't seem to be answering the question you asked, they're probably answering something you should know about or that your subconscious is mulling over. When certain cards appear, you should take nothing for granted. Even if you don't know, the cards do! So pay attention to what they have to say.

The Least You Need to Know

- ◆ The Major Arcana cards can show the lessons you need to learn at this point in your life.

- ◆ The Minor Arcana cards can show the lessons you need to learn today.

- ◆ You shouldn't wait for a crisis to consult a Tarot reader.

- ◆ What cards you're most and least drawn to can reveal a lot about you.

- ◆ The Tarot can help you break through your destructive patterns and ideas.

- ◆ There is no such thing as good cards or bad cards!

Chapter 6

Learning to Use the Tarot Deck

In This Chapter

- ◆ "Wearing in" your Tarot cards
- ◆ Upright and reversed cards
- ◆ Your Tarot journal

Your relationship with your Tarot deck is the beginning of a beautiful friendship and, like any friendship, a little mutual respect and care will go a long way. In this chapter, we're going to explore ways to enhance the energy you and your Tarot deck will share so your beautiful friendship will move beyond that beginning into a long and exciting future.

Your Personal Energy and the Tarot Deck

When you do a Tarot reading, it's important to be objective. This means opening yourself to the possibilities of the Tarot and not allowing your preconceived notions to sneak in.

Let's say, for example, that a client of Arlene's, a Querent, asks her, "Will I win the lottery tonight?" Lots of people *do* ask questions just like this one. But let's say Arlene thinks gambling is a waste of time. She doesn't let her judgment cloud a reading.

Instead, she might let the Querent know why she's obsessed with winning the lottery. She might tell her, if a Major Arcana card comes up, that there could be a deep, soul-level issue that she's working through.

In the Cards

Doing a Tarot reading is a lot like teaching: You can learn a great deal from the readings you do for other people by connecting to their personal energy. After you do a reading, you might feel a tingle. That means you've gotten in touch with your own higher energy, that healing psychic power we all possess.

The most important thing is to let the cards talk. Let them come out. Read what they say, not what you feel about them. Let people experience their own souls, even if it means they have to go "to the edge." Take *yourself* out of it, in other words. The information you provide should help the Querent instigate her own power. Your role is to channel information constructively: Be the High Priestess, sitting between logic and emotion—objective.

Rather than judge if someone's concern is "good" or "bad," always bear in mind that the Querent should be allowed to pursue her own particular issue. That's how she'll get to learn, in the case of gambling, for example, that she can't always win—and that she can't use a medium, like Tarot, to make herself win.

When people put too much stock in something, their very obsession with obtaining it can push it away. One Tarot reader we know has always been struck by people she sees at the racetrack, carefully marking their tip sheets and calculating odds. When she bets on a horse, she picks it by its name or just on some hunch (if you're one of those people with the tip sheets, we know you're shuddering now!). Interestingly, she wins at least as often as those people with their tip sheets—and sometimes more often.

The lesson here is sometimes called beginner's luck. What beginner's luck really means is that if it's not a big deal to you, you win. Beginner's luck occurs because you approach something with no preconceptions, with the honesty and innocence of the Fool. Such pureness of intention, uncolored by fear or bias, can result in big payoffs, while obsession can result in misdirected or negative energy. Think about it!

Can You Read Yourself from Your Own Deck?

When you read from your own deck, the most important thing, again, is to be objective. Take your time, and don't demand that the cards reveal some meaning to you. Preconceived ideas can result in missed messages, so it's important to not let what you *want* to see color what you really see in the cards.

The reader, even when it's you reading for yourself, should always tell the truth and always do so in a nonthreatening way. You might know on a subconscious level what's going on, but it's the cards that will show you the truth. With a good ear and a good heart, you can find a new way of seeing, for yourself as well as for others.

"Wearing In" the Cards

Part of getting all you can from your Tarot deck is helping the cards help you and the Querent, and one way to ensure that this happens is to "wear in" or "season" your cards on a weekly basis. Arlene does the following affirmation exercise every Sunday evening before she begins another week of readings.

Separate your deck into its four Minor Arcana suits and its one Major Arcana group. Your cards won't necessarily be in order, but Wands will be with Wands, Cups with Cups, Pentacles with Pentacles, Swords with Swords, and Major Arcana with Major Arcana.

After you've divided your deck into these five stacks, spend some time with each individual stack, clearing the cards of the past week's readings and opening them up for the readings to come. You should use an affirmation, which is a positive sort of prayer, to do this; here's the affirmation Arlene recites each week as she contemplates her five stacks of cards:

My wish for these cards will be to read for the next person well, with confidence, the best intentions, and for the highest good.

"Season" your cards this way at least once a week, taking the time to do an affirmation for each of the five stacks. When you're finished, reshuffle your stacks back into each other, as if they were parts of a new deck. Shuffle at least six or seven times, and the cards will be ready for another work week.

Seasoning your deck clears both the cards' energy and yours, renewing it so the readings of one week will not be influenced by the readings of another week.

What's the Deal If Cards Are Reversed (Upside Down)?

You mean there's a difference between upright and *reversed* cards? Some readers say there's not, but we feel there is—yet it's not necessarily a negative thing. Reversed meanings can reveal that the lessons of a particular card may be more challenging for this Querent or that he is fighting himself on this issue. The Querent will also need to evaluate his issues when a reversed card appears in his spread.

All the cards—both the Major and Minor Arcana—have both upright and reversed meanings, and this can scare some people. For one, reversed cards don't look right to us; they don't sit right with our brain, which seeks to put everything upright and in order so it looks and feels "normal." Anything reversed seems scary to us, as if its energy was somehow negative instead of positive. But once you realize that reversed cards allow you to know where you might have delays, false starts, indecision, ambivalence, or frustrations, you begin to see that they're helpful rather than dangerous cards. At the same time, they can let the reader know when a Querent is having difficulty handling a particular situation, and so help her help you—or you help her, as the case may be.

So although reversed cards might *appear* to be negative, in fact they're just another way the cards tell us what's happening or could happen. Reversed cards are crying, "Pay attention!" loud and clear. We should listen to their message.

Card Catalog

Reversed cards occur when the lessons of a particular card are more challenging for a Querent or when a Querent is fighting himself on an issue.

In the Cards

Reversed cards are usually noted in Tarot texts, including this book, with a capital R following the cards' names.

When we turn the Hanged Man upside down, it looks as if he is in perfect position to step down and walk into a new future!

All in a Day's Energy: A Tarot Exercise

We like to do daily spreads and record them in a Tarot journal to review later. If you'd like to try this, you should use a Three-Card Spread like those we've mentioned in earlier chapters or like the one that follows.

In the morning, take out your Tarot deck and shuffle it, asking the question, "How's my day going to go?"

Think about this question as you shuffle and then, when you feel you're ready, divide the deck into three stacks. Select three cards, either all from one stack or one from each, and put these three cards out, face up. Write down the cards in your journal, and also write down the date. Don't look up the cards' interpretations now. Just let them speak to you, without demanding any meaning from them.

You can do this daily for a week, a month, or forever. The purpose of this exercise is to look for patterns. If you miss a day or two or three, don't worry about it. There's nothing rigid about this exercise; it's meant to help you understand yourself.

To help you see how this works, the following table shows five days from one person's daily readings.

Date	Card 1	Card 2	Card 3
March 23	8 of Wands R	7 of Wands	High Priestess R
March 24	Queen of Pentacles R	2 of Cups	Knight of Wands R
March 25	8 of Cups R	9 of Swords R	Fool R
March 26	7 of Wands	6 of Swords	4 of Wands R
March 27	Queen of Swords	King of Wands	8 of Swords

Take out your own Tarot deck and assemble the readings as shown in the table to get the picture of the week. Don't look up the interpretations of these cards just yet. Instead, look at the patterns you see. Quite a few 8s and 9s are present, as well as a lot of reversed cards (those followed by R), including the two Major Arcana cards that appear. By the end of the week, though, the reversed cards have disappeared, and two Swords come up in March 27's daily reading. In fact, Wands and Swords seem to be the energy of this particular week. Remember this reading when we talk about the specific energies of the Minor Arcana suits in Chapter 12.

Your Own Daily Readings

Now it's time to start doing your own daily readings, if you'd like. Use the following table to record the cards you find for any five consecutive days.

My Daily Readings

Date	Card 1	Card 2	Card 3

Again, don't look up the interpretations for these cards. Instead, wait a few days, weeks, or months; then go back and look at what you've recorded. You might want to take out the cards again and place them as they first appeared, so you can note their visual impressions on you.

Note, too, any patterns you see, such as whether they're suits, numbers, or reversed cards. As you get to know the cards, you'll intuitively know what these patterns mean to you, and you'll be able to come back to these first daily readings and understand just what they meant for you then—and now.

Feeling the Synergy of Card Combinations

For this exercise, we're going to put out our first Celtic Cross Spread. We'll be discussing this spread in detail in Chapter 19, so if you'd like to know more about it now, sneak a peek ahead. Here's a form for recording the cards, which we'll be using throughout the book to record this particular spread.

Shuffle the deck as many times as you want, asking whatever question you want to ask. Your question can be as general as "What's going to happen in the next six months?" to a more specific "Will I find the job I want?"

When you're ready, select 10 cards from the deck, either from the top of the deck or from a fanned-out spread. Lay the cards you choose face up in the pattern shown in the figure, placing the first card at 1, the second card at 2, and so on.

After you put out the 10 cards, take a moment to study them. We want you to *feel* the cards first, noting how they mix, match, or alternate. Try to answer these two questions as well:

- Do the cards seem to belong together?
- Do the cards feel as if they don't combine well?

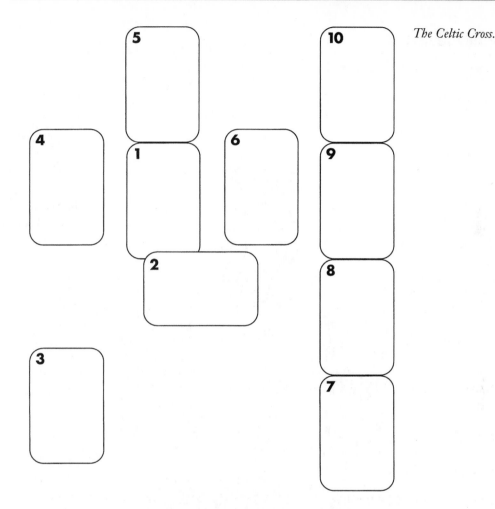

The Celtic Cross.

Look at the pictures first before checking the cards' interpretations; that's where you'll find the synergy of the cards (the energy of the cards together).

Sit back and spend at least five minutes considering how you feel about these cards and this combination of pictures. If they feel confusing to you, your answer is about confusion. If you feel a harmony, then the answer's harmonious.

Be sure you feel the cards' energy before you read about what the cards mean in later chapters of this book. Open your intuitive sense to the cards, and see what they have to say. Don't be surprised that you're not surprised when you look them up—you may have already found what you needed to know.

A Sample Spread

Now let's look at a sample spread to help get you started.

Diane's Sample Spread

Celtic Cross

October 9, 2002

Question: "What's happening in my love life now?"

Card 1: King of Cups R

Card 2: Queen of Pentacles

Card 3: Judgement

Card 4: 5 of Wands R

Card 5: The Tower

Card 6: The Sun

Card 7: 4 of Wands

Card 8: 6 of Cups R

Card 9: The Chariot

Card 10: The Fool

In the Cards _____

If five or more cards in a Celtic Cross Spread are Major Arcana, something's going on in your life at a karmic level that's destined to be learned or to happen. When this occurs, you're working with other forces or people for these things to happen, and they're going to happen no matter what, so you might as well cooperate. Such a spread helps explain why sometimes you can't seem to get your mind off certain people or situations. Some things are bigger than we are, and we need to accept them when they come along. But it's not necessarily something to worry about!

Without looking up the cards and ignoring the five Major Arcana just for the moment, take a look at the Minor Arcana in Diane's reading. What do you see? First, there's the King of Cups reversed and the Queen of Pentacles up, which would be Diane and the relationship she is now working on. That leaves us with the 5 of Wands reversed, the 4 of Wands upright, and the 6 of Cups reversed. These three Minor Arcana show Diane's thoughts and energies toward what her question is.

Diane asked about her romantic life because she was questioning what was going on with her present guy. With a question like this, you look at the Minor Arcana to get a feel for what the Querent would like to have happen. In this case, Diane does want good things: The three Minor Arcana cards say that she wants peaceful, harmonious energy, while the 6 of Cups reversed represents her nostalgia for a heart-centered relationship like she had in her teenage/college years.

The King of Cups reversed in her spread represents her present fellow. Because the card is reversed, it seems that Diane's guy is not sure whether or not he wants a permanent relationship or commitment at this time. He is kind and heart-connected, but by showing up reversed, he shows ambivalence or fear of commitment. Perhaps he has some emotional baggage from his past that bothers him as well.

Diane is represented by the Queen of Pentacles upright and in opposition to him. This suggests that she wants a commitment and is ready for what he is ambivalent about. (After Arlene had read the entire spread, Diane told her that she was ready for marriage!) The upright position of the card shows that she is very focused and clear about what she wants in a relationship.

Looking at the Major Arcana cards—all five of them—we can get a clue about Diane's destiny regarding the question asked. She has been working on her life's lessons and goals for quite a while and has been trying to find a compatible relationship that will lead toward marriage (represented here by the Sun card). In fact, Diane noted this was her original thought as she shuffled the deck. This many Major Arcana cards indicate that she is not only ready for marriage but is ready to find the right relationship that will lead to marriage.

The last card, the Fool, represents that Diane will become open to finding that right person. It might or might not end up being the King of Cups, because, as the Fool tells us, Diane will remain open to new possibilities (and new men) in the very near future.

Now It's Your Turn

But you don't want to look at someone else's reading, do you? You want to do one of your own. So shuffle the cards and lay them out, using the Celtic Cross form we provided earlier. If you already did a Celtic Cross Spread in the earlier "Feeling the Synergy of Card Combinations" section, you can use those cards for this exercise. But if you want to do another, you might be surprised to see how closely it resembles that first spread. Either way, record the cards you choose here.

My Celtic Cross Spread

Date: _____

Question: "What's happening?"

Card 1: _____

Card 2: _____

Card 3: _____

Card 4: _____

Card 5: _____

Card 6: _____

Card 7: _____

Card 8: _____

Card 9: _____

Card 10: _____

Now look at these cards. What do you notice?

◆ Are there a lot of Major Arcana cards?

◆ Are there more of a certain suit or number?

◆ What about the pictures themselves? Are there a lot of men or a lot of women shown?

◆ Do certain pictures or shapes occur more than once?

◆ Does there seem to be a pattern of harmony or of conflict?

After you've spent some time contemplating the cards, go ahead and look up what we have to say about them later in Parts 3 and 4. You may very well find that the interpretation is not so very far from what you already knew yourself!

Start Your Own Tarot Journal

Keeping track of Tarot spreads is as important as the spreads themselves. Writing them down means you won't lose any of the spreads you have done. Even Cancers (who are known for their good memories) can't commit *that* many cards to memory!

How and where you keep your Tarot journal is up to you. You can choose a spiral notebook or a pretty journal you got for Christmas. (A word of warning about those pretty journals, though: You might be hesitant to write in them.) If you're computer-savvy and prefer to keep your Tarot journal on your computer, that's fine, too. This is *your* journal, so however and wherever you want to keep it is what's important.

> **Wheel of Fortune**
>
> Get creative with your Tarot journal! Make it a picture journal, for example. Photocopy your spreads and collect them in a three-ring binder, or draw the cards in your journal. (You might want to write down the name of the card, too, especially if you're no Picasso!) If you're journaling on your computer and feeling really creative, scan some of your cards or find pictures of cards you like on the web and save your spreads on your computer.

Keeping Track of the Cards

You don't have to keep your journal in pretty books if you don't want to. An 8½×11-inch sheet of paper with the date and time you did the reading, your question, and a line for each card is fine. You can make 40 or 50 copies of the form we have here and then save your recorded readings in a spiral notebook or set up a database on your computer and record your daily cards there. You can use any format you want, in other words, but be sure to save each reading as you do it.

Daily Tarot Reading

Name: _____

Date: _____

Question: _____

Card 1: _____

Card 2: _____

Card 3: _____

Thoughts:

_____

_____

_____

_____

_____

_____

_____

_____

_____

_____

_____

_____

_____

_____

When you return to look at these spreads three or six or however many months later, you'll find that the cards say much more than you first realized or imagined. Saving a page for each reading provides a visual record and assists your memory, which has enough to remember, after all. With your journal in front of you, you can pull the cards out again and see what they have to say to you now. When you record every spread you do in some form, you're sure to learn a great deal when you look back, and you'll be recording your own history in the process.

Recognizing Patterns

One of the things you should record in your "Thoughts" section for each daily reading is what's going on that day. Do you have a doctor's appointment? Are you behind in your bills? Did your daughter bring home a straight-A report card? Was your Christmas bonus much bigger (or smaller) than you'd been expecting? Just scribbling down a few words about what's going on will bring the emotions you were feeling at the time of the reading back for you—and, with the perspective of three or six months, you'll begin to see a pattern in which cards appear when you're feeling certain things.

At the same time, when you look back at readings you did over a period of time, you'll begin to notice that certain cards seem to recur much more often than others. One of us, for example, seems to have a lot of Queens show up, which she attributes to all the positive feminine energy of her co-authors, her book producer at Amaranth, and her friends.

If a certain Major Arcana card appears frequently, whether upright or reversed, remember what we said in Chapter 5: That card represents a lesson you need to learn. If the card is upright, you're doing just fine, but if it's reversed, it could be that you're resisting its message—or the messenger.

Practice, Practice, Practice

In the course of learning something new, homework is always part of the process. When Arlene says this to her students, some of them always say, "Oh no! Homework?" Their faces show some chagrin, as if they are going to be tested. As Arlene tells these students, however, the only way you can become good at anything is to practice and study the subject matter over and over.

The more Tarot readings you do, the more fascinating the Tarot will become. Even new students can go out into the world and ask their friends or family—even a total stranger—if they would like a reading. "I'm a Tarot newbie," they might say, "and I need to practice the process of throwing spreads to become good at reading them."

Arlene believes "homework" is the best way to continue the lessons from this book or from a Tarot class. One assignment all of Arlene's students find helpful is to read an article or listen to a news report and then immediately do a reading on or about what they've just read or heard. You can try this yourself. Chances are, the cards will reflect not only the report but show future developments—and perhaps even the outcome as well.

If you try this exercise, write down the cards you get or file them away in your computer. Arlene's favorite way of saving a reading is to record the whole reading on tape. Add your comments and any other thoughts you'd like, too. When you play the tape back later, you will be amazed to see how close you came to the actual outcome of that particular news flash.

When you're recording a reading, it's just as important to record what you see and feel from the cards as the cards themselves. No matter how good your memory is, it's hard to remember everything you saw or felt later on, so recording these emotional reactions can be the perfect method of "practice makes perfect." You can judge for yourself how accurate you were or whether you need to rethink the meanings you get.

Last, nothing is wrong with reshuffling the cards and rethrowing the spread if you didn't feel clear about the first reading. Tarot cards will reflect and reveal more to you the more you practice. Like playing the piano, learning to dance, and, yes, riding a bicycle, the more you repeat the process, the more satisfying the results.

In the same way, lots of Arlene's students ask her if they'll ever be as good a reader as she is. Arlene always tells them, "You might be even better." Arlene knows that as much as any of us practice, some of us are natural Tarot readers and some of us are natural at whatever we are attracted to. With practice, you can be a good Tarot reader, and some of you will be great ones, if you've got that innate Tarot talent. Time—and practice—will tell.

The Least You Need to Know

- Think of your Tarot deck as a friend you want to take care of.

- Objectivity for yourself and for others is key in any Tarot reading.

- A reversed card can mean you're resisting that card's lesson. Designate reversed cards with an R, as in 3 of Pentacles R.

- Record your Tarot spreads in a daily journal so you can go back to them again and again.

- Practicing with your Tarot cards can help make you a better reader.

Part 3

The Major Arcana: A Fool for the World

The Tarot cards themselves are divided into 22 Major Arcana cards and 56 Minor Arcana cards. By the time you've traveled through the 22 Major Arcana cards, you've completed a journey from beginning (the Fool) to end (the World) and encountered both the best and worst of life in the process. Discover the interrelationship between fate and Free Will and how the Tarot can help you empower your life.

Chapter 7

Don't Be an Idiot, Be a Fool

In This Chapter

- ◆ The Major Arcana cards
- ◆ The significance of lots of Major Arcana cards in a reading
- ◆ Some Major Arcana cards in combination
- ◆ Destiny vs. Free Will: Who's in charge here?

Where are you in your journey of life? From those first baby steps to the wisdom of maturity, every day of life is a celebration, and we find ourselves participants in an arc of experience. As Muhammad Ali once said, "The man who views the world at 50 the same as he did at 20 has wasted 30 years of his life."

The Tarot deck's Major Arcana cards are visual metaphors for each step in the experience of human life, for each lesson to be learned in a continual movement toward self-actualization. These cards represent your life's journey toward enlightenment and depict situations of major significance. Think of them as the many forks along your own particular road. How, when, and if these archetypal cards appear in a reading can show you where you are on life's highway, what you already know about life, and what you still have to learn.

Take the 22 Major Arcana cards out of your Tarot deck and examine their names. As you'll notice, these names alone—like the Emperor, the Empress, the Chariot, the Hermit, and the Tower—suggest ancient mysteries and myths. What do they have to do with you? Everything! These "mysteries" are as relevant today as they ever were!

Using the Universal Waite Deck, let's take a look at the pictures, symbols, colors, and numbers of each of the Major Arcana. Come along with us and enjoy the beauty, color, awakenings, and challenges of experience that we're sure to find.

The Fool Looks for Signposts of Experience

Sometimes just realizing that we don't know everything or understand everything there is to know and understand about life can open us to whole new worlds and ways of thinking and growing. As the Fool (key 0) sets off to learn about the World (key 21), he's full of confidence and anticipation, but it's clear he's not the most practical observer. Ah, youth! This guy's not afraid of falling into the valley beneath him or even aware that there might be any danger at all. He's dazzled by the strong light of the Sun (key 19).

Little by little, as we grow older and accumulate experience, we learn life's lessons and achieve the compassion and empathy we need to guide others. The strong light of the Sun enters our souls, and we become the shining signposts for the youth who stands bedazzled on the mountain crag, poised to fly and fall—that is, if we're willing to fully experience the journey of life ourselves. We can be wise guides if we dare to challenge our notion of ourselves, to question the ways of the world, to push the envelope of what we know, to face life's darker side (both in ourselves and in others), and to tear it all down and build it all up again.

THE FOOL .   THE MAGICIAN.   THE SUN .

From 0 to 21

The path of life is indeed exciting, and the Major Arcana's archetypes contain a variety of metaphors for unlocking it. Whether you think of it as the Yellow Brick Road or the Fellowship of the Ring, a metaphor can help you better understand your own travels. We'd like to take you on a tour of the Major Arcana, following a progression of Jungian archetypal signposts. (For those of you into numerology and astrology, we've provided that information here as well.)

The Fool, key 0. Number: 0. Astrological sign: Aries. Here's where the journey begins, with the Divine Child archetype. In this myth, an infant, such as the baby Jesus, is sent by God to enlighten the human race.

The Magician, key 1. Number: 1. Astrological sign: Aries. Here's where the Fool discovers his creativity and talent for using various tools to achieve his goals. The Jungian archetype for the Magician is the Trickster, such as the Native American coyote.

The High Priestess, key 2. Number: 2. Astrological signs: Pisces and Virgo. Although the Magician can control the material world, another world is out there—the hidden, intuitive side of everything. The High Priestess sits between logic and spirit and is associated with the Jungian archetype of the Wise Woman, such as Grandmother Spider in Navajo myth.

The Empress, key 3. Number: 3. Astrological signs: Taurus and Libra. Now that he's learned about his own two sides, the Fool meets the first of the parental archetypes. The Empress represents the Earth Mother and fertility, healing, feeling, and giving. According to Jungian theory, the Empress is the anima, or the feminine side of the self.

The Emperor, key 4. Number: 4. Astrological signs: Scorpio and Aries. Just as the Empress is the feminine, the Emperor represents the masculine side of each of us, the animus. This card is about responsibility, authority, and reason, all ideas we associate with a father figure. Picture Hamlet's father, the king of Denmark, from the Shakespearean tragedy.

The Hierophant, key 5. Number: 5. Astrological sign: Taurus. Society's larger traditional values are represented by the Hierophant, sometimes called the Pope. Jungian psychologists assign the archetype of the persona to this card, the social mask we all wear when we are out in the world. This concept is also associated with your astrological ascendant, or rising sign. For example, if you're Libra rising, the "mask" you wear for the world will have a Libra balance and sense of diplomacy.

The Lovers, key 6. Number: 6. Astrological sign: Gemini. It's time for the Fool to learn about sex! The Lovers represent yin and yang, attraction, desire, and romance. A variety of archetypal equivalents exist for this card, including Romeo and Juliet and Tristan and Isolde. Mythological lovers are often fated to heartache because even love is not without its difficulties, as we all know.

The Chariot, key 7. Number: 7. Astrological sign: Sagittarius. Here's where the Fool encounters the two sides of any issue and learns about compromise and balancing conflicting forces. In Jungian terms, the Chariot represents the struggle between light and shadow. We all possess the Tolkien character Frodo's heroic goodness, for example, but Frodo's shadow, Sauron, lives buried in our hearts as well.

Strength, key 8. Number: 8. Astrological sign: Leo. After encountering his dark side, the Fool needs to learn to trust himself and develop self-confidence. This card can be equated with the Jungian hero or heroine, the mythological self.

The Hermit, key 9. Number: 9. Astrological sign: Virgo. It's the Fool, but instead of looking skyward while he walks toward a cliff, he's looking inward, where he'll learn about the benefits of meditation and reflection. The archetypal equivalent here is the Wise Old Man, or Tolkien's Gandalf.

The Wheel of Fortune, key 10. Number: 1. Astrological signs: Aquarius, Taurus, Leo, and Scorpio. Having completed the personal aspects of his journey, the Fool now encounters the outside forces associated with it. The Wheel of Fortune is all about destiny, the things of life that are beyond his control. This is exemplified by the Serenity Prayer "God grant me the courage to change the things I can, the serenity to accept the things I can't, and the wisdom to know the difference."

Justice, key 11. Number: 11/2. Astrological sign: Libra. Some aspects of life might seem beyond the Fool's control, but at the same time, justice does prevail. The Justice card is about learning our lessons, being rewarded for the good we do, and, likewise, being punished for the evil we do.

THE HANGED MAN.

The Hanged Man, key 12. Number: 3. Astrological sign: Pisces. Hanging by a thread, the Hanged Man is learning the lessons of letting go and of not being ruled by the material or the mundane. Here's the Fool searching for spiritual enlightenment and psychic revelation.

DEATH.

Death, key 13. Number: 4. Astrological sign: Scorpio. Here's one of the hardest lessons the Fool must face: the knowledge of his own mortality. But this is also where he will learn that death is not an ending but a beginning and that new things cannot be started without old ones coming to an end.

TEMPERANCE.

Temperance, key 14. Number: 5. Astrological sign: Cancer. With transformation come the lessons of moderation and perspective. Temperance is all about tolerating differences, learning patience, and waiting rather than rushing in headfirst.

THE DEVIL .

The Devil, key 15. Number: 6. Astrological sign: Cancer. Even with all his newfound knowledge, the Fool continues to harbor internal demons, petty things that could undermine his existence, such as obsessions, doubts, or impulsiveness. This card is to remind us once again of our shadow side and the evil we can do to ourselves.

The Tower, key 16. Number: 7. Astrological sign: Aquarius. Lightning can strike without warning, and the Tower serves to remind us that sometimes change can come out of the blue. Sometimes it's change for the good, and sometimes it can be more difficult. Here's a wonderful haiku that puts the Tower into perspective: *Until I lost my rooftop I could not see how The Moon floats along the sky.*

The Star, key 17. Number: 8. Astrological sign: Aquarius. The last five Major Arcana cards can be found in the heavens and, as the haiku of the Tower card reminds us, there's always hope no matter how dark the road might seem. The Star represents the idea that hope, courage, and inspiration will bring the promise of better days to come.

The Moon, key 18. Number: 9. Astrological signs: Cancer and Pisces. By the light of the Moon, things aren't always what they seem. The Moon reminds us that illusions and hidden forces can obscure what's really happening. But this card also represents our psychic, imaginative, or emotional sides, the Pisces or Cancer in us all.

The Sun, key 19. Number: 1. Astrological sign: Leo. The darkest hour is just before dawn, and in the light of the Sun, the Fool has come out of that darkness into a new awareness and strength. Revitalized by the power of life's journey, he is at his strongest, ready to shine.

Judgement, key 20. Number: 2. Astrological sign: Scorpio. Archetypally, Judgement means resurrection, the rebirth that comes with spiritual awareness. Arriving at this step on his journey, the Fool understands the possibilities of transformation that can come with change. The Fool reaches for enlightenment.

The World, key 21. Number: 3. Astrological sign: Capricorn. At the end his journey, the Fool has achieved wholeness and understands his place in the world. The World card is the card of achievement and success, where the Fool understands that life encompasses much more than himself and his own journey. He is ready to begin again on a new cycle of learning: the process of reincarnation from the world of experience to the innocence once again of the Fool.

Where Are You on the Journey?

We asked a friend to take the Major Arcana cards, mix them around, and shuffle them well, separating the cards into three piles. Then we asked her to pick three cards that would indicate where she stood on the Fool's journey. Here's what came up: the Hanged Man (key 12), Justice (key 11), and the Fool (key 0). Then we asked her to pick another card to represent her current challenge: Death (key 13) reversed.

Like the Hanged Man, our friend is in a state of questioning everything, barely hanging on to the old order of things. With the exuberance of the Fool, she needs to trust her intuition and let go—with the assurance that Justice will prevail and she won't fall on her head! She needs to resist the temptation to fight against the rebirth that will come if she has the courage to let go and allow herself—and her life—to change. Notice the numbers of her cards: 11, 12, 13, with a return to 0 for a little bit of courage of heart to keep moving on the path and to find the new beginning that awaits her.

Try this exercise yourself. Record your cards.

My Current Signposts

Card 1: _____

Card 2: _____

Card 3: _____

My challenge:

_____

_____

_____

What do the cards tell you about your position on the Fool's journey?

The Universal Mysteries of Life

Life. Death. Sex. Violence. Rock 'n' roll. (Well, maybe not rock 'n' roll.) But certain things in life remain mysteries despite science's greatest efforts to explain them. But are they really mysteries? Let's look at a few of them from a mythological point of view and see if they begin to make a little more sense:

◆ **Birth.** We've seen those _Life_ magazine pictures, too: the mystery of birth revealed in living color! But do we _really_ understand how a little fun on Saturday night can lead to a little bundle of joy nine months later? If you've ever been present at any birth—whether an animal's or a human's—you've probably used the word *miracle* to describe this event.

Being born is a lot like the Fool beginning his journey: We arrive innocent, with clean slates, waiting for our lives to write our lessons. Myths from Adam and Eve to the birth of Venus on a half-shell explore this innocence, too, helping to demystify this particular mystery.

◆ **Death.** Yup, that Horseman of the Apocalypse. That nasty skeletal face you can just make out under that black cowl—the Grim Reaper. The black-armored skeleton on a white horse at key 13 (!) of the Tarot deck. All these images and ideas share a common theme: After we die, we go somewhere else.

Now, sure, science can't "prove" that. Yet every great religion—both modern and ancient—insists that this is so. Some call it heaven and some call it Valhalla, but the fact remains that our myths provide an "answer" to death's mystery; namely, that it's not an end, but a beginning.

◆ **The Unexplained.** At times, events seem to come out of the blue. Where, for example, did September 11 come from? Why are there events like that, when after they've happened, your life is never the same? You might respond by saying that we are not meant to know certain things, because if we knew and couldn't do anything about them, what would that do to us?

When Arlene's marriage ended, one of her best teachers asked her, "If you were to have known the outcome, would you have gone through with the marriage?" "Of course not!" Arlene responded. "Then you would have passed up an opportunity for growth or completing a karmic duty." That was when Arlene understood that there were good things within that marriage as well as good growth. Whatever happens, no matter how difficult, it will always have some good in it as well. With that in mind, meet the Tower (key 16) in the Tarot deck and expect the unexpected.

In the Cards

Joseph Campbell (1904–1987), master of comparative mythology, showed how seemingly unconnected societies share the same mythological motifs. These include "creation stories," such as the one in Genesis at the beginning of the Judeo-Christian Bible and the Navajo story of how The People came up from The World Below. Flood myths are another example, like that of Noah in the Bible and of Pyrrha and Deucalion in the Greek tradition. It's written in Ecclesiastes 1:9 that "There's nothing new under the sun." When we look at the myths of various peoples, we find that this is definitely true.

As you can see, although science is still trying to answer these mysteries, our myths explained them a long time ago. We think the Tarot can help, too. Its images, after all, are rooted in these very myths.

What Do Lots of Major Arcana in Your Reading Mean?

As we discovered in Chapter 6, when a lot of Major Arcana cards show up in a reading, much of what's going on is fated to happen, whether you work with it or not. A reading with many Major Arcana cards infers that the answer to the question at hand is not under your, the seeker's, control. Instead, many other surrounding circumstances are affecting its outcome.

When this happens, you really can't change what's already in motion, because the cards reflect a process that started before you even asked. In other words, the wheels are in motion, so you're just gonna have to go along for the ride!

The specific Major Arcana cards that show up are the particular lessons you're learning about the question at hand. Major Arcana cards tell you that something is going on that you need to pay attention to—even though you won't be able to control the whole outcome. In fact, the outcome is usually in someone else's hands, as is the case for the following two readings.

> **Wheel of Fortune**
>
> An upright Major Arcana card shows that you've been successfully mastering the card's particular lesson, that you're ready to accept it. A reversed card shows that the lesson is meeting resistance, and so setbacks, delays, or other difficulties might be occurring.

The Major Arcana in Combination with Minor Arcana Cards

When you look at a Tarot spread, you should look at the whole spread, because meanings of cards can change depending on the cards surrounding them. If Temperance R is next to Judgement, for example, you might be impatient for the answer you're waiting for. Here are two spreads with Major Arcana in combination for you to contemplate.

What Are Deanna's Karmic Lessons About Her Biological Father?

Deanna came to see Arlene about her biological father, whom she's never met. Deanna was concerned not only about finding and meeting him, but what *karmic lessons* there might be around their relationship.

Card Catalog

Karmic lessons refer to things one must do in this lifetime because of what has happened in past lives. *Karma* is Sanskrit for "work." A good way to think of karmic lessons is "what goes around, comes around."

Celtic Cross for Deanna's question: "What are my karmic lessons about my biological father?"

Card 1: Ace of Swords R

Card 2: 3 of Wands

Card 3: 9 of Cups

Card 4: Wheel of Fortune

Card 5: 7 of Pentacles

Card 6: The Magician

Card 7: Justice R

Card 8: The Tower R

Card 9: 9 of Swords R

Card 10: The Sun

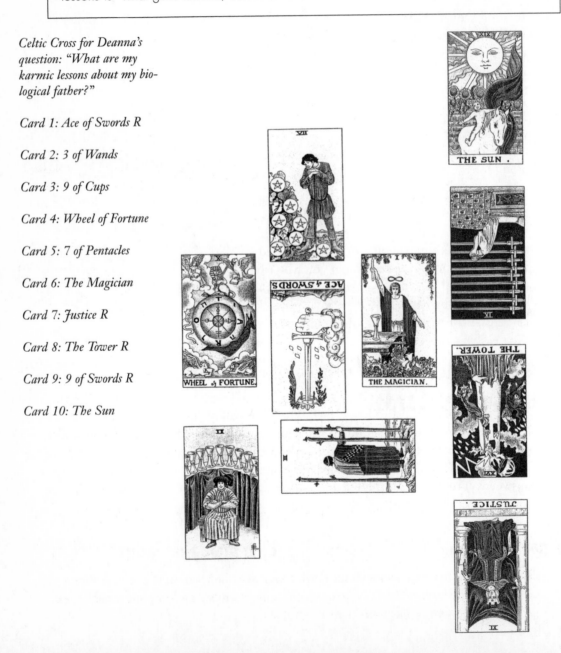

The Ace of Swords reversed begins this new venture for Deanna, of not only getting to know her "new dad," but also of how to communicate with him when they do meet. It's difficult to know how she will be accepted, after all: Even though this is her biological father, she's never met him before. Deanna will need to take things slowly and not behave too assertively.

Things start out a little rocky with other people around the situation. Both Justice reversed in the seventh position and the Tower reversed in the eighth position suggest the opinions of others are mixed and some people feel threatened. Still, the 3 of Wands in the second position and the 9 of Cups in the third show the relationship will be good for both Deanna and her biological father and that her wishes—wanting to know about her past and the family she was born into—*will* happen.

More than anything, Deanna wants to know *who* her biological father is and what he's like, a wish that would take the unknown out of her imagination. The five Major Arcana cards in this reading indicate that this question relates to a destined situation. This suggests that not only will Deanna find her biological father, but it's destined to work out. No rejection is shown on either side, as the lessons here are related to the Magician upright in the sixth position and the Sun upright in the tenth position.

The reversed Tower and Justice Major Arcana cards in the seventh and eighth positions relate to other people not quite accepting this new relationship. Deanna said she knows who these people are and that she has to accept and relate to her biological father with the understanding that others might feel threatened by a new person (her) in their family.

The easy lesson is that Deanna's birth father will feel good about the meeting and knowing about his birth daughter. The harder lessons will come with how others feel about their connection. No rejections take place in this reading. In fact, with the Sun upright in the tenth position (outcome), we would say that Deanna and her birth father will not only get to know each other, but will be able to develop a solid relationship Deanna can feel good about. This, in turn, can help her feel focused and centered in her life. When the "maybes" and "I wonders" are gone, these cards say to Deanna that she has the freedom to move on with her life.

Will Charlene's Investments in the Stock Market Go Up in 2003?

Here is another example of Major Arcana being the primary focus of a reading. The upright and reversed cards in this spread indicate the roller-coaster cycle of the stock market. Charlene was nervous about her stocks and really wanted to know about the cycle of profit at least to get a feeling about how the market might go in 2003 so she could get a sense of what to do with her money.

Celtic Cross for Charlene's question: "Will my investments in the stock market go up in 2003?"

Card 1: The Sun

Card 2: 9 of Wands

Card 3: The Chariot R

Card 4: The Emperor R

Card 5: Strength

Card 6: 7 of Pentacles R

Card 7: The Devil

Card 8: 10 of Swords

Card 9: 2 of Wands

Card 10: The Moon R

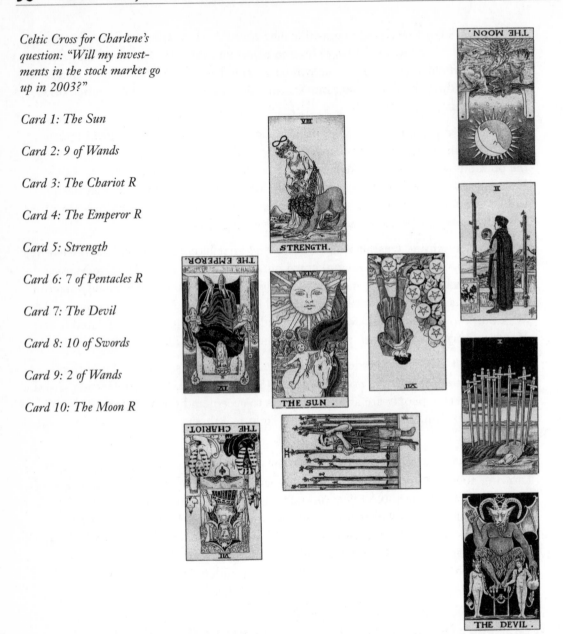

Although in the past, Charlene's investments had done well and her profits had looked satisfactory, recently she (like all of us!) had losses in her stocks, as shown in the Emperor reversed in the fourth position. With the slow economy and the volatility in the stock market, Charlene wondered if this trend would continue.

The cards are not looking very good for the year 2003. It might have been Sunny for Charlene before, but it's going to take Strength to get through this more Devilish time. Some profit might be there for her (7 of Pentacles R), but the overall theme looks like less profit than the year before.

Arlene always tries to advise rather than control anyone's thoughts about their money. In this case, Arlene suggested Charlene put her money in lower-risk stocks or into something that would allow her more control of them. Arlene also suggested that Charlene try not to listen to everyone getting upset about the marketplace, but instead either take a class on this subject or work with the people more closely involved with her stocks because the Moon reversed relates to her need to get back into awareness or control of her money and stocks.

Because of her reading, Charlene is now doing more things to protect her money. She needed to take a more personal approach to her portfolio and "pay attention to the signs of the times," as Arlene advised her. Caution and a conservative approach to her stocks and the stock market should serve Charlene well!

Destiny vs. Free Will

Looking at the previous two examples, you're probably wondering who's in charge here. Whatever happened to the idea of Free Will? Don't we have *any* control over our destinies?

Of course we do, and when we talk about the Minor Arcana cards (in Part 3) you'll see how those choices are shown in the cards. Some things, though, are karmic lessons we're destined to learn, and although we have choices about whether we learn these lessons the easy way or the hard way, we're going to learn them no matter what.

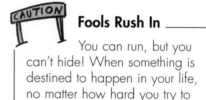

Fools Rush In

You can run, but you can't hide! When something is destined to happen in your life, no matter how hard you try to avoid or deny it, it's going to happen anyway.

Travelers on the Road of Life

We're all travelers on the road of life, just like our archetypal counterparts Frodo, Dorothy, and the Fool. The journey the Major Arcana illustrate is nothing to be afraid of. No matter what shows up, you can handle it!

As we discussed in Chapter 6, a reversed card doesn't necessarily equal a reversed meaning. Major Arcana cards represent your life lessons, and if a card appears reversed, it could be because you're resisting that particular lesson.

In fact, until you learn that lesson, that card will show up again and again. Sometimes it will be upright—"Ah, you're really trying," it says. Then it will appear reversed again—"Fighting your lesson again, aren't you?" Both of us seem to get Temperance pretty regularly when we're waiting for a situation that's out of our control to resolve itself. "Patience," it says, "patience." If only we could actually learn that lesson!

So if the Devil appears in your spread—upright or reversed—don't worry. The Devil is a lesson you'll learn as you travel along the road of your life. Pay attention to what that card has to say, and soon you'll be the Star!

The Least You Need to Know

- ◆ The Major Arcana cards reveal the things that are destined to happen in your life.

- ◆ The Major Arcana cards show how events already in motion will play out.

- ◆ The Major Arcana cards reveal the lessons you must learn in your life.

- ◆ A lot of Major Arcana cards in a reading mean the outcome of a situation is not in your hands.

- ◆ Each Major Arcana card is a step along the journey of your life.

Chapter 8

Setting Off on the Life Path

In This Chapter

- The Fool (key 0)
- The Magician (key 1)
- The High Priestess (key 2)
- The Empress (key 3)
- The Emperor (key 4)
- The Hierophant (key 5)

As any Fool knows, all enterprises and adventures require a beginning, and the first six Major Arcana cards depict all that can happen whenever we start anything new. Whether it's the spontaneity of the Fool or the constraint of the Hierophant, though, the lesson of each card will be what you make of it.

At last—it's time to set off on the life path of the cards themselves! Former First Lady and Senator Hillary Clinton is known for quoting the African proverb, "It takes a village to raise a child." In this chapter, we'll learn about the Major Arcana cards that nurture and guide the Fool in those crucial early years of childhood development.

Let the Cards Tell You What They Mean

We've provided you with keywords and archetypal characters for each card, but we encourage you to let each card "tell" you what it means as well. Here's a *meditation exercise* for you to do just that.

Before you read about each card, find that card in your deck and place it in front of you. Don't even look at the keywords or archetypes we provide. Instead, just look at the picture on the card. What do you see? Consider any or all of the following:

Card Catalog

Meditation exercises are ways of helping you use more than your logical, analytical left brain to look at things. Looking at Tarot cards without preconceived ideas and allowing the images to "tell" you what they mean is one such exercise.

- ◆ Colors
- ◆ Figures (both human and animal)
- ◆ Shapes
- ◆ Landscape
- ◆ Vegetation
- ◆ Heavenly bodies
- ◆ Symbols

Write down what each card seems to be showing you. Only then should you go on to read what we say about it. We bet you'll be pleasantly surprised when you find just how in tune your own High Priestess is—before you even read a word!

The Fool (Key 0): Open to All Possibilities

The Fool (key 0).

Your initial reactions to the Fool:

_____

_____

Keywords:	Beginnings
	Innocence
	Naïveté
	Look before you leap!
Archetypes:	Toto
	Neil Armstrong's leap for humankind
	Charlie Brown (especially when Lucy's holding the football for him)
	"A babe in the woods"

Numerology and astrology: The Fool is represented by the digit 0, which represents a continuum of life. In other Tarot decks, it can be placed as 22 or as the last card in the Major Arcana. Aries is represented by the Fool because of the open-minded and adventurous spirit of both the card and the zodiac sign.

Upright imagery: A carefree young man in yellow boots and a flowing tunic looks up at the bright yellow sky, about to step off a cliff. In his left hand, he carries a white rose; in his right, a satchel on a pole. His little dog dances at his feet, just as happy, carefree, and unaware as he is.

Upright meanings: What you do with this particular adventure—whether it be life, a new job, or a new relationship—is up to you. You're entering into the situation with excitement and childlike wonder: The Fool is full of optimism, hope, and the freedom to explore without any preconceived notions. Upright, this card means a fresh start, a clean slate, and a wonderful beginning.

If you've been trying to decide whether to take a leap of faith, the upright Fool's appearance suggests you've already taken it. This card can also come up when you've completed one project and are about to embark on another. When the Fool appears, the time for something new is nigh.

Reversed imagery and meanings: When we look at the Fool reversed, we see the same desire to seek new freedoms, start anew, and explore different horizons, but the journey could be unsatisfying or fraught with foolhardy actions. Look at the imagery in this reversed position: Upside down, the satchel will lose all its contents, the rose

Wheel of Fortune

Remember, reversed cards don't necessarily mean the *opposite* of upright ones. A reversed card can indicate delays, more difficulties than expected, or a lesson that needs to be worked on. The reversed card reminds you that you'll grapple with this particular lesson again and again—until you get it right. "If at first you don't succeed, try, try again!"

will fall out of the Fool's hand, and the sun is setting instead of rising. This Fool looks like he'll fall off the cliff headfirst. And the little dog, poor pup, can't help his master, because he's falling along with him!

The Fool reversed might mean that the path you're now on will have delays and troubles or that you'll make unwise choices along the way. Foolhardy or thoughtless actions can lead to unsatisfactory experiences, and wanting freedom—or anything— too fast or too soon can mean you won't be able to handle what's coming into your life later on down the road.

The Magician (Key 1): Unleashing Your Creative Power

The Magician (key 1).

Your initial reactions to the Magician:

_____

_____

Keywords: Creative power

Manifestation

Turning an idea into reality

You already know the magic words!

Archetypes: The Wizard of Oz

Gandalf

Dumbledore

Georgia O'Keeffe

Numerology and astrology: The Magician is represented by the number 1, which is the beginning of creation and the initiation of materializing your ideas. As an Aries card, the energy is indomitable and forward-looking!

Upright imagery: The Magician stands with his wand in his right hand pointing toward heaven and his left hand pointing toward earth. All the tools of his trade are on the table in front of him, representing the suits of the Minor Arcana: the cup (imagination), the sword (ideas), the wand (enthusiasm), and the pentacle (materials). And these are the same items he carried in his satchel as the Fool. Note, too, the figure eight, which represents the continuum that is life, and the red roses of passion and white lilies of thought that surround him.

Upright meanings: The Magician represents our ability to create our own reality. Because of the Magician in all of us, we're able to turn ideas into something tangible. The writer writes it down on paper (or types it into the computer), the architect draws the design to build that new house, the artist paints the watercolor, the mathematician figures the equations, and the musician sounds it out on her instrument.

Sometimes the Magician comes up for someone who wants to have a baby or find a new direction in life. This card always indicates that something great is developing because something is being created. Ask and you shall receive—because you already have the power in your own hands.

Reversed imagery and meanings: Turned upside down, all the Magician's tools fall off the table, which leads to scattered ability and inadequate use of talent. Your mom might say, "You can do better than that!" and she's right. The reversed Magician indicates that your ability lies hidden, or that you're not using your hidden talent—or the talent that's visible either. At the same time, the roses and lilies can't grow as well upside down, and the Magician's wand is pointed down instead of up, indicating improper use of power.

With nothing to hold them to the Magician's table, the cup, sword, wand, and pentacle all fall down. The Magician is upside down as well. Like any of us, he can't get much done standing on his head. This means that you haven't yet realized your full potential. Sometimes the Magician reversed can describe a situation that's not developing correctly or one that's hampered by a lack of enthusiasm for following through on the original idea. This card might also show up reversed to describe mediocre workmanship.

The High Priestess (Key 2): Trusting Your Own Intuition

The High Priestess (key 2).

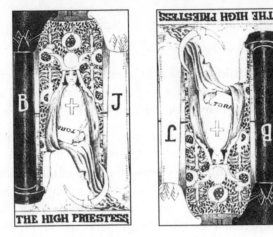

Your initial reactions to the High Priestess:

_____

_____

Keywords: Intuition

Developing your psychic skills

The sixth sense

Go with your gut!

Archetypes: Glinda, the Good Witch

Pearls of wisdom from your grandmother

Whoopi Goldberg in *Ghost*

Numerology and astrology: The High Priestess is represented by the number 2, denoting the need for the balance between logic and emotion that you can achieve by using the intuitive part of your nature. She incorporates the Pisces/Virgo polar opposites as she sits between the pillars of feeling and reason.

Upright imagery: Sitting between the pillars of Boas and Joachin with pomegranates (fertility) and palms (intuition) on her silkscreen, the High Priestess represents the world of the unseen and the mystery of what's "behind the veil." She holds out the Torah of Divine Law, representing truth, half-hidden and half-exposed to your view.

The crescent moon at her feet and the full and crescent moons on her crown represent the power and the ability of your own intuition: Through your third eye (the High Priestess), you can know more than what's visible to your other two eyes. The High Priestess represents the lesson of psychic development at its beginning stages.

Upright meanings: The High Priestess appears in a reading to get you to open your intuition and feel energy being sent or received in ways you might not be accustomed to. The High Priestess reminds you of your own ability to see beneath the surface of what's happening around you. She's the psychic intuition within each of us, neither male nor female, left brain nor right brain; the High Priestess is simply the part of you that at some level knows the answer to your own question.

The High Priestess uses psychic insight to discover that answer instead of what we westerners might call "rational thought." If you're doing too much analyzing or are too emotionally attached to an issue, chances are you're not using your High Priestess energy. This card is telling you to listen to yourself, because the High Priestess just knows—and so do you, if you listen to her.

Reversed imagery and meanings: Reversed, the High Priestess creates an image of confused psychic energy. Now she can be less than honest about the information she's about to give you because the pillars are on the opposite sides of the card. Sometimes students of the Tarot see these reversed pillars and feel that the black pillar is more dominant or ominous in this position than when it's on the left. In any event, the High Priestess reversed can't give accurate information; instead, information might be delayed or, worse, because the Torah is dropping away from her, the truth leaves her entirely, so that what you see might not be what you get.

Superstitious, cautious, and not very trusting, the High Priestess reversed can suggest that things are not right or not accurate. Here, she teaches us that all that "appears" might or might not be true or real: There's more to this than meets the eye. So be cautious when you get the High Priestess reversed; she has the power to manipulate psychic energy toward personal gain—and not necessarily your own.

In the Cards

The High Priestess is the first incarnation of Goddess figure in the Tarot. You'll find this imagery again in the Lovers, the Star, and the Moon cards. Here Goddess is represented in a practical way, as the beginning of your connection to your higher self.

The Empress (Key 3): Abundance and Fertility (Mom)

The Empress (key 3).

Your initial reactions to the Empress:

_____

_____

Keywords: Abundance

Fertility

Nurturing

Your garden runneth over!

Archetypes: Aunt Em

Gaia—Mother Earth

Yin

Your mom

Numerology and astrology: Represented by the 3, the Empress connects spirit to body, which brings forth creation and new life. She is the trinity of spirit over matter and then manifestation. Taurus and Libra are represented by the Empress because the planet Venus is within this card.

Upright imagery: The Empress sits on her cushioned chair with a scepter in her hand. Her crown of 12 stars represents the 12 signs of the zodiac, and Venus, the planet of affection and love, is represented in her heart-shape shield. The Empress is surrounded by wheat, trees, and all that Mother Nature has to offer. She's clearly content and ready to bring forth abundance, new life, and prosperity.

Upright meanings: Happiness to come! From her chair, the Empress assures that she can be of help and service to the earth and humankind. The archetypal Earth Mother, she represents fertility to would-be parents, a happy home and marriage to couples, and contentment with life to all. The Empress brings comfort and a peaceful lifestyle, along with the help of supportive women and the nourishment they can bring in all its forms.

When the Empress appears upright, it can mean a cycle of prosperity is about to begin. This could mean a new home or new conditions in the home that are peaceful and filled with an abundance of the good things in life. The Empress indicates good resources from the land. It's harvest time!

Reversed imagery and meanings: Reversed, the Empress sits decidedly uncomfortably in the same field. Nearly earthbound, the power of her scepter is no longer strong, and growth and development have stopped. When this card appears reversed, the lesson may be one of poverty or a lack of security. The heart-shape shield of Venus is not as prominent and hence has less power.

A reversed Empress can indicate infertility or that the home or environment is lacking in some way. It might represent a troubled home or marriage, inadequate resources, low income, environmental pollution, or contaminated land or environment. This card could mean a bad year for the farmer, a loss in the family, or a lack of understanding between family members. Dissatisfaction with the family or a dysfunctional family could also be indicated. The lesson here might be to pay more attention to one's home life before it becomes a problem.

The Emperor (Key 4): Authority (Dad)

The Emperor (key 4).

Your initial reactions to the Emperor:

_____

_____

Keywords: Leadership

Problem-solving

Yang

Logic and strategic planning

Archetypes: Rudy Guliani

Zeus

Martin Luther King Jr.

Your dad

Numerology and astrology: The Emperor is represented by the number 4, which is solid, logical, realistic, and concrete. Everything is 4 square with the Emperor! Scorpio and Aries represent him because the planet Mars is within this card.

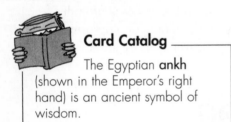

Card Catalog

The Egyptian **ankh** (shown in the Emperor's right hand) is an ancient symbol of wisdom.

Upright imagery: The regal Emperor sits on his throne wearing the emblems of war (rams' heads and the planet Mars), with the Egyptian *ankh* in his right hand and the globe of dominion in his left. Everything about this card suggests power and authority, from his determined visage to his suit of armor. Behind him are mountains—pillars of strength—and his red robes and purple throne are the colors reserved for royalty.

Upright meanings: The Emperor dominates the patriarchal world and, just as the Empress is the active mother archetype, the Emperor is the active father archetype. When the Emperor shows up in your cards, he represents the need to develop leadership and the lesson of using good logic and reasoning ability. The Emperor is a thinker, a problem-solver, and analyzer. He leads everyone else into whatever confrontations may be necessary for their own good.

When the Emperor shows up, you'll learn to develop your leadership skills and the masculine side of your nature. This card gives you the power to use logic and reasoning well and to receive good counsel and advice. The Emperor upright means you can use your authority to gain positive recognition and are learning to develop your powers.

This card might predict government connections or authority figures you'll need to deal with, whether it's your boss, your doctor, the president, or your father. This card will come up for women as well as men, because don't we all have to master our ability to lead, govern, or analyze situations? Concrete knowledge is as essential a tool as the nurturing the Empress provides.

Reversed imagery and meanings: The reversed Emperor is falling from his place of comfort and can't hold on to the position any longer. When you turn the card over, you can see how the armor on his legs is more evident, and with good reason—he's much more guarded and careful now.

This card can indicate immaturity when dealing with those in power, or with someone who's dictatorial because they fear losing power or being out of control. Character can become weak here (or at the very least, timid) in the face of problems. A lack of leadership, abusive conditions, or the feeling of being put in a very uncomfortable situation might be present. The Emperor reversed is cautioning you to take a careful look at things before proceeding to make sure you're safe.

The Hierophant (Key 5): The Lure of Conformity

The Hierophant (key 5).

Your initial reactions to the Hierophant:

_____

_____

Keywords: Conventional wisdom

Conformity

Traditions

Don't rock the boat!

Archetypes: Your country

Dorothy's Kansas

The pope

Public education

Numerology and astrology: The Hierophant is represented by the number 5, which is a turning point number, changing your life by recognizing the process of ritual or tradition. You are more enlightened after you have educated yourself! The Hierophant is Taurus, helping you connect to your extended family and community.

Upright imagery: The Hierophant (or Pope) sits in an attitude of blessing the two priests kneeling at his feet. The crossed keys between the priests represent the kingdom of heaven and earth in communion. Note, too, the gold of his mitre, or triple crown (the kingdom of heaven), and the red of his sacred vestment, or robe (the kingdom of earth). The vestment's white trim symbolizes the purity of God, while the triple cross in his left hand, the *crosier*, represents the Trinity.

Card Catalog

In the Roman Catholic Church, the **crosier** can be traced back to the walking staffs used by the 12 apostles. Ancient Roman astronomers also used staffs similar to those carried by bishops of the early Church.

Upright meanings: The Hierophant is the educator or the rabbi, who teaches the tribes one common language so all can communicate. He also teaches a common way to deal with philosophy and religious practices. The main idea of the Hierophant upright is to connect the masses through one common language, religion, or even one common denomination of money for trade.

At the same time, this card represents the need for social approval. If this card appears in your reading, you're learning how to conform to a given situation, whether it's the ways of the present society or culture you live in, or living with conventional ideas. Marriage, public education, and traditional medicine are all ruled by the Hierophant upright, too. We do a lot of things in life to be accepted by others and so we all get to learn how to be conventional at different times in our lives. What's good for the whole is good for you, this card says—sometimes whether you like it or not!

Reversed imagery and meanings: How does the Hierophant feel to you when you turn him upside down? Feelings about the card are very important. Suddenly, the two priests are at the top of the card. Are they questioning the Hierophant and his authority? What are those upside-down Y's at the top of the card? Those were the priests' vestments when the card was upright. Is the Hierophant hanging by a thread?

The Hierophant reversed indicates unconventional behavior and unorthodox ideas—the flower child, the rebel, and the nonconformist. Nontraditional circumstances can be found when this card appears reversed, as well as unconventional ways of going about your life. You might have a different focus than the rest of society or be interested in nontraditional practices such as holistic medicine, metaphysical studies, or unconventional marriages or partnerships. Are you bohemian? A rebel? A "defiant youth"? Or are you just marching to the beat of your own drummer?

Fools Rush In

If you've ever stood in line for your driver's license, waited in your doctor's lobby, or argued with your parents or your children about anything, you've confronted the Hierophant we all must deal with in our day-to-day lives. What this card is trying to tell you is that it does no good to butt your head against authority—it's there for a reason. Remember, Father knows best!

The Least You Need to Know

- The first Major Arcana cards represent your early life lessons.

- The Fool stands for the innocence of new beginnings and the start of your journey.

- The Magician represents the tools and creativity that will help you on your way as you aim to reach your full potential.

- The High Priestess gets you in touch with your intuitive side, your psychic power, and your hidden talents.

- The Empress is your mothering instincts, your nurturing feminine side, and the abundance of nature.

- The Emperor represents your masculine, paternal instincts as well as power and authority.

- The Hierophant is about understanding the need for and conforming to social values. It's all about how you deal with authority.

Chapter 9

What Kind of Fool Are You?

In This Chapter

- The Lovers (key 6)
- The Chariot (key 7)
- Strength (key 8)
- The Hermit (key 9)
- The Wheel of Fortune (key 10)
- Justice (key 11)

Getting through life consists of a lot more than those first baby steps, and many more issues must be considered as well. We're faced with choices and decisions every day, and how we deal with those choices will help determine just what kinds of Fools we are—and aren't.

The second six cards of the Major Arcana represent the many choices we all must make as we journey through our lives. From relationships (the Lovers), to reflection (the Hermit), to the vagaries of chance and society's rules (the Wheel of Fortune and Justice), this sequence of cards reminds us that learning can only come with experience and that the best way to learn a lesson is sometimes to first make a mistake.

Gaining Knowledge Through Choice and Experience

As you did with the first six Arcana cards, look at these next six one by one. What do you see? What discoveries do you make in their colors and images?

The people in these six cards include lovers, strong men and women, and solitary men and women. Choices are also present, especially in the Lovers and the Wheel of Fortune cards. This part of life's journey represents the choices we all must face as we gain more and more experience about our lives.

The Lovers (Key 6): Choices in Paradise

The Lovers (key 6).

Your initial reactions to the Lovers:

_____

_____

Keywords: Choices offered

                Romance

                Inspiration

                Temptation

Archetypes: Will and Grace (soul mates means more than sex …)

                Romeo and Juliet

George and Mary Bailey (from *It's a Wonderful Life*)

You and your soul mate

Numerology and astrology: The Lovers card is represented by the number 6, which stands for responsible relationships of all kinds and the desire to relate personally— but with a sense of duty or obligation. The Gemini zodiac sign is represented by the Lovers just as the two people/twins or similar souls reflect each other's needs/desires.

Upright imagery: A nude woman and man stand beneath the arms of Raphael, the angel of Air, who gives them his blessing. Behind the woman is the Tree of Knowledge, and behind the man is a tree bearing the 12 signs of the zodiac. The man, who looks toward the woman, represents the conscious mind and reason. The woman represents the subconscious and emotion, and so it is she who can look up to the angel Raphael.

Upright meanings: The Lovers upright is about making choices in love and romance. With this card, there's always the possibility of a new romance or a new direction for the heart. The angel Raphael indicates inspiration from above, and so, love at all levels—spiritual, physical, and emotional.

This card also points toward harmony with others around you. Family and personal relations are very important to you, and you want all your relationships to be balanced and intimate. You might be trying to make choices and decisions for the highest good in your life. Or you might find new love or love for something that is starting in your life. The Lovers card is all about learning the ways of the heart, attraction, and the desire for cooperation.

Reversed imagery and meanings: When we turn the Lovers upside down, the mountain becomes prominent and seems to divide the couple, representing obstacles or division. The upside-down angel has no power to give the couple energy from above, making developing the relationship more difficult. Consequently, you might find delays in attaining a desired result with someone or something you love.

This card might indicate indecision, or that you're making a choice that won't fulfill you. You might be involved in an unsatisfactory relationship. The lesson of the Lovers reversed is to learn how to make the right choices for where you are now in your life. Make sure you're ready for this; it could be a difficult or rocky beginning— though the end might be worth the struggle.

The Chariot (Key 7): Victory Through Adversity

The Chariot (key 7).

 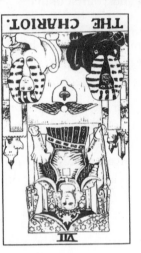

Your initial reactions to the Chariot:

_____

_____

Keywords: Success and conquest

Victory after hardship

Stamina

Good health

Archetypes: Young Obi-Wan Kenobi

Spiderman

Wonder Woman

"My hero!"

Numerology and astrology: The Chariot is represented by the number 7, which suggests dedicating oneself to a goal or an ideal. Wisdom will be developed through the number 7. The Sagittarius zodiac sign fits in well with the Charioteer, for Sagittarius is always aspiring to seeking the answers and shooting for the stars.

Upright imagery: In this card, a prince, carrying his wand of will and authority, rides in a chariot under a starry canopy that represents celestial protection. Although the astrological symbols and celestial hieroglyphics indicate he has protection from above, he must use his own will and fortitude to win the day, however. The black and white sphinxes represent the negative and positive energies in the world, and the charioteer has control over them for now. But notice the Chariot has no reins: His control comes from his stamina and his focus on the goal at hand.

Upright meanings: The upright Chariot indicates success and victory through hard work and effort, ending in triumph over enemies of any kind. When this card appears in a reading, it shows you have a responsible and kind nature but might be very intensely focused on your goal and concentrating on victory. You have the perseverance to maintain focus and the inner strength to achieve the desired success.

This card often comes up in relation to travel. After the journey, the hero, like Homer's Odysseus, is welcomed home safe and sound. Excellent health and the ability to overcome adversaries are also indicated when the Chariot appears upright.

Reversed imagery and meanings: When the Chariot appears reversed in a reading, you might have difficulty maintaining focus and stamina. Perhaps you're too weak to fight or feel like just giving up. Maybe the battle has been too long and hard, and you're finding it tough to stick with the program. Sometimes the Chariot reversed can represent poor health, a lack of vigor, or mentally giving up the fight. You might feel at loose ends, as if you can't find your way out of the situation.

Despite the desire for change, there's just too much that overwhelms the Chariot reversed. But take heart: "Tomorrow is another day." Rest, recuperate, and regroup before you go out to fight this one again. Once you relax, you'll be better equipped to decide if the battle is worth it. So retreat and stay calm. Give yourself time to think about further action, and the Chariot will soon be traveling forward again.

In the Cards

We all must struggle to control the light and dark in our own natures. Jung called this the "balance of shadow and light," and the Chariot, in both its upright and reversed positions, illustrates this principle beautifully. Even the black and white pillars in this card represent this idea.

Strength (Key 8): Learning Fortitude and Compassion

Strength (key 8).

Your initial reactions to Strength:

_____

_____

Keywords: Love wins over hate

Inner resolve

Calmness

Compassion

Archetypes: The Cowardly Lion

Hermione in *Harry Potter*

Lisa Beamer (author of *Let's Roll: Ordinary People, Extraordinary Courage*)

Your best friend

Numerology and astrology: Strength is represented by the number 8. Both loops of the figure eight, or leminscate, are representations of growth through facing difficulties. Abundance and gifts will come after taming one's fears. The Leo zodiac sign is represented by Strength as well, as we can see the woman is with the lion.

Upright imagery: The woman of Strength has flowers in her hair and around her waist. Calmly, she closes the lion's mouth and actually seems to be petting him. This card is showing us unconditional love and spiritual courage by teaching us how to face our fears. The lion represents our fears of the unknown or anything that's wild to us. The cosmic figure eight above the woman's head (remember the one above the Magician's head in Chapter 8?) represents her confidence to calm a fear.

Upright meanings: We need strength and courage to face our fears, and because love is always stronger than fear or hate, the ability to develop courage despite overwhelming odds is an outgrowth of love. Facing your fears can, in turn, help you evolve: As you free yourself of your fears, you become freer to do more with your life.

In the Cards

The Cowardly Lion as a symbol of Strength? Yes, we say, exactly. This card is all about overcoming fears to find the courage to face what might seem at first too frightening to consider. Does that sound like a lion we all know from our journeys down the Yellow Brick Road?

Strength upright is all about unconditional love and understanding. The woman of Strength doesn't need physical force to make her point, and neither do you. Like her, you have inner strength already. This card reminds you to use it.

Reversed imagery and meanings: As several students have said, when the card is reversed, the lion is in control! He's at the top of the card, representing a fear that's getting to you. Thus, when Strength is reversed, you feel out of control. The woman has the power, but it seems to be leaving her in this position. You might be feeling out of control because fear has taken over. You need to be careful that discord and confusion don't result.

Strength reversed can also indicate fear of overwhelming passions or intense emotions leading to uncontrolled action. You might be paying too much attention to the material or physical side of life or you might lack the courage to face a problem. This card is telling you to pay attention to that lion. Calm him down; get yourself back upright again. Remember, that lion's just a kitty cat at heart!

The Hermit (Key 9): Timeout for Inner Truth

The Hermit (key 9).

 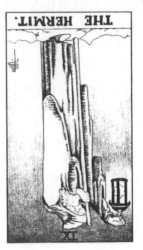

Your initial reactions to the Hermit:

_____

_____

Keywords:	Seeking truth
	Wisdom offered
	The inner voice
	Silence is golden
Archetypes:	Thich Nhat Hahn, Vietnamese monk
	Galadriel
	Your mentor
	The voice of Obi-Wan Kenobi telling Luke Skywalker, "The force is with you!"

Numerology and astrology: The Hermit is represented by the number 9: to be content and at peace with the knowledge he has attained. He is universal now, able to share what he has learned with others. The number 9 represents the desire to complete a cycle of growth and think about how far you have come. The Virgo zodiac sign is represented by the Hermit because analyzing introspectively is Virgo's greatest attribute.

Upright imagery: The Hermit stands alone, high on a snowy peak, waiting and watching for others who come along the path. He holds the Lantern of Truth, which contains a six-pointed star. Look at him closely: He's the Fool, much older and wiser. "Where I am, so shall you be," the Hermit seems to be thinking. He has experienced many lessons and now wants to share them with you. Even though he's alone, he's not lonely: Even though we're often surrounded by others, we always must follow our own paths.

Upright meanings: The Hermit upright indicates silent counsel and wise advice given and received. You've learned many lessons thus far, and now you have the experience under your belt to know much more clearly which way to turn in your life. The Hermit card shows open-mindedness and a willingness to be of help, and it can represent that either you will seek counsel or someone wants to help you on your path of life. Either way, you have the maturity and wisdom of your own truth to decide for yourself.

Like the solitary Hermit, you might need to withdraw to meditate on what's going on in your life. Patience is a virtue and leads to a studied conclusion rather than a hasty one.

Reversed imagery and meanings: When the Hermit is reversed, the Lantern of Truth is about to go out. As the light fades, the Hermit feels the cold in the air, and the snow falls down upon him. Then the light goes out, and when this happens you may need to review a few lessons you might have missed. Upside down, no one is listening to the Hermit, so he feels truly alone in the darkness. Even his walking stick can't balance him anymore.

In his reversed position, the Hermit suggests that wisdom is disregarded. Perhaps you're not listening to your own advice or not paying attention to others who have been there for you before. History can repeat itself, remember, and your refusal to learn from your past can lead to foolish decisions. This card can also indicate a tendency to daydream or to wish for something to happen without taking any action. The Hermit reversed can mean your head's in the clouds so you're unaware of how dark it really is outside.

Wheel of Fortune (Key 10): Taking Your Chances

Wheel of Fortune (key 10).

Your initial reactions to the Wheel of Fortune:

_____

_____

Keywords: Luck

                     The ups and downs of fate

                     The dartboard of life

                     Fortune

Archetypes: The gambler

                     Beginner's luck

                     Pat and Vanna

                     You've won the lottery!

Numerology and astrology: The Wheel of Fortune is a combination of the numbers 1 and 0, recognition that life is a wheel and its ups and downs are now evident. Life includes change, and the acceptance of this change is the number 10. At the four corners of this card are the Aquarius, Taurus, Leo, and Scorpio zodiac signs. These four fixed signs of the zodiac represent the ups and downs of our lives, and the four elements these signs represent—air, earth, fire, and water—are part of the focus of our lives.

Upright imagery: Like a wheel, life keeps turning, and the Wheel of Fortune represents the inevitable ebbs and flows. The four creatures represent the four fixed signs of the zodiac: Aquarius (the angel), Scorpio (the eagle), Taurus (the bull), and Leo (the lion). These show that spiritual reality is unchanging even though your personal life changes constantly. Also on the wheel are the letters TARO. Where have we seen these before? The mystery of life through the tool of the Tarot shows that TARO destiny is at work.

Upright meanings: When the Wheel of Fortune appears upright in a reading, you're entering a lucky period or cycle in your life. You get to turn the Wheel of Fortune and have great things come up. You're very lucky now no matter what you want to do; things just seem to go your way. In fact, nothing can stop you now!

There could be new conditions in your home or business, the possibility of financial improvement, or a change in environment for the better. No matter what, the Wheel of Fortune always indicates a positive change. When this card appears in a reading, the laws of chance are in your favor.

Reversed imagery and meanings: When the Wheel of Fortune is reversed, what comes up must go down. The four fixed creatures are about to lose their books of knowledge, which are falling away from them. The wheel itself has come to a grinding halt, and not even the snake, jackal, and sphinx can keep the wheel moving with the correct momentum. Situations are in disarray, and the lucky cycle has come to a halt.

Chances are you've got a feeling of stagnation, where there's no action or momentum anymore. Because the cycle has turned downward, it's best to relax and slow down. Remember, the Wheel of Fortune will eventually come back up again. It's wise to know when to stop action and when to start up again. Have the courage to pull away and say better luck next time—or at least to know there will be a better time later.

Wheel of Fortune

May I buy a vowel? Or get a different card? The answer to both questions is yes, but you shouldn't ignore what the cards are trying to tell you. If the Wheel of Fortune reversed comes up and tells you your luck has turned, you need to relax and wait for it to come back up again. The wheel never stays in one place for long—it's a wheel, after all.

Justice (Key 11): Being Fair and Honorable

Justice (key 11).

Your initial reactions to Justice:

_____

_____

Keywords: Fairness

Pros and cons

Balanced judgment

Equilibrium

Archetypes: The Wizard of Oz

Supreme Court Justice Ruth Bader Ginsburg

Mediators

Your own sense of fairness

Numerology and astrology: The Justice card is represented by the numbers 11/2, the need to maintain fairness, balance, and honor. The number 11 is a master number having to do with maintaining the law of man and the law of heaven. The Libra zodiac sign with the balanced scales fits this card perfectly! Libra acknowledges the need for mediation, negotiation, and cooperation.

Upright imagery: Justice holds a sword in her right hand and the scales in her left, and because she has no blindfold, she can see everything clearly. Behind her are the same pillars we've seen in the High Priestess and the Hierophant cards. Justice sits between them to give us balanced and fair judgment.

Upright meanings: Fair and honorable, Justice will make certain the right thing is done in the end. Lawsuits will be fair, and the system will give an honest assessment with no preconceived notions. With Justice in a reading, open-mindedness will be present to weigh the pros and cons, and fair decisions will be made to the satisfaction of all parties.

Justice is a card of cool, rational, decision-making, where intellect is key. All things being equal, Justice will say, "This is the decision I have made." She comes to a conclusion with all the evidence present, and so her decisions will always be just ones.

Reversed imagery and meanings: When Justice is reversed, her sword is pointed downward and the scales are no longer balanced. Because it's difficult for her to keep the sword and the scales in her hands, the result can be decisions that haven't been thought through.

Justice reversed might indicate inadequate counsel, unwise decisions, or simply the unfairness of dealing with the system. This card can also suggest an unfair outcome of events, perhaps as a result of prejudice, discrimination, difference of opinion, or legal complications. No matter what the root cause, things will seem unfair when this card comes up because they're *not* equal. Justice seeks a balance in all things, as should you.

Fools Rush In

If you come to your Tarot reader and ask about the outcome of a court case that's already in progress, chances are the Justice card will come up in your reading. But don't assume that just because it's upright that things will go your way—or that if it comes up reversed, things won't. Many factors are involved in any case, and sometimes Justice belongs to the other party.

The Least You Need to Know

 ◆ The Lovers reveal what's going on in your love life and with all your relationships.

 ◆ The Chariot gives you the fortitude and energy to achieve success and reach your goals.

 ◆ Strength is all about finding power and courage you might not have known you possessed.

♦ The Hermit gives you time for the solitude, reflection, and soul-searching that are necessary to make better decisions.

♦ The Wheel of Fortune represents the hand of Fate in your life, your lucky cycles, and your not-so-lucky ones.

♦ Justice comes into play when decisions must be made. Justice will prevail with a verdict of honesty and fairness.

Chapter 10

The Fool in Dante's Dark Wood

In This Chapter

- ◆ The Hanged Man (key 12)
- ◆ Death (key 13)
- ◆ Temperance (key 14)
- ◆ The Devil (key 15)
- ◆ The Tower (key 16)

No experience is without its problems and setbacks, and the Major Arcana cards for keys 12 (the Hanged Man) through 16 (the Tower) metaphorically represent the various ways such issues may manifest themselves. Whether it's the transformation of Death, the tolerance demanded by Temperance, or the unexpected surprises represented by the Tower, the cards in this sequence signal questioning, spiritual grappling, and coming to terms with our demons. It's time for the Fool's midlife crisis.

"Midway Upon the Journey of Our Life ..."

Up until now, the Major Arcana have pretty much let us go our own way. With the innocence of the Fool and the tools of the Magician, our path has been cleared for the success of the Chariot (whose charioteer seems so adept at balancing the light and dark sides) and the luck of the Wheel of Fortune. Now, though, we come to the dark, middle part of the journey, where we encounter "lions and tigers and bears"—Death, the Devil, and the Tower.

Written 700 years ago, Italian poet Dante Alighieri's (1265–1321) profoundly beautiful poem, *The Inferno*, continues to challenge us. It was translated by Henry Wadsworth Longfellow in the nineteenth century and again recently in a collaboration of twentieth-century poets that included, among others, Seamus Heaney, Mark Strand, Amy Clampitt, Robert Hass, and Robert Pinsky. At the beginning of the poem, Dante finds himself lost:

> *Midway upon the journey of our life*
> *I found myself within a forest dark*
> *For the straightforward pathway had been lost.*

To reach enlightenment, Dante (the Fool) must journey through the underworld, with the ancient Greek poet Virgil (the Magician) as his guide. At some point, we all stumble upon Dante's dark wood. How we find our way through it can make all the difference on our life journey. Are you ready to look deeper into your own Jungian dark side?

Dante in the dark wood.

(Engraving by Gustave Doré, 1861)

Those new to the Tarot often find this sequence of cards frightening, and we'll be the first to say we can well understand why. But Death doesn't mean death literally, and you can't meet that tall, dark stranger without experiencing the unexpected events the Tower represents. Change isn't easy—especially major, transforming change—but with the Tarot tools you've already acquired up to this point, you can make it past those lions and tigers and bears—and witches and dark forces, too.

As you did in Chapters 8 and 9, look at the cards here and let them speak to you before you read more about them.

The Hanged Man (Key 12): Sacrifice and Release

The Hanged Man (key 12).

Your initial reactions to the Hanged Man:

_____

_____

Keywords: The gift of prophecy

Self-sacrifice

Hanging by a thread

Letting go

Archetypes: Dr. Martin Luther King Jr.

Jesus

Confucius

Yourself at the crossroads

Numerology and astrology: The Hanged Man is represented by the number 12 or 3. The desire of the number 3 is to find contentment on a physical, spiritual, and karmic level, and the trinity of number 3 focuses the need for all three levels of your life to be in harmony. The Pisces zodiac sign fits well with the Hanged Man card because Pisces knows how to sacrifice and learn that only in giving up something can something else come in. Pisces and the Hanged Man know that letting go of the old lifestyle is not easy but necessary at times.

Card Catalog

A **nimbus**, represented by a halo or bright disk around someone's head (this is often seen around the heads of saints in religious paintings from the Middle Ages), stands for someone's spiritual aura. People crowned with a nimbus are blessed and protected by a higher power.

Upright imagery: The Hanged Man is being held on a T-cross of living wood with one leg free. His position looks similar to the yoga tree pose, which lets God come in. At the same time as he contemplates his former life, he desires a more uplifting or spiritual one. Around his head there's a *nimbus*, or white light, and his face expresses contemplation or meditation of some kind.

The Hanged Man is contemplating making sacrifices for a higher good, and he's certain that heaven will lead the way. Whatever comes will come, after all, and the Hanged Man is ready to accept the next direction in his life for his own highest good as well as for others'. The color red represents his passion for life, the blue stands for his deep thoughts and contemplation, and the yellow and white surrounding his head are vitality and spiritual desire.

Upright meanings: In its upright position, the Hanged Man card represents spiritual growth and surrender to a higher wisdom. By accepting the situation he's tied to, the Hanged Man is finding his enlightenment. Heaven has many things to offer, and the Hanged Man is ready for the new direction being shown to him. He could be looking toward a complete reversal of lifestyle, or he might be making sacrifices that he hasn't made in the past. In any event, he's definitely giving up and letting go.

Put another way, the Hanged Man means that you're finding your place in the spiritual universe. You want to stay on the earth plane to do good work to benefit others, but you may develop a psychic or prophetic ability in order to do so. The Hanged Man is tolerant of everyone else's ideas and philosophy; this is a card about being open to possibility as well as being ready for it.

When this card appears in your reading, you're at a point where it's time to leave the past behind and move on to the future. You could think of the Hanged Man as a present moment of stasis, but you can't remain there forever, or even for very long.

Reversed imagery and meanings: The Hanged Man reversed stands on one foot and so is still quite literally in touch with his former life. He can move his hands away from his back, and he can come off the living T-cross of wood and walk away. He wants to change, in other words, but he's still holding on to the past. He's not quite able to totally let go and let things be yet.

Reversed, the Hanged Man delays himself from the eventual outcome. When this card appears in your reading, you need to remember that it's okay to let go. You don't need to worry about the past anymore; once you really change consciousness, you can't go back there anyway. That's what growth is all about.

The desire of the Hanged Man reversed is to slow down the progress of events that are, in the end, inevitable. He's hung up (pun intended) on the past and hung up on the future, indecisive and vacillating between them. The Hanged Man reversed is stuck on maintaining his old image rather than what he's become. He has a fear of making a sacrifice, a fear of letting go and letting God or the other side help. This card can also indicate a resistance to spiritual teachings or other lessons that might help you.

In the Cards

The archetype the Hanged Man represents tends to be reserved for those we hold in high spiritual acclaim, like Jesus, Buddha, Muhammad, and the Dalai Lama. To move on to a new phase, you must first accept what's come before. Acceptance of what you're going to leave behind is one of life's hardest tasks. It's no wonder we revere those who've accomplished it.

Death (Key 13): The Power of Regeneration

Death (key 13).

Your initial reactions to Death:

_____

_____

Keywords: Transformation

Rebirth

Renewal

Time to move on

Archetypes: The Wicked Witch of the West

Sauron

The King is dead! Long live the King!

Your big move

Numerology and astrology: The Death card is represented by the number 13 or 4. The number itself suggests the closure of something old with something new arriving to replace it. Death represents a transitional process with the certain outcome of a new start and a new life. The Death card represents the Scorpio zodiac sign, the most mysterious sign of all. Rebirth, transformation, and change for one's highest good are represented by this sign. Scorpio knows that transition and rebirth can only mean better things to come.

In the Cards

"Oh no! The Death card!" If you haven't said this yourself, you've probably heard it from someone else when this card came up in a reading. The truth is the Death card comes up a lot whenever people are going through a change of attitude or lifestyle, as they realize that their old way is truly obsolete. Death signifies that it's time to move on, for the old to make way for the new. Arlene never predicts the death of a loved one or the Querent in a reading, and neither does the Death card. It might help to think of this card as one of transformation and beginnings rather than one of finality.

Upright imagery: A black-armored skeleton rides an armored white horse toward a priest, a woman and child, and the fallen king. He carries the banner of life, and the five-petalled rose in the banner signifies change and rejuvenation. Note that although death and destruction lie at the horse's feet, the sun is rising yellow and hopeful, and the priest seems to feel that death offers the promise of a new day.

Upright meanings: When Death appears upright in a reading, it signifies renewal, transformation, or a total change in your life cycle. An old chapter is coming to a close when this card shows up. For one thing to live, another must die, and Death is really about major change and the leaving behind that comes with it.

You can't live in the past if it no longer has any substance or application to where you are now. After "Death," the birth of new ideas follows. You'll take off in your new direction, and the horse will go between the two pillars and find the sun again. When Death appears in a reading, we can truly say that the old will be gone and the new will follow.

The Death card depicts the cycles of life and death, and the ebbs and flows that go along with these cycles. The symbolism here is the constant circulation of the life force. Even if we aren't aware of it, life has a constant flow of change, a circular flow, always returning to its source.

Think, for example, about how people say, "When I was a child, we didn't do things this way. My, how things have changed since my generation!" Your parents said it, their parents said it, and soon, if you haven't already, you'll be saying it, too. That's because the cycle repeats itself over and over again, from generation to generation. The Death card reminds us that the more things change, the more they stay the same, but sometimes it takes a major transformation to get there.

Reversed imagery and meanings: When Death is reversed, the horse can no longer move well, and his lack of action means there's no movement ahead. The skeleton will fall off the horse, and his banner won't be seen by anyone.

Death reversed indicates stagnation, inertia, stalemates, complications, political upheaval, or that what you're doing seems to have come to a standstill. Revolution or strife may be indicated by this card. The crisis continues, it says, and there seems to be constant battling, with no end in sight. When Death reversed appears in your reading, you probably have the desire to call it quits, but the event itself won't quit. Instead, the war goes on, the tension continues to mount, and the horse doesn't die but is instead sick or immobile, and you meet blockages at every turn.

This card suggests that you regroup and see if you really want to take this particular path. Perhaps you should just stop, camp out, and rest until dawn. For now, the warrior (you) is tired of trying to initiate a change. Death reversed can mean the future is delayed, but a new start, new treaty, or new direction is coming. Sometimes this card comes up when someone is very enthusiastic about something. When this happens, it might mean delays and stagnation will occur in the projects they want to initiate.

Temperance (Key 14): Patience and Adaptation

Temperance (key 14).

Your initial reactions to Temperance:

_____

_____

Keywords:	Patience
	Adaptation
	Self-discipline
	Cooperation
Archetypes:	Penelope (Odysseus's wife)
	Aunt Em
	Nelson Mandela
	Your dog

Numerology and astrology: The Temperance card is represented by the number 14 or 5—to change and transform again and again, but this time with patience. Temperance suggests the need to adapt and cooperate with conditions rather than give them up. The Cancer zodiac sign represents this card. The two cups in Michael's hands, moving the water back and forth again and again, show that he needs to keep the water in the cups and be patient with the process. Patience is a virtue—both in this card and in life!

Upright imagery: In the Temperance card, Michael, one of the archangels, is pouring the essence of life from a silver cup to a golden one. Symbolically, the water flows from the subconscious to the conscious, from the unseen to the seen and back again. The archangel is coordinating the flow of the past to the present into the future. The square on the angel's breast is foursquare reality (earth), and the triangle with the square is that of spirit manifest on earth. Michael is well balanced, with one foot on the water and one foot on land; water (emotions) and earth (logic) are perfectly balanced in this card.

Upright meanings: When Temperance appears upright, it indicates self-control or a good sense of balance with people management. Temperance is able to coordinate the work of many and to work in harmony with others. This card indicates good management skills and an understanding of other people's skills.

When this card appears in your reading, its lesson is to have patience with others; work with and not against them. Harmony can prevail if we all work together, after all. To have good balance in your feelings about life, you need to learn patience and develop an understanding of where other people are coming from. Temperance tells you to learn to go with the flow. Patience and perseverance are what's at stake here—learn them and prosper.

> **Wheel of Fortune**
>
> Someone we know (hint: her first name is Arlene) kept getting Temperance reversed in her readings. "Again?" she always asked her reader. Arlene kept getting this card because *she needed to learn its lesson,* namely, *patience.* Arlene still gets Temperance reversed sometimes; some lessons are just particularly hard for us to learn, no matter what the cards tell us!

Reversed imagery and meanings: When Temperance appears upside down, the rainbow around the angel's head is not strong and the wings no longer have the power to take flight. The balance of land and water has changed, too; the water, which represents our emotions, seems to be the focus. The water will fall from the two cups as well, again representing emotions out of control.

Temperance reversed can indicate impatience or intolerance of others. This might result in poor business management due to not listening to other people's complaints, or unfortunate combinations in business or personal life. A lack of good judgment might also be present.

Perhaps you want everything to move fast, or you're getting pushy in order to get things done your way. Others might seem to be in the way of your ideas, or it might appear to you that they're moving way too slowly. Although various obstacles may be causing things to take too long, remember that if you run too fast, you might miss something great. Take it from two speedsters who get Temperance reversed far too often—slow down and smell the roses!

The Devil (Key 15): Confronting Materialism

The Devil (key 15).

Your initial reactions to the Devil:

_____

_____

Keywords: Bondage to the material world

Temptation

Addictions—to anything

Obsessions

Archetypes: The Wicked Witch of the West's flying monkeys

Anthony Hopkins as Hannibal "The Cannibal" Lecter

The Black Riders from *Lord of the Rings*

Those who seek to control you

Numerology and astrology: The Devil card is represented by number 15 or 6, the condition of obligation or of being tied to others through fear. Obsessive-compulsive lessons are being learned with this card. The Capricorn zodiac sign represents this card as well, and—as any Capricorn can tell you—people in this sign can become deeply entrenched in responsibility and obligations. Therefore, a need exists to form sometimes deeper, heavier bonds than necessary. The highs of ecstasy to the depths of despair are both part of what this card represents.

Upright imagery: The Devil sits on a half-cube, which signifies the half-knowledge we have if we look only at the material side of life. There's nothing wrong with having a little fun, but this Devil wants to keep the couple we saw before in the Lovers chained to something, such as fear or ignorance. The Devil's batwings and the inverted pentagram represent the sensory side of life. And those chains? Well, remember Aretha Franklin singing, "Chain, chain, chain … chain of Fools"?

Upright meanings: In its upright position, the Devil card represents sensuality, bondage to fears, or sexual energy that seems a little out of control. It could indicate an addiction—to anyone, anything, or the way things ought to be. Maybe you're obsessed with an old boyfriend or girlfriend, or obsessed with a fear. It could be you're paranoid or somehow focused on one thing and one thing only.

This card can also indicate the wrong use of force or abusive conditions. This is where we find the dark side of humankind, the controlling of others for the purpose of self-gain. If you have an addiction to anything from sex to drugs to rock 'n' roll, the Devil probably made you do it.

Although the figures are chained to the Devil, those chains can easily be released. The Devil is really that part of ourselves that likes to delve into the dark side once in a while to find out about human nature in its most possessive form. We've all been obsessed with something or someone before—and we will be again. That's what the Devil reminds us of.

Reversed imagery and meanings: Reversing the Devil means letting go of obsession, letting go of your fears of the dark side, or freeing yourself from an addiction. In the Devil reversed, the inverted pentagram becomes a star, so the goodness comes back into the card. When this happens, you don't have to let fear control you. You have the power to release the chains of bondage at any time in your life.

Sometimes this card can come up if you're being weak or ineffectual or if you're starting to get yourself back together again after a long battle. This could be due to an addiction, fear, or something that's taken control over you in the past.

The Devil reversed gives you the freedom to go into your future with no chains, with nothing holding you back. This card means you're free of your own self-imposed prison or restrictions. It's only when you lose your fears that true freedom comes. When it does, the Devil will be just a figment of your imagination. Remember, the Force is with you.

The Tower (Key 16): Facing the Unexpected

The Tower (key 16).

Your initial reactions to the Tower:

_____

_____

Keywords:	Expect the unexpected
	A bolt from the blue!
	Surprise!
	You could have knocked me over with a feather!
Archetypes:	Dorothy's house in Kansas (that killed the witch)
	The lightning bolt of Thor
	The tall, dark stranger
	Your wildest dreams

Numerology and astrology: The Tower card is represented by the number 16 or 7. This number represents a sudden, out-of-left-field change. Whoa, didn't see that one coming! Sometimes when change happens in our lives, it sends us into an introspective state. At those times, the card becomes 7, or the surprise brings us to some kind of deep search prompted by asking "Why?" The Tower card is also represented by the astrological sign Aquarius, the sign of sudden change and enlightenment. Erratic and unpredictable, the Tower and Aquarius open our minds to the "What if?" and "How on earth did that happen?" questions.

Upright imagery: Man, oh, man, look at this card. A bolt of lightning has struck a gray tower, setting it on fire, knocking off the king's crown, and sending everybody flying. Raindrops are flying, too, in the form of the Hebrew letter yod, which is symbolic of the hand of God. The symbolism of this card can be thought of as a fall from grace or banishment from the Garden of Eden. All in all, things aren't looking good.

Upright meanings: This card used to be called the Tower of God or the Tower of Babel. It represents the unexpected events that can change your life or your perception of things. The clearest aspect of this card is the element of surprise, but it's no surprise that this card has come up for global events that shocked the world. For this reason, the energy of this card can represent the events of September 11 and similar cases around the world about which we had no control or prior knowledge of. The Tower indicates a rude awakening of some sort, whether it's your old way of life coming suddenly to an end or a release from a situation in which you were stuck.

But the Tower may also forecast a wonderful unexpected event, such as a new baby. It might be "Some Enchanted Evening" when "you might see a stranger/across a crowded room." The Tower might be the accident that forces you to reevaluate your values or lifestyle, or the wrong turn that causes you to end up in Oz's Emerald City. Life is full of these dramatic surprises, which in turn make us look at our own lives. After the Tower card happens—whether to us or our community—we never are the same again. Still, it has a good side: The events of the Tower card often lead us to connect with others in our community. As a teacher of Arlene's once said: Crisis brings out the humanity in all of us.

The Tower can also be something that no one expected or an upsetting event of some kind. If you thought you had that new job and then the company decided not to follow through on the offer, the Tower, sometimes called a reversal of fortune, is at play. You can't plan for what the Tower will offer up, though, because there's no way to know what it will be. That's why it's called "unexpected," right?

Reversed imagery and meanings: When you turn the Tower upside down, the people are flying up instead of down. The bolt is coming from below, from—you guessed it—the Devil in key 15. The people still don't look entirely happy, but it's quite possible that all is not lost. Something that initially shocked you might be coming to an end soon, or maybe you'll soon be able to start over, putting the chaos and disruption behind you.

The Tower reversed can also indicate a feeling that life isn't giving you a fair shake. Maybe you feel as if circumstances are conspiring against you, and that no matter what you do, you'll never come out on top—as if you were, like these people, trying to fly without wings. You might feel backed into a corner or stuck in a situation with no way out. This card is telling you to pay the piper and listen to the music. It's time to face what you've been avoiding so you can get on with the rest of your life.

The Least You Need to Know

- The Hanged Man slows things down while you make your decisions to move ahead. He helps you let go of the old so you can make way for the new.

- Death represents your major, transformative, life-changing experiences.

- Temperance reminds you to be tolerant and patient as you go through life.

- The Devil stands for your base instincts, the things that are not so good for you but that we all have to face once in a while.

- The Tower is all about unexpected change, both good and not so good. This card reminds us that we can't plan for everything.

The Fool in Tune with the Universe

In This Chapter

- The Star (key 17)
- The Moon (key 18)
- The Sun (key 19)
- Judgement (key 20)
- The World (key 21)

By the time you arrive at the last five cards of the Major Arcana, you've earned the right to the hope and success they assure you. There's no question your journey's been fraught with trial and error, bumps and false starts, but now you get to reap what you sowed along the way. The Star, the Moon, the Sun, Judgement, and the World are the cards of the Fool's successful return to the fold after his hero's journey into the great unknown. Here is where the Fool tunes in to that celestial music, the harmony of the spheres!

Look to the Skies

Just as the ancients looked to the skies for divine inspiration, the last five cards of the Tarot's Major Arcana archetypically represent the rewards you'll find at the end of the Fool's long, arduous journey. From the hope of the Star to the completion signified by the World, here's where you'll find the fruits of your labor and the affirmation of your goals.

What do these cards hold for you? Take a few moments to respond to them on your own before you read our interpretations.

The Star (Key 17): Hope and Faith

The Star (key 17).

Your initial reactions to the Star:

_____

_____

Keywords: Hope

Faith

Over the rainbow

When you wish upon a star …

Archetypes: Dorothy from Kansas

Cinderella's fairy godmother

Princess Diana

Your hopes and wishes for *your* life

Numerology and astrology: The Star is represented by the number 17 or 8—hope and prosperity of the spiritual kind. Although the difficulties will be known, the lessons of hope, faith, and charity will prevail. The zodiac sign that represents the Star is Aquarius, the sign that is connected to humanitarianism and understanding that we are all human.

Upright imagery: A beautiful woman kneels at a pond's edge, holding two urns of water. She pours one on the land (the material universe or earth) and the other into the pond or pool of water (emotions and imagination). This card tells us to dream is to create. The water of life the woman pours will bring new life through new hope.

The woman of the Star is inspired from above by the eight-pointed radiant star of spiritual energy and truth. The seven smaller stars represent the wisdom she has; she's already realized, for example, that life has many miracles, and her experiences have never taken away her faith about life or humankind. There's always hope, the Star assures us, and to confirm this, the sacred ibis rests in the tree of the mind and sends messages from heaven to focus and concentrate on her wishes.

Upright meanings: The Star upright always focuses on affirming a positive attitude toward whatever you want to accomplish. Courage, hope, and inspiration from above are this card's messages. She believes all things (including any wish you might have) can come into being and anything can manifest simply because you wish it so. Whether it's good health, good energy, or an optimistic attitude, the Star will win the day and make things happen.

In the Cards

The Star card is often used as a card of meditation. To calm down after a hard day, take out the Star card and meditate on it for a while. It really does calm the heart and mind. Its cool water, tranquil skies, green fields, and peaceful, relaxed state will make you feel the same way. Say to yourself, *I believe things will improve,* and just as Dorothy was whisked back to Kansas, you'll find the Star's peace and tranquility are also yours. That's because the Star doesn't just *think* things will get better, she *knows* they will. So use the Star's faith to bolster your own.

The Star also indicates that great love will be given and received. An insight is being made here into the meaning of life, and with that knowledge, the Star continues to create more for everyone. She believes plenty of worldly goods exist for all and that everyone can share in life's abundance—or at least have the faith that anything can change for the better.

Reversed imagery and meanings: When we turn the Star over, the stars are now falling away from the woman, and her waters are falling back into the urns. It's almost as if good energy is being taken back or that water and earth will mix together and create a muddy mess. The stars in the sky are dimming, too, so not much hope exists here. It feels as if she's no longer flowing with the universe.

When the Star appears reversed in a reading, it can indicate that, at least for now, all hope is dashed. The lights fade, the bird stops singing, and it's altogether much too quiet. The woman appears nearly sullen or moody, and it may be necessary to apply reserved energy here. Something you've hoped for might not happen as you idealized. The Star reversed may mean you're doubtful, pessimistic, stubborn, or ill at ease about a situation. Or you may be confused or lack faith that things will work out. A loss of friendship could also be indicated with this card or sometimes it represents a health problem, either physical or mental.

You might feel as if nothing will ever change when this card comes up for you. But instead of becoming more despondent, let this card encourage you to read, meditate, or ask for help from others who will encourage you to reach a higher state of mind. You need to move past your lack of confidence and find the faith that your life—and the Star card—will turn around.

The Moon (Key 18): Nurturing Imagination

The Moon (key 18).

Your initial reactions to the Moon:

_____

_____

Keywords: Imagination

Psychic development

Unforeseen changes

Things aren't always what they seem

Archetypes: *The Secret Garden*

Mother Nature

The knowledge Dorothy had all along

Your hidden side

Numerology and astrology: The Moon is represented by the number 18 or 9, which suggests the need to master a high level on the psychic realm. "Can you read the group consciousness?" the Moon and number 18/9 ask. "Can you feel the energy of many people's emotions?" Universality and the desire for attunement to our imaginative side are represented by 18/9 as well. Is it real or it is an illusion—that is the question! Not surprisingly, Cancer and Pisces are the zodiac signs that rule this card of psychic and emotional attunement. Feelings and sensitivity to human emotions and human needs are intrinsic to both Cancer, Pisces, and the Moon card.

In the Cards

The Moon and the High Priestess are sisters in the Major Arcana. When the Moon appears in your reading, it means you've just gone a notch higher in your development. Just as the High Priestess is a young goddess archetype, the Moon represents a more mature one. You could think of the High Priestess as Dorothy before she gets to Oz, and the Moon as Dorothy when she gets back to Kansas with all her newfound knowledge about herself.

Upright imagery: A dog and a wolf bay at the Moon in its full phase, representing the domesticated and the wild, the tamed and the untamed. The pool of water represents the imagination and the subconscious, and a crayfish crawls from the pool—is he friend or foe? Will that crayfish walk away, or is he going to bite? In other words, is he disciplined or undisciplined?

The two pillars again represent the theme of duality—in this case, good and evil. The path goes between the pillars because in life we walk through a lot of different emotional experiences, with the ups and downs emotion inevitably brings. In the Spanish tradition, *la luna*—the moon—is sometimes psychic and sometimes crazy, and this is a good metaphor for this card. It's well known that both people and animals react to the full moon every month and that when the moon begins to wane, everything calms down again.

Upright meanings: When the Moon appears upright, it can herald unforeseen events or a new turn of events already in motion. Sometimes it can mean a disagreement with the one you love or an emotional outburst over something very little—making a mountain out of a molehill. The Moon intensifies everyone's emotions, just as it pulls the tides in and out.

The Moon also reflects psychic ability, dreams, and intuitive powers. It gives you the ability to prophesize universally. When you feel something big is coming, whether it's a change of residence, career, or in your own emotions, the Moon will appear to confirm your intuition. This card also indicates nocturnal activity, or things that happen at night.

Reversed imagery and meanings: Now here's a card that seems to shine a lot more light in its reversed position. That's because instead of being full, it's now a *new* moon. A new moon indicates harnessed imagination, and when this card is reversed, the moon is setting rather than rising. The dog and wolf seem to have calmed down, the crayfish goes back into the water, and the animals rest now.

When the Moon appears reversed in a reading, it indicates that your imagination will be harnessed by good common sense. You'll take practical considerations into account and be cautious not to make any rash decisions. Any change that occurs now won't be disruptive.

Reversed, the Moon allows all truth to come to the surface. This means that people will tell you what they're really feeling—without theatrics and without being overly emotional. The Moon reversed assures us that love and understanding will win in the end and that all misunderstandings will be cleared, thank goodness. Communications will have clarity, and good psychic information will come forth as well. This is a card that clears the slate.

The Sun (Key 19): Enjoying Contentment

The Sun (key 19).

Your initial reactions to the Sun:

_____

_____

Keywords: Contentment

Enjoying a peaceful life

Happy unions/partnerships

Pleasure

Archetypes: Snoopy

The Munchkins

Your children and grandchildren

Your own inner child

Numerology and astrology: The Sun is represented by the number 19 or 1, the initiate who begins a new life aware of all the lessons learned on the earth plane. Happy and content with life and living is 19/1. He maintains his individuality while cooperating with others. The Leo zodiac sign rules this card of happiness and success in home, family, and career. All is well and prosperous for the proud lion and his family in this card.

Upright imagery: A big, brilliant sun shines down upon a little boy on a strong horse. The child is open, with nothing to hide, and carries the red banner of life. He holds the banner in his right hand (the subconscious) and passes it to his left hand (the conscious). He's been successful in learning his lessons. "You did it!" this card says; you've learned a skill well.

What lessons the child (yes, the Fool, again) has finally mastered! The four sunflowers represent the four elements of the Tarot—air, earth, fire, and water—which we'll soon be seeing more of in the Minor Arcana. These sunflowers are turned toward the boy and horse to continue their development, because that's where the brightest light is. The horse represents the freedom of movement, travel, and progress toward goals. The walled garden reflects the growth and development of humankind.

Upright meanings: The upright Sun promises happiness and success in all your lessons. You'll have a good marriage, a good home life, and success in all you do. Success is also indicated in such areas as higher education, agriculture, the sciences, and the arts. You've become a master of your talent, the Sun says. Your studies in life are completed. Congratulations, you've graduated!

Happiness and pleasure come from within, so enjoy your success and happy memories of your childhood. You can reflect on the past, review how well you've done, and bask in your well-earned glory. Travel and the freedom to move around are also represented by the upright Sun, and this could mean new career offers or simply happiness with the good life, satisfied and content.

Reversed imagery and meanings: The Sun doesn't shine as well when the card is reversed, and the child and horse don't have the same movement or momentum. The sunflowers can't grow and develop correctly either. The Sun reversed indicates delays in getting a lesson, so the future will seem clouded and accomplishment far away.

Fools Rush In

Is your partner not talking? Is the textbook you're studying a little over your head? Is your goal stubbornly just out of reach? The Sun reversed is telling you to ask someone for direction. The Yellow Brick Road is not far away; all you need is for someone to point you in the right direction.

The Sun reversed might indicate trouble understanding what a delay is all about. Perhaps your home life or marriage is at a crossroads. It's likely that development and growth in this particular phase have stopped. You might be stuck on some childhood memory or be suffering from low self-esteem.

The path you're on is rocky, and you feel you haven't completed or mastered the situation correctly—or at least not enough to make you feel satisfied. When the Sun appears reversed in a reading, counsel and optimism are needed. The issue might require more study so you can figure out what needs to be corrected.

Judgement (Key 20): The Awakening

Judgement (key 20).

Your initial reactions to Judgement:

_____

_____

Keywords: A cosmic wake-up call

The great *a-ha!*

Clarity

A change in consciousness

Archetypes: The Force

Dorothy's ruby slippers

Beethoven's *Ode to Joy*

I have seen the light!

Numerology and astrology: The Judgement card is represented by the number 20 or 2, and it signifies a cooperation with the higher spiritual forces in your life. With this card, you come into communion with your religious or spiritual ideas and practice them daily. You walk your talk, so to speak! Apply all of what you have learned and then even more understanding comes of your own journey. The Scorpio zodiac sign is represented by this card as well. Scorpio is about resurrection to a higher level, seeking the mysteries of life and discovering them. What insight Scorpio brings to life: Open the door and the truth is revealed!

Upright imagery: In this card, the angel Gabriel is blowing seven blasts on his horn to awaken humankind from its earthly state. "Look up," he says. "All things will be known!" Aroused by the music from above, people rise from their coffins to realize there's more to life than meets the eye; a greater purpose exists for everything we do and how we do it.

The cross on the angel's banner is red and white. The red represents a passion for life, and the white, spiritual attainment and purity of spirit. This banner represents balanced forces in nature and heaven. As above, so below.

Upright meanings: In its upright position, Judgement signals an awakening, a coming alive to a change of awareness. This card indicates self-actualization, a life well lived, and work well done. You're on the verge of blending with the universe and have renewed energy now that you're so close.

This card often comes up when you're trying to improve your health or well-being. It indicates a desire for something higher or better than where you are now. We call it the great aha of life because you'll be saying, "Oh, now I've got the picture," "I didn't realize that," or "Gee, I never thought I'd learn something new, but here it is." All these statements reflect your own awareness toward life and its mystery. Judgement represents that you'll understand something you hadn't or that you'll suddenly realize something existed that you'd never thought of before. Cool!

Reversed imagery and meanings: Judgement reversed is a card in which the people don't have control over the ocean or the coffins and don't know whether or not to listen to the seven blasts of the horn. They can't hear the true nature of a situation, and confusion is taking place on the seas of life.

Gabriel is still blasting away, but when Judgement is reversed, he's not being heard by the one who has this card. Are you denying the inevitable? Do you have a fear of failure or a fear of being judged? Judgement reversed might be trying to tell you to listen.

Fools Rush In

Some people are afraid of this card because of how it looks. Maybe it has something to do with the old Armageddon thing, the end of the world as we know it. But what *is* Armageddon anyway? It's a condition that's happened on earth over and over again throughout history, an old way making way for a new one. The unknown is always scary, but where would we be if brave folks hadn't ventured out into it before us?

Judgement reversed can indicate a fear of losing control or a fear that you won't find happiness. Sometimes it shows a lack of interest or awareness in the spiritual side of life, or possible losses or delays in realizing a higher spiritual calling. This card cautions you to take care not to be superstitious, but instead to believe that all conditions of life have a higher purpose. There's a reason, in other words, for everything—even though some of those things are not very pleasant.

The World (Key 21): Attainment and Self-Actualization

The World (key 21).

Your initial reactions to the World:

_____

_____

Keywords: Final attainment

Triumph in all areas

Karmic lessons complete

Liberation

Archetypes: The winner and still champion

The Return of the King

Dorothy getting back to Kansas

You have it all!

Numerology and astrology: The World card is represented by the number 21 or 3. It stands for the culmination of work well done, life well lived, and the accomplishments you have worked toward, as well as blessings from above and from the people you have worked with. The number 3 is associated with knowing that your skills and lessons have been mastered, so the Capricorn zodiac sign is represented by the World card as well, because the positive side of Saturn-ruled Capricorn is to climb every mountain and continue with growth. You will make it to the other side of the mountain. Business success and personal achievements are the focus of Capricorn—all of it!

Upright imagery: A maiden is dancing, holding two wands in her hands. One wand is the power of involution and the other is the power of evolution, so she has the power to connect to all the lessons previously learned. Now she's ready to understand why she's here and what she's accomplished, and she's ready to grow into a new phase of life, accepting the responsibility of life on this earth.

The four mystical creatures from the Wheel of Fortune are here, too, now evolved into their full potential in the World card. The wreath surrounding the maiden represents universality and blending with a global perspective.

Upright meanings: In its upright position, the World promises the fulfillment of all desires and goals as well as an understanding of all the lessons you've been through. Here's the freedom to move ahead and continue your growth the way you want to. You now have all the talents and all the tools, so go for it!

You have the ability to make others happy and are aware of what their gifts are. A change could be taking place for the better in your home or career, or you may be arriving at a cosmic state of consciousness. There might be travel—in comfort, now that you've arrived. The World upright indicates the freedom to come and go as you please. You've earned the path of liberation, your karmic reward.

Reversed imagery and meanings: When the World is reversed, the maiden will lose her wands and her scarf will come off. Energy or power leaves, and a failure to learn or integrate the former lessons occurs. Upside down, she's no longer totally aware of what's going on around her. There might be a fear of change, or the home might be threatened in some way.

The World reversed can indicate a lack of vision or a refusal to learn from your experiences. It's possible you could walk off the path you were on. At any rate, your journey is postponed or frustrated for now. It could have been better—and it still could be—but more concentration is required and more work must be done first. This is not a traumatic card or a negative card reversed, but it does indicate that more must be done or more must be accomplished before you attain the upright position of security. Total self-actualization—the World upright—can be yours. You're almost there already!

The most important use of the Tarot is to make us think about our lives and reach toward our goals with patience. The Tarot gives us an understanding that anything good takes time and some introspection. The lessons of the Major Arcana are lessons we learn again and again as we journey throughout our lives.

The Least You Need to Know

- The Star represents your wishes come true and your dreams fulfilled. This card promises hope and faith for the future.

- The Moon puts you in touch with your intuitive and emotional natures. It fires the imagination.

- The Sun promises success—a bright, sunshiny day and an optimistic outlook.

- Judgement helps us see things we haven't seen before. This card is one of rejuvenation and renewal.

- The World is the card of universal attainment and mastery. It is the journey's end, the culmination of the Fool's efforts.

Part 4

The Minor Arcana: Wands, Cups, Swords, and Pentacles

The 56 Minor Arcana cards stand for the events in every person's archetypal day. Through their symbolism, these cards represent everyday events and the things you have choices about. Minor Arcana cards are divided into four suits, which represent the four areas of life:

- ◆ Wands: Enterprise

- ◆ Cups: The emotional

- ◆ Swords: Conflict

- ◆ Pentacles: The material

Together these cards add up to anything that can happen to you.

Chapter 12

Everyday Cards

In This Chapter

◆ The Minor Arcana cards

◆ Free Will and your everyday choices

◆ Some Minor Arcana in combination

◆ The four suits: Wands, Cups, Swords, and Pentacles

Now that you've successfully completed your journey through the Major Arcana, you're ready to deal with life on a day-to-day basis. That's what the 56 *Minor Arcana* cards of the Tarot deck are all about. These cards deal with every eventuality a life can offer, from careers to relationships, from emotions to cold, hard cash. They represent the choices we make in our everyday lives.

Where should I go for lunch? Should I buy that suit? How about a date with so and so? Should I accept that job in sales? All these questions are addressed by the Minor Arcana cards, the Tarot cards of your own Free Will.

The Small Mysteries

Our study of the Minor Arcana returns to the four elements—fire, water, air, and earth—Tarot uses to represent the human condition and the use of your Free Will. The elements are also important in a study of astrology. Each element, and each of the Minor Arcana suits, represents an area of life:

Card Catalog

The astrological **elements**—fire, earth, air, and water—represent the basic qualities of the signs and of life.

- ◆ **Fire** is represented by Wands and is connected to enterprise and project development.

- ◆ **Water** is represented by Cups and is the element of emotions and matters of the heart.

- ◆ **Air** characterizes Swords and is all about mental activity and decisive action.

- ◆ **Earth** is represented by Pentacles and is the element of the material and earthly world.

Element	Astrological Signs	Minor Arcana Suit
Fire	Aries, Leo, Sagittarius	Wands
Earth	Taurus, Virgo, Capricorn	Pentacles
Air	Gemini, Libra, Aquarius	Swords
Water	Cancer, Scorpio, Pisces	Cups

In the Major Arcana cards, these astrological equivalents can be found: Leo, the lion, for fire; Scorpio, the eagle, for water; Aquarius, the angel, for air; and Taurus, the bull, for earth. We've already seen astrological signs in the Wheel of Fortune and World cards, and we'll be seeing a lot more of them as we make our way through the Minor Arcana.

Every Choice You Make

We know you've got questions, and we also know you often can't remember what those questions are when it comes time to ask them (we know *we* can't!). So we've devised a set of questions for you to use when you want to ask the cards to address those matters closest to your heart, your wallet, your ego, and your mind:

- ◆ Do you need help making a decision about your job or career? Your answer will be found in Wands, the cards of your goals and ambitions.

- ◆ Are you wondering whether a relationship is worth your efforts? Your answer will be found in Cups, the cards of your emotions.

- Does it seem as if a situation you're in is full of conflict or problems? The answer will be found in Swords, the cards of how you act and interact.

- Are you worried about money or trying to decide about an investment? The answer will be found in Pentacles, the cards of the material things in your life.

More Free Will Cards Exist Than Destiny Cards

Out of the 78 Tarot cards, the Minor Arcana consists of 56 cards, which represent humankind. In these cards, you'll find your ability to choose or select conditions to work with as you live your day-to-day life.

In any life, many choices will be made. We like to think of these as choices along the road. Do you take the high road or the low road? The little winding lane or the free-way? The left fork or the right? When it comes to decisions like these, you have the Free Will to choose, and the Minor Arcana represent those choices that *you* make.

So although the 22 Major Arcana cards represent things that are destined to occur or karmic issues you've got very little choice about working on in this life, the 56 cards we're looking at now allow you to make choices, to choose your fate. Using your Free Will, those choices shape the lessons you *choose* to learn. So there you have it: Not everything is written in stone. Only a few guidelines are available for how to live your life; you get to choose the rest.

In the Cards

Does it seem sometimes as if you keep butting your head against the same lesson over and over again? When that happens, you're dealing with something you're *fated* to learn, a Major Arcana issue of karma. Whether it's consistently picking the wrong type of partner or always misplacing your car keys, if it happens again and again, it's a Major Arcana issue. Although the Minor Arcana can help you learn how to make better choices about these things, they are lessons you have to learn—with or without your help.

What Suits You?

In addition to being correlated with the elements, the suits of the Minor Arcana have their equivalents in the regular deck of playing cards. Thinking about the meanings of these suits can help you identify them more easily. Each suit has a keyword and an image associated with it, as shown in the following table.

Tarot	Playing Cards	Keyword	Image
Wands	Clubs	Enterprise	Waving a magic wand
Cups	Hearts	Emotion	A cupful of joy
Swords	Spades	Action	A sword fight
Pentacles	Diamonds	Money	Counting your money

As with learning anything new, remembering what each suit represents takes time. We hope these words and pictures will help reduce that time a little. We'll repeat them for you as we talk about each suit individually, too.

All About Wands

Keywords: Enterprise, growth

Key image: Waving a magic wand

Element: Fire

Corresponding astrological signs: Aries, Leo, Sagittarius

Go ahead; take that Wand. Its power belongs to you.

Card Catalog

Wands are the suit of enterprise, growth, and development.

Wands represent our ability to dive into our work world, our ambition, growth, and development. These are the cards of our enthusiasm for life and our enthusiasm for living it.

Wands were originally called staffs, which were used to carry fires at night. Wands brought light into wherever the darkness was and are also a symbol of authority or personal power.

Wands are associated with the element of fire and are made out of green wood that still has a few twigs, which represents growth. In the Minor Arcana cards, Wands are used for everything from clubs for fighting, to staffs to carry victors' crowns, to walking sticks to lean on. With this in mind, it's easy to see that the position Wands take within a reading will tell us whether they'll be used for a constructive or destructive outcome.

Wands are associated with the world of creation and ideas, with manifesting something to make it real, just like a magic wand. *Poof*—it appears! Wands are helping us create this book, and Wands are helping you use it for good purpose.

All About Cups

> **Keywords:** Emotion, sensitivity
>
> **Key image:** A cupful of joy
>
> **Element:** Water
>
> **Corresponding astrological signs:** Cancer, Scorpio, Pisces

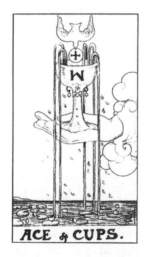

Drink from the Cup and get in touch with your feelings.

Cups stand for how we perceive our emotions. Here's where we find our feelings and sensitivity for others, our joys, our artistic selves—and a good, old-fashioned cry. Cups indicate matters of the heart.

The suit of Cups is associated with water, which is the symbol of the subconscious mind and instincts. Cups represent the heart-centered connections we have, such as attachments to people, animals, or anything we have an emotional response to.

Card Catalog

Cups are the cards of emotion and sensitivity.

The association of Cups with water, and of water with emotional issues, is rooted in the fact that cups hold water. Cups are filled with water from above, the symbolic wine of life. This represents the joys—and the sorrows—of living, and Cups are in fact called the happy suit, although they're sometimes the sadder suit as well because they deal with all human emotion. If you're looking for love, Cups is the suit you'd like to see come up in your spread.

All About Swords

Keywords: Action, mental ability

Key image: A sword fight

Element: Air

Corresponding astrological signs: Gemini, Libra, Aquarius

Grab that Sword and get ready for action!

Swords represent our mind and mental ability, including how we think, our logic and reasoning, and our ability to know what to do through the use of good, old-fashioned common sense. At the same time, Swords can be symbolic of strife or aggressive behavior, but remember, these also start in the mind.

Card Catalog

Swords are the cards of mental activity and action.

When we look at the cards in the Swords suit, we often find fighting, acts of aggression, or people in some kind of misfortune. Sometimes these cards can be graphic, and it's for a reason. Swords can cut two ways: for either constructive or destructive purposes.

Swords symbolize what we can do to each other when we're fearful or threatened. In these circumstances, we can either act or react in a way that causes trauma instead of enlightenment.

All About Pentacles

Keywords: Money, possessions

Key image: Counting your money

Element: Earth

Corresponding astrological signs: Taurus, Virgo, Capricorn

Take possession of that Pentacle and count your riches.

Pentacles represent our connection to the material world and focus us on financial issues and goods, on shelter, and on earthly things like clothing, home, and financial success. Pentacles can indicate material gain and abundance of the land, or they can represent difficulties with handling finances; it all depends on the cards and their placement.

Except for the 5 of Pentacles, this suit shows people working away at developing resources or enjoying the fruits of their labors. Pentacles are actually the coinlike discs shown in these cards. They're inscribed with pentagrams, which are five-pointed stars that are symbolic of man's earthly presence.

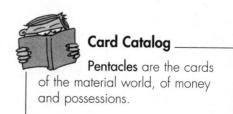

Card Catalog

Pentacles are the cards of the material world, of money and possessions.

Pentacles represent the financial success or material gains you can develop in your life. Here is where you'll find your riches or your prosperity. Labor, hard work, and industrious efforts pay off and bring Pentacles into your spreads. These cards might appear when you ask a question about money, future money, wealth, or security. Pentacles also show up when you're gambling or thinking about investing.

The Minor Arcana in Combination with Major Arcana Cards

Between the 56 Minor Arcana and the 22 Major Arcana cards, you have the full spectrum of your talents and abilities, your karmic lessons and your Free Will, and the choices you'll make to try new ideas and learn the lessons of fate. How these cards appear in combination can help you understand exactly what's going on in a given situation.

As we discussed in Chapter 7, when the majority of cards in a reading is Major Arcana (5 or more in a 10-card Celtic Cross Spread is a majority), the answer to the question is not in your hands. It might be in the hands of other people or already in the works, but you can't do much about changing anything now. Lots of Major Arcana cards in a reading signal that you're in a learning curve, so going with the flow is important. At the same time, the reader pays close attention to the fact that you're doing something with a higher purpose than you realize.

When the majority of cards in a reading is from the Minor Arcana, though, you have a lot of Free Will or choice in deciding which way the reading could turn or how you want to pursue it. More Minor Arcana cards put matters in your hands—and your fate is what *you* make it.

> **Wheel of Fortune**
>
> Do you consistently receive a lot of Minor Arcana cards in your daily Three-Card Spreads? Some people think this means that nothing significant is going on in their lives, but that's not the case at all. A majority of Minor Arcana means that *you* hold the cards, at least for now. Have a good time plotting your course!

Although Major Arcana cards represent karmic issues you must deal with whether you like it or not, you still have the Free Will to decide how you will deal with those issues. In other words, Free Will is the rule, and you use it to your advantage or detriment in dealing with karmic issues of life. So even though you might not be able to choose your "lessons," you *can* choose how you evolve or grow through them. For example, if your lesson is to break free of destructive or addictive relationships, you can choose to develop the power to do that or you can choose to remain in that lesson, even repeating it into the next life. The choice is yours!

Rising to the Challenge

Are you ready to accept the challenge of learning something new about your life? Are you ready to know what's happening on a deeper level than you knew before? Are you curious about what's at the other end of the Yellow Brick Road? Well, Toto wants to take you on a fabulous journey, so turn the page and let's get started!

Put your Wand, Cup, Sword, and Pentacle—and Dorothy's ruby slippers—in your knapsack; grab your trusty canine friend; and let's hit the Fool's road!

The Least You Need to Know

- Wands speak for your choices about growth and enterprise, your goals and ambitions. They are connected with the element of fire.

- Cups are your emotional choices, keeping you in touch with your day-to-day ups and downs, and are connected with the element of water.

- Swords point to your mental choices about action and interaction and are connected with the element of air.

- Pentacles indicate money and your material choices and are connected with the element of earth.

- When the majority of cards in your reading is Minor Arcana, your fate is in your own hands. The Minor Arcana cards represent your everyday choices.

Wands: The Fruits of Your Labors, the Tools of Your Trade

In This Chapter

◆ Wands represent enterprise, growth, and development

◆ Royal Wands: strength, energy, and new efforts

◆ Everyday Wands: how you work through things

The first Minor Arcana suit we'll be exploring is Wands. As we discussed in Chapter 12, Wands are the suit of your enterprise, growth, and development. Here's where you'll find the ways in which you approach anything new that comes into your life, whether it's with the excitement of the Ace of Wands, the fear of the 5 of Wands, or the impatience of the Knight of Wands.

The Royal Court

Royal Minor Arcana cards, or *court cards*, often take on more meaning than simply speaking for events. Sometimes they can be people in your life or an aspect of yourself. Royal cards might reveal some role you're currently playing or a role you *should* be playing in order to deal with a situation.

As you might recall from Chapter 12, Wands represent the element of fire, which in turn is connected to the Aries, Leo, and Sagittarius astrological signs. The King, Queen, and Knight of each suit correspond to those astrological signs more directly, as you'll find out in the following paragraphs.

King of Wands: Leadership and Ambition

King of Wands.

Astrological sign: Aries

Upright imagery and meanings: What do you notice first when you look at the King of Wands? We see the lions and salamanders decorating his robe. These represent growth and new beginnings, and the lion has the pride and passion to follow through on those beginnings, too.

The regal King of Wands has the element of fire as his realm, and he holds it in a torch (wand) in his left hand. This indicates that he's a man of authority and personal power, confident in all he does. Like the astrological sign Aries, the King of Wands has an enthusiasm for life and also encourages growth and potential in others. This is a king who says, "With a positive outlook and confidence, you can do anything your heart desires."

The King of Wands is a proud, confident, enthusiastic, and kind soul, with the presence that comes with those qualities. He's also a proud father and eager to be of help—always forthcoming with advice when someone asks. The King of Wands is passionate about all he believes, and he carries himself well. He has excellent leadership qualities and can delegate well. Think of him as a mentor or father figure, good at getting people to see their own potential.

Reversed imagery and meanings: When we turn the King of Wands upside down, we find the same power—but not the same enthusiasm. Reversed, the King of Wands can represent a lack of confidence in his ability to follow through, low self-esteem, or a lack of focus for getting things done.

The King of Wands reversed has a tendency to let everything fall away because of pessimism or doubt. He's insecure and unsure of himself or others, and he might be temperamental. The King of Wands reversed can scare people away with his big roar, but like the Cowardly Lion, he's not as harsh as he seems. All reversed court cards exhibit uncertainty and fear. There might be feelings of inadequacy, hastiness, or a short fuse. The King of Wands reversed, for example, appears to be grumpy and detached.

But remember, even though they're court cards, these are still Minor Arcana. When you receive a reversed court card, *you* have the power to right yourself if you work on the issues, because *these are Free Will cards.* Just because you've received a reversed Minor Arcana in a reading doesn't mean you'll stay that way. Reversed Minor Arcana indicate momentary reversals or may be specifically about a reversal for the question asked. Unlike the Major Arcana, the Minor Arcana *can and will change to their upright positions* if and when you change consciousness.

Card Catalog

Royal Minor Arcana **cards,** or **court cards,** can stand for various aspects of yourself or for those around you. Sometimes they also stand for certain times or seasons. The royal cards are the King, Queen, Knight, and Page in each of the four suits.

In the Cards

The King of Wands used to be called the Country Gentleman because he loves the outdoors and all types of sports. He is also enthusiastic about change and development. The King of Wands loves to see things grow, too, and he adores both animals and children.

Queen of Wands: Self-Assurance and Personal Magnetism

Queen of Wands.

Astrological sign: Leo

Upright imagery and meanings: The regal Queen of Wands has lions and sunflowers on her throne. These show her strong personality and her desire for growth and development. The black cat at her feet represents her intuition and her ability to assume a role of catlike observation.

The Queen of Wands sits facing us and has strong features, which show us her power of command and her power to create new directions. Action and movement will take place when she's around. Ambition, growth, and development of any idea or plan are the name of the game here.

The Queen of Wands is honorable and respectable and can be a strong leader in business or at home. *Dominant* is a good word to describe her presence, and in fact you can sense her in a room. Just like the astrological sign Leo, she's affable, cordial, and sometimes just a little aggressive, but above all enthusiastic and motivated. The Queen of Wands is kind to animals and children, and she enjoys growing and/or developing anything into something greater. She has an outgoing personality and overall is agreeable and strong.

Reversed imagery and meanings: When we turn the Queen of Wands upside down, the black cat is on top. The cat is the aggressive, passionate side of the Queen of Wands, as well as the sometimes pushy part of her personality. Reversed, the Queen of Wands is almost too forceful with her ideas, words, and actions. In addition, she can be overly temperamental and easily agitated.

The Queen of Wands reversed can be quite strict and domineering. Sometimes immature emotions come through and she seems bossy, pushy, or arrogant. This kind of fire, in both the King and Queen of Wands, can be hurtful. But as with all Minor Arcana, this position can be reversed if you work at it.

Knight of Wands: Off to the Races!

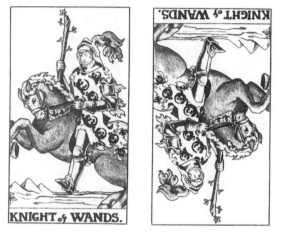

Knight of Wands.

Astrological sign: Sagittarius

Upright imagery and meanings: The brave young Knight of Wands is going off on his own journey, and—lucky him!—he has a strong and gallant horse to carry him through all sorts of territory. The Knight's armor and robe are decorated with salamanders, which protect him as he goes on his journey.

Like the astrological sign Sagittarius, this Knight is hasty in all that he does and takes action where others would not. The Knight of Wands carries his wand, which gives him the power to manifest his goals, and the three pyramids in the background represent body, mind, and spirit.

Although he's sudden and impatient in all he does, the Knight of Wands is strong and always enthusiastic nonetheless. These days we might call him a little hyper, but he just wants to get on with it and get going; he doesn't like to dillydally!

The Knight of Wands can be a generous friend or lover and always does everything in a big way. This card can also represent a change of residence, a journey that you're about to undertake (sometimes an unexpected one), a new adventure, or an approaching major change in your life for which you'll want to be ready. Because it's upright, any change it heralds will be terrific!

In the Cards

According to myth, a mythological lizard resembling the salamander lived in fire. In Paracelsus's alchemical system, the salamander's spirit could be called on for protection.

Reversed imagery and meanings: The Knight is upside down! Poor horse! Everything is falling away, the horse is lame, the wand of fire falls away (the Knight's power has left him), and even the pyramids are upside down, reversing all energy that was constructive when they were upright.

In the Cards

Any time we see a horse in a card, it signifies movement, action, or a change in the wind, and news to come of a new beginning. All knights have horses, of course, so Knight cards herald such things. But these are not the only cards where horses appear, so be sure to notice them when they ride into your spread.

The Knight of Wands reversed comes up when things are awry, disorganized, out of control, and chaotic. Perhaps the journey is postponed or not worth taking. Maybe messages are not being delivered correctly or things are out of control at the office, in a business deal, or at home.

Jealousy, personal conflict, insecurity, self-doubt, and *vulnerability* are just a few of the words that describe the Knight of Wands reversed. He can be narrow-minded, argumentative, and downright ornery. But as with all reversed Minor Arcana cards, *you* have the power to turn this Free Will card upright again.

Page of Wands: Enthusiastic Messenger

Page of Wands.

 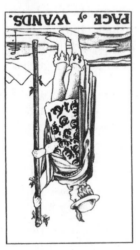

Upright imagery and meanings: As the messengers of the Tarot, all Pages relay messages of concern. This can take the form of a phone call, fax, e-mail, regular mail, or just good old-fashioned conversation. When we look at the Page of Wands, we see that, like the Knight of Wands, he's next to the three pyramids of the body, mind, and spirit. He's studying his wand, possibly reading a message he's just received.

The Page of Wands is often contemplating and studying messages and information because he brings you good news. It might be a message confirming your new job or that you just passed your exams. When he's upright, the Page of Wands always brings news of the best kind.

This card can also represent a child or young person who's still considered dependent on family or friends. This could be a grandchild, a new baby coming into the family, or your own child who's a good communicator.

The Page of Wands has great enthusiasm for life. He loves adventure and is often interested in travel to foreign lands. With his strong and dynamic personality, he can prove to be a good friend, one who will always tell it the way it is.

Fools Rush In

You know how you feel full of energy and really motivated one week, and then just pooped out the next? When everyday Wands come up reversed, they're reflecting those times when you're just not that motivated. Wands, upright for energy and reversed for lack of energy, reflect the changeability of life we all experience at times.

Reversed imagery and meanings: When the Page of Wands is reversed, the messenger isn't able to deliver his news correctly. This could mean delays in receiving the message or that the contacts are not made. Things might be waylaid, or delays or disappointing news may be on the horizon.

The reversed Page of Wands usually brings a message you don't want to hear, but as you know, that happens sometimes. This message might not arrive in time, and warnings are often being given when the Page of Wands is reversed.

If this card represents a person, he's likely to be theatrical, overzealous, superficial, or image conscious. The Page of Wands reversed is trying to let you know that you should be on the alert for some delays or disappointing news. But remember, you can turn the card back up if you desire.

Everyday Wands

The everyday Minor Arcana are the cards that show the routine events and day-to-day feelings we encounter in our lives. These events might be happening at the time of the reading or about to happen in the very near future. Like the royal Minor Arcana, these are Free Will cards, so we have control over how things unfold.

Everyday Wands explore your daily work, as well as any new projects you might be considering, including travel. Reflecting the energy of their fire element, these cards stand for your creativity and enthusiasm, as well as your ambition and competitive nature. Here's where you'll find the passion and the power to get what you want done.

Each card has its own energy and power. Wands represent how we get up in the morning and go about our day. This suit shows exactly what your energy is today and tomorrow.

Wave Your Wands: An Exercise

Place the Ace through 10 of Wands cards in front of you on a table to see how the energy grows and develops as you make your way through this suit. It's fun to look at the whole suit in this way: You can see the green leaves blooming from each card and the development from the Ace to the 10 of Wands.

Now reverse the same 10 cards. When you lay them out this way, you can see that all the green leaves are pointing down. Not much growth is occurring, and the downward-pointing leaves can represent setbacks and a lack of ambition and enthusiasm. Except for the 5 of Wands, which has more problems in its upright position (more on that a little later in this chapter), all the others have slowed down, with their energy at a halt.

Try this exercise as you go through each suit and watch what happens as you make your way from the Ace through the 10 of Wands, Cups, Swords, and Pentacles. You can actually watch the story of each suit unfold!

Ace of Wands: A New Beginning

Ace of Wands.

Upright imagery and meanings: In the Ace of Wands, a Hand (and we capitalize that Hand of God intentionally!) comes out of the clouds holding a flowering wand. Like all ones (Ace = 1), this represents the beginning of new energy, renewed courage, good self-esteem, and being ready to face a new day. The Ace of Wands shows a desire to initiate a new direction in life as well as the energy to start a new project. You'll have plenty of ambition and motivation to get started, too.

A fresh start in a new direction can represent anything—from a new job offer to a new attitude about something or a situation that you approach with renewed energy. A new baby might be on the way, but even if that's not the case, a birth of some kind is definitely in the works.

Reversed imagery and meanings: How does this upside-down Ace of Wands look to you? For starters, the Wand pointed downward is a sure sign of false starts or low self-esteem. The fire in the wand is almost out when it's reversed. But remember, you have the matches to ignite that fire again!

The Ace of Wands reversed lets you know you must look for something you're missing. Is it something you didn't do right? Are you not as motivated as you appear or are too tired to accomplish what you set out to do? This card suggests that you need to start over again, to regroup and see what you need more of. "It's time to go back to the drawing board," says the Ace of Wands reversed. "Do not pass Go. Do not collect $200."

> **Wheel of Fortune**
>
> Aces always mean new starts or new conditions entering your life. Aces show that you have the motivation, power, and enthusiasm to get on with your projects. So take those Aces by the horns, er, by the cards!

2 of Wands: Waiting for Results

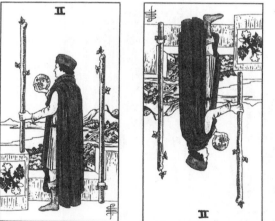

2 of Wands.

Upright imagery and meanings: The 2 of Wands shows a man holding one wand, and a second wand is here as well. The man has a globe in his hand (*"He's got the whole world in his hands ..."*) and is looking toward the world he's already put some energy into. Maybe he's started a business or project and is now waiting for his ships to come in. In any event, he's looking with anticipation.

The 2 of Wands indicates that you're waiting for results. Upright, this card shows the patience and focus of your intent. You've set things in motion, so they'll surely develop, and you can patiently wait for your rewards.

The 2 of Wands can also represent someone who'll help you along the way. As your new enterprise grows and develops, things are starting to move along. It's beyond just an idea; now you get to see how things start to materialize.

Reversed imagery and meanings: When the 2 of Wands is reversed, the globe is falling away from the man, who's standing on his head, and he has control over only one wand in this position. Is he going back to square one? Reversed, the 2 of Wands *is* back—to the Ace of Wands. Because the man can't hold on to both wands at the same time, backward action or motion is indicated.

The 2 of Wands reversed suggests that no movement is being made toward your goal. A lack of follow-through or harmony might be taking place, but in any event, your venture will have many delays and frustrations. It could mean that help hasn't come, that the partnership isn't balanced, or that global conditions aren't helping at this time. It might be time to go back and regroup or change the plan, or you might have to start over entirely.

3 of Wands: Partnership and Cooperation

3 of Wands.

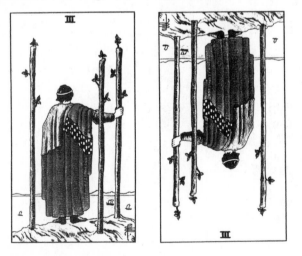

Upright imagery and meanings: Here we have the same man from the 2 of Wands, but now he's looking toward the future of his developments. Look with him toward the sea, and you'll see, just as he does, the boats of his labors coming back to him.

They're full of new resources to fulfill his next goal. Threes represent synthesis, after all, and the coming together of resources.

When he arrives at the 3 of Wands, the man feels more established in business and education. He can tell events are moving along much better and that the momentum has increased. He knows he'll benefit from his efforts and receive the rewards of the hard work he's put forth. He's also rightfully proud of his accomplishments.

The 3 of Wands often comes up when you're being offered help. It indicates good partnerships and solid cooperation with others. In business or education, support can be found all around you, and everyone involved wants to either help out or support your efforts. Success can't be too far away when you have that kind of backup and positive thoughts from others!

Reversed imagery and meanings: Reversed, the 3 of Wands can indicate the same desire for accomplishment and the same amount of focus as its upright position. But when it's upside down, the two wands slip away, so we're back to square one and the Ace of Wands (only one wand is left in his hand) all over again. Reversed Wands are starting to sound a lot like "One step forward and two steps back," aren't they?

When we turn this card over, the sea and boats are hardly noticeable. The 3 of Wands reversed represents that your talents and skills aren't as fine-tuned as they should be, and the competition or conditions around you might be stronger than your own efforts at this point.

Sometimes this card shows energy being wasted or too much attention being given to details at the cost of the big picture. It could mean you're preoccupied with other conditions or have too many irons in the fire. The 3 of Wands reversed wants to remind you that pride or overconfidence isn't the right way to go. These can make the ships come back to you without the proper cargo or resources, leaving you high and dry, with inadequate resources or information.

4 of Wands: Celebration Time!

4 of Wands.

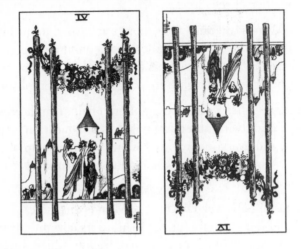

Upright imagery and meanings: What a beautiful card this is! Students in Arlene's classes often say they'd love to find several 4 of Wands in the deck. This card shows a celebration after hard work, a gathering of family and friends to celebrate a joyful time in life, and garlands welcoming people into the peaceful setting of home and garden.

Harmony, peace, and fulfillment of your ideals are occurring at this time in your life. This card means a bountiful harvest for the farmer, a wedding celebration, a graduation, or a reunion with the ones you love. Here you'll find the work well done suggested by the number 4 and satisfaction to enjoy your rewards. Your home life is content, your garden is growing, and your children are developing their own talents. The foundation of a good life and stable conditions at home or work are evident here, so "Celebrate, celebrate, dance to the music!"

Reversed imagery and meanings: This is a good card either way! The 4 of Wands reversed represents that, although the celebration isn't as big or spectacular, congratulations are due nonetheless. When the 4 of Wands is reversed, you're learning to appreciate the little joys of life, such as the first flower to blossom in spring, the first step a baby makes, a breath of fresh air, or the final mortgage payment.

These are the blessings in life you often see but sometimes don't notice. The 4 of Wands reversed represents thankfulness for the people and conditions around you, and happiness that the basics are secured. It's time to give a little thanks for what you *do* have, no matter how big or small.

5 of Wands: Confusion and Struggles

5 of Wands.

Upright imagery and meanings: In the 5 of Wands, we see men fighting. They all have issues with each other it seems, and the 5 of Wands, like all the other fives upright, indicates competitive action. In this card, the wands are all over the place. Nothing is organized or has any particular focus, so the energy is scattered. The men look as if they just woke up to something they hadn't planned on. It's likely they were caught off-guard and are reacting defensively.

This card represents opposition or struggles. These fellows are not exactly sure what they're fighting against or about, but they feel the need to defend something. Maybe they're confused, overly agitated, under constant stress, or simply disorganized. Whatever it is, these men need to release or understand what threatens them.

When this card comes up in a reading, you should remember that something's gone awry. This is a difficult situation, and more clarity must be found before you make any further movement. This card can represent legal issues, and the need for advice is very evident now. Don't let yourself get struck down!

Reversed imagery and meanings: Because the number five is positive in its reversed application, here we have the opposite of strife: Harmony will once again prevail. The men put down their wands and sit down to talk and discuss their problems. This card comes up a lot for problem-solving through dialog rather than physically fighting about things.

In the Cards

Fives—the midway point of the numbered Minor Arcana cards—represent turning points. In their upright positions, they often show confusion or disunity. Reversed, though, fives are more positive and represent more creative approaches to problem-solving and getting over those humps.

When the 5 of Wands is reversed, the men put down their wands. This indicates your "fights" will be constructive and you'll find a way to work out your differences using good old common sense and have a constructive outcome. Everyone involved will agree to sit down and talk about the problem, and with good energy applied in the right way, your goals will end in victory.

This card represents a win-win situation. Be prepared for exciting new opportunities coming your way, such as a new idea you never thought of to help you through a difficult situation. Compromise and negotiations are successful here.

6 of Wands: Coming Home to Success

6 of Wands.

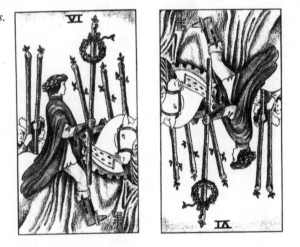

Upright imagery and meanings: In the 6 of Wands, a horseman comes home to victory, wearing a laurel wreath on his head and carrying another on his wand. Five other wands surround him, as well as townspeople who applaud him on his return.

This card describes the recognition you receive when you come through a difficult time successfully; you've won a battle and become a good example for others. It can also represent upcoming good news and success right around the corner; sixes are cards of idealism and committed responsibility. Relationships will improve when the 6 of Wands appears, too, and all problems, whether personal or business-related, are in the process of being solved.

Guests or family might be arriving soon, or a group or organization reunion may be in the works. This card also predicts the possibility of a safe journey out of town, with successful results for the reason you traveled in the first place. It's good news all around!

Reversed imagery and meanings: In the reversed 6 of Wands, the horseman and wands have turned upside down. This indicates delays or that the opportunities are not available. You might feel like you just can't pull off the victory; you're tired, world-weary, and in need of some rest and relaxation.

Whichever way you try to go, you'll be met with frustration and obstacles. Stress and tension seem to be building up, and you should try not to overreact to events that seem to be at a standstill. Here the need is to develop patience and ride out the storm. A planned journey might be postponed or delayed for some reason, but anything delayed will someday be shown to have been for the best.

> **Wheel of Fortune**
>
> The 6 of Wands reversed could indicate that someone or something is stronger or more victorious than you are at the moment. It's a time to be introspective and think about your next step. Time's on your side, and it's just what you need right now—time to reflect before you make your next move.

7 of Wands: Spurred by Competition

7 of Wands.

Upright imagery and meanings: In the 7 of Wands, we see a man in a defensive stance, holding his own against some unseen enemy. Standing atop a hill, he looks as if he's not sure whether to strike or stand his ground. Notice he has the advantage of being just a little above the crowd, though.

When you get this card, you have the inner strength and stamina the 7 represents, as well as the ability to stand your ground whatever the circumstances. Your courage is evident, and you can work through adversity and all sorts of pressure. Stiff competition in business or in personal issues might be indicated, or someone or something might feel like an enemy.

The man is protecting what he believes in and feels the need to fight for those ideals and beliefs. His courage is developed by maintaining his position.

Reversed imagery and meanings: The 7 of Wands reversed is actually better than its upright position. The man hangs on to the one wand he holds, but the threatening wands will fall away from him. This indicates that the threats have passed by. His enemy is gone, and the feelings of insecurity have passed.

With the 7 of Wands reversed, your position is upheld and you're stronger for it. You might have won a legal case or the acceptance of others, had some kind of near-hit, or found that the competition wasn't as strong as you thought. Your fears should leave you now and you'll realize that you've overcome a rough time in your life. You'll have patience and make slow progress toward your original goals because the storm has passed.

8 of Wands: Clear Sailing

8 of Wands.

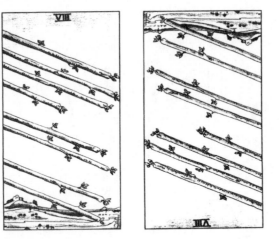

Upright imagery and meanings: The 8 of Wands is a simple scene of eight wands traveling through the air across an open countryside. Success on your travels! Success with your new love interest! Success for the goals you now have in mind! The number 8 represents success, and in this card, it's shown beautifully.

With the 8 of Wands, everything will take flight and land in happiness and pleasure. The movement is in the right direction, and you'll get what you've desired. Progress is being made toward a goal, a business idea, a new education, a new relationship, or possibly a positive change in the environment. This card indicates your goals are within reach, so keep moving in the direction you've planned. All your actions are encouraged at this time.

Reversed imagery and meanings: With the 8 of Wands reversed, the arrows fall out of the sky. Your new love interest is waning, your journey is postponed, or arrows of conflict or jealousy may arise. You might need to control some unruly emotions or you feel apprehensive or insecure.

Anger can develop with this card, so don't let your feelings get out of control. Learn to not force an issue if the 8 of Wands reversed comes up in a spread. It's time to slow down like these slow-moving wands and take the time to reorganize your goal. Stand back and observe what's going on rather than jump in and force something to happen.

9 of Wands: Prepared to Handle Adversity

9 of Wands.

Upright imagery and meanings: The 9 of Wands shows a man with a bandage on his head, leaning on his wand and waiting for someone or something that appears to be an enemy. Behind him are the eight wands we've seen before, now seeming to protect him from an enemy from behind. The bandage represents wounds from past conflict. You are wiser now from the experience and know what it takes to keep your life in order.

The man is well prepared to handle adversity and hostility. He protects all that he's worked for, including his home, livelihood, and the friends and family who've been loyal. He has strength and stamina in reserve and is able to maintain control over his own interests.

"So far, so good," says the 9 of Wands. As with any 9, you're on your way to greater success. You've earned your standing in society and will fight to maintain the rights and livelihoods of others. Hold on to what you believe in and the philosophy you've developed through your experience. Perseverance, stamina, strength of character, and the ability to defend yourself or others are indicated with this card.

Reversed imagery and meanings: The 9 of Wands reversed still represents the desire to protect and be of help to others, but the man can barely take care of himself. Most of the time, the reversed 9 of Wands indicates the lack of stamina and physical strength to see things through. You've been beaten down either mentally or physically, and your health isn't good enough to follow through on the difficult tasks ahead.

You need to rest and recuperate, rather than go out and fight the battles again. You're not prepared and need to check on things before you make your next move. You could be vulnerable, too weak to fight, or just plain exhausted. Sometimes this card comes up when you feel let down by others or are worried about something. The 9 of Wands reversed suggests it's best to regroup and calm yourself before taking another step.

10 of Wands: Shouldering the Burden

10 of Wands.

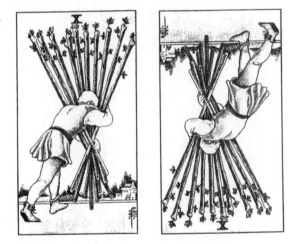

Upright imagery and meanings: The 10 of Wands shows a man bent over from carrying 10 flowering wands to the marketplace. Not only has he taken on many responsibilities from all areas of his life, but he's chosen to take on others' responsibilities as well. Now he has too many wands to carry. The 10 of Wands indicates an oppressive burden, both physically and mentally.

The 10 of Wands indicates that you want to help others, but at what cost? Maybe you're taking on the burdens of your immediate or extended family. You might shoulder these burdens well, but not for long. You need to look at how much you're carrying and decide which wands are important to keep and which wands you should drop. The 10 of Wands reminds you to keep your priorities straight.

Reversed imagery and meanings: In the reversed 10 of Wands, we finally see someone letting the burden dissolve! The man is letting go of the guilt or pressure he once felt: "Whew! That was heavy! I didn't realize how much I was carrying around on my shoulders!" The burden was there for so long he didn't realize he could drop it. Or maybe he didn't know how or if he could drop the extra tasks he was doing.

Sometimes this card represents someone who can manipulate others into carrying a heavy responsibility; the reading will tell us which way this card should be read. This could be a clever person trying to unload his burden onto someone else or shifting responsibility to others—delegating, but with a hidden agenda.

The 10 of Wands reversed can indicate the burden is finally lifted and that you're free to go. But it also reminds you that the right approach would be to take responsibility for these burdens and resolve them yourself, rather than dumping them on someone else.

Fools Rush In

The 10 of Wands is the card of the codependent. Sometimes it appears that you like carrying this burden. Maybe you're such a good caretaker it seems as if you can handle anything. But remember, this card represents too much stress, which can ultimately affect your health. So don't overburden yourself with other's problems; *your* well-being or health can truly suffer.

The Least You Need to Know

- The fire energy of Wands represents your enterprise, growth, and development.

- Royal Wands are your strength and determination to begin something new.

- Everyday Wands give you the energy to work your way through your projects.

- Wands can be used to further your enterprise or to stall it.

14

Cups: Life, Creativity, Emotions

In This Chapter

- ◆ Cups explore your emotional life and creativity
- ◆ Royal Cups: the nature of your heart and soul
- ◆ Everyday Cups: your interaction with others

Whereas Wands are concerned with your growth and enterprise, Cups are the cards of your heart and soul. Here's where you'll find your emotional nature, the way you interact with others, and your creativity as well. From the strong-hearted faith of the King of Cups to the happily-ever-after 10 of Cups, these cards show the path to—and from—your heart.

The Royal Court

The watery Royal Cup cards reveal your emotional nature. As we all know, our emotions can be as changeable as the weather, and that's why we have both the King of Cups with his fatherly love, and the Queen of Cups with her motherly, more maternal love. Then we have the romantic, young Knight of Cups and the eager and gentle Page of Cups, both harbingers of good things to come in your love life. Because Cups are the cards of emotions, they are connected to the water element as well as to the Cancer, Scorpio, and Pisces astrological signs, as you'll learn in the following paragraphs.

King of Cups: A Kind and Devoted Leader

King of Cups.

Astrological sign: Cancer

Upright imagery and meanings: The King of Cups sits on a turbulent ocean from which a dolphin jumps. Looking out, we can see a ship at anchor as well. The King appears peaceful as he experiences the conditions around him. He holds the Cup of the water of life, knowing that he has to handle and deal with emotions and heart-centered issues. He also wears a golden fish on the chain around his neck, signifying his dominion over the sea.

Like the astrological sign Cancer, the King of Cups is a man of devotion, introspection, and kindness in all that he does. When he speaks, it comes from the heart, and he has a quiet power. He can be a great leader in religion, at home, or as a counselor. Above all, he wants to do humanitarian work or some kind of work with people. He can handle the rocky emotional side of humankind, and he does so with compassion.

The King of Cups is also very interested in the arts, music, or careers related to the ocean, fishing, nature, and the home/environment. The main concern of this king, though, is to understand and share human feelings and sensitivity. He covers his emotional nature with a calm exterior and enjoys watching progress from behind the scenes.

Reversed imagery and meanings: The reversed King of Cups has fallen into the ocean; his throne is tossed upon these turbulent seas! Upside down, the King of Cups still has his feelings, but they're being tossed around, causing emotional upheaval or unsteady conditions.

When the King of Cups is reversed, your affections might be undergoing some stormy weather, as there's no control over what's going on in your home or family. Because the environment is emotionally volatile, you might lose your sense of perspective. Maybe you're suffering from some loss and are naturally reacting very moodily or seem detached. You are being asked to rise up and face an emotional issue with wisdom and maturity, but you don't feel up to it.

Sometimes this card comes up reversed to tell us of deep-seated emotion and sensitivity, but the King can't express it or handle it at all. Instead, he'll stay detached, not tell the truth about an issue, or become reclusive, almost Hermitlike.

> **CAUTION**
>
> **Fools Rush In**
>
> When the King of Cups is reversed, emotions are turned inward, so you can easily be misunderstood. You're certainly not saying what you're *really* feeling. You need to express yourself better and express your true feelings—before it's too late!

When the King of Cups is reversed, secrecy or shyness may be indicated, but the other cards around it can tell us more about him. Just remember, the King of Cups is emotional whether he's upright or reversed, but when those emotions are upside down, they can prove hard to handle.

Queen of Cups: Nurturing Creative Intuition

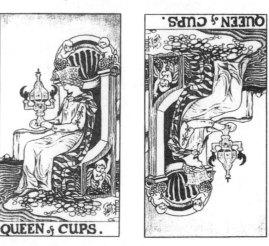

Queen of Cups.

Astrological sign: Scorpio

Upright imagery and meanings: The Queen of Cups sits on her beautiful throne, gazing into the cup of her imagination. Notice that this cup is closed, showing us that, as with the Scorpio astrological sign, her thoughts are in the realm of the unconscious. The Queen is on the beach, with the quiet waters ebbing and flowing around her, showing that beauty and love surround her.

This sensitive Queen devotes herself to matters of the heart. Her attachment to others is strong and her desire to nourish and help others is evident as well. She's usually a good wife, a loving mother, and devoted to whatever she's committed herself to.

The Queen of Cups is willing to be of help and is concerned with the welfare of others. Among the possible careers for her are caretaker, nurse, home-care worker, artist, or writer. Her imagination, in fact, can be one of her most powerful talents, and art, music, home, or family careers are most attractive to her.

Poetic and dreamy, the Queen of Cups is sensitive and relies on her intuition more than logic and reason. She feels everything and wants to know what's going on at a deeper emotional level. Usually soft-spoken and good natured, she wishes to please above all.

Reversed imagery and meanings: Reversed, the Queen has lost her cup, the ocean has become rough, and the tide is coming in too fast. This Queen has developed an overworked imagination. She's always worrying and concerned about things over which she has no control.

The Queen of Cups reversed can exaggerate the conditions around her by her emotional outbursts. She means well and wants to be of help, but she's out of balance emotionally and can't see clearly through the turbulent conditions.

When the Queen of Cups comes up reversed in a spread, you need to take a deep breath and take a moment to think about what's going on instead of reacting. Just go within that cup and meditate on the best thing to do, without reacting at all. Sometimes this card comes up for a secretive nature or a self-deceptive personality, but mostly you need to harness your emotions. Remember: This, too, shall pass.

Knight of Cups: The Romantic Dreamer

Knight of Cups.

Astrological sign: Pisces

Upright imagery and meanings: The Knight of Cups is a handsome young man who sits on a gallant horse traveling across the countryside. This card reminds us of the white knight who's come to save the day. This Knight wears a winged helmet, the sign of the imagination, and he and his horse are about to cross a river into a romantic adventure.

The Knight of Cups is a man of genuine character who's offering an invitation or proposal, and this card can represent the beginning of romance and falling in love. Skilled in the arts and music and with a good understanding of human needs, this is one Knight who knows how to romance!

The horse symbolizes an issue or condition being brought closer to you, and for this young Knight, this means an issue of the heart, or learning to develop relationships of a heart-centered nature. Action in the heart and emotions are being brought to the fore when this Knight appears in a spread. Also considered a romantic dreamer like the astrological sign Pisces, the Knight of Cups is full of ideas that can open your heart and make you look at your deepest feelings.

Fools Rush In

Look before you leap into this situation, warns the Knight of Cups reversed. Caution is advised before committing to what's being offered when this Knight shows up. This could suggest that you need to look more deeply at the reality of what you're being offered, including a new romance that might not turn out as you'd like it to.

Reversed imagery and meanings: The reversed Knight of Cups has fallen off his horse, and that will postpone the offer or proposal. In romance, it means turbulent times and that emotions aren't being shared equally between two people.

Upside down, the Knight of Cups doesn't relate well with others around him. The horse can't carry him across the water of his subconscious, so a fear of getting involved with others or a fear of commitment is represented here.

All these fears and overworked emotions have left this Knight tired and weary of relationships. Sometimes the Knight of Cups reversed is a person who will hesitate or not tell the whole truth about what he or she feels.

Page of Cups: Messenger of Love

Page of Cups.

Upright imagery and meanings: This little Page holds a cup outward to us, from which a mischievous fish, a symbol of the emotions and the imagination, peeks out. The Page of Cups brings attention to love and feelings in our lives. "Wake up and notice there's love in the air and in your heart," he reminds us.

The Page of Cups upright can indicate a message concerning romance, help from others, and devoted friends and family. This young Page wants to offer help and cooperation, and he has a gentle and good nature. When he appears in a spread, he brings joy, happiness, and a good omen that your life is changing for the better.

The Page of Cups offers gentleness, sweetness, kindness, and the desire to make you happy. Romantic or encouraging letters might be arriving in the mail, and music, the arts, and poetry come with this young Page as well. He could also bring news of a birth of a child or happiness in family conditions, with a young person bringing the good news.

Reversed imagery and meanings: When the Page of Cups is upside down, the fish and water fall to the ground. Either messages don't arrive or a happy message is delayed. Plans might be postponed, or the desire to plan ahead isn't there. Sometimes this page is just too emotional to say much. He can be moody, brooding, or detached, because he's feeling sorry for himself (or herself).

In the Cards

Congratulations! The Page of Cups comes up quite often when young people are graduating from school or receiving awards or some sort of recognition. The news is always happy and positive when the Page of Cups arrives in your reading—so accept your just rewards!

When the Page of Cups is reversed, not much action is taking place. Instead, he withdraws from people, preferring to be alone. If this is a child in your life, try to get him to talk about his feelings so he won't overreact to conditions in the future. You know how difficult it can be for a child to sort through all those confusing emotions, but you can help.

Even though the Page is reversed and prefers not to communicate right now, the child needs to say something to relieve the built-up emotion that will eventually express itself, and it's up to you to encourage this. The Page of Cups reversed can represent an oversensitive child or a situation that calls for calmness and introspection. Assert your free will and turn the Page upright again!

Everyday Cups

Everyday Cups take us on a sensual, emotional journey, as represented by the element of water. We begin with the unfolding of the heart in the Ace of Cups and continue through courtship, joy, dancing, and dreams. Sometimes the heartache of the 5 of Cups occurs, but as we get older, the old loves of the 6 of Cups can find us. And in the end, we all can achieve the happily-ever-after ending the 10 of Cups promises.

Ace of Cups: New Love

Ace of Cups.

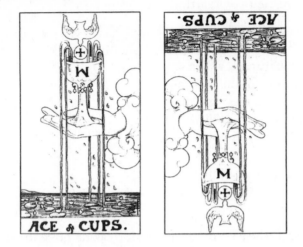

Upright imagery and meanings: With this card resonating to number 1, we have the beginning of the opening of the heart. Five streams of water, symbolic of the five senses, come out of a cup being held by the great Hand and fall into a pond. Water lilies, which symbolize psychic unfolding, float on top of the pond. Meanwhile, the dove of spirit descends, holding a wafer.

Spirit is manifest in soul, and you're in a cycle of opening your heart to new emotions or perhaps beginning a new romance. No matter what, it's the beginning of something wonderful! Joy surrounds the start of this new venture, including an openness of the heart and a desire for happiness. The Ace of Cups can promise new spiritual insight, a new awareness toward love, or a breakthrough in spiritual understanding.

In this card, we find blessings from above. It can also represent fertility and the conception of a child, for above all, this card stands for joy, happiness, and good health to come.

Reversed imagery and meanings: When the Ace of Cups is reversed, all the water is spilling out, so a rushing out of emotion is taking place. Soon the cup will be empty, which can represent a heart that's not as open to love as it should be or the insecurity of a new relationship. This card can suggest the fear of starting over in a relationship or insecurity concerning a new person who's arrived in your life. Sometimes out of low self-esteem, we act selfishly and are preoccupied with ourselves rather than others, and this card can point that out.

The Ace of Cups reversed can also indicate that you're bored or tired of the same old conditions. You might have a desire for something or someone new, but a new relationship won't take shape at this time. In addition, delays might stall attaining contact with someone or frustration occurs with a new start.

Wheel of Fortune
If the Ace of Cups reversed comes up for the beginning of your new relationship, it likely means the relationship will take a while to get off the ground. You might have a sense of feeling unwanted or uncared for and be moody and hesitant about putting yourself in the vulnerable position of giving away your heart. Remember, though, that the reversal of this Free Will card is up to you.

2 of Cups: Harmony in Partnership

2 of Cups.

Upright imagery and meanings: The 2 of Cups heralds the beginning of a friendship, with two people pledging their devotion. The couple on this card has decided to make a commitment to friendship and to begin to share their feelings with each other. The serpents are twined around a staff, an emblem of life's male and female energies, and the lion has the wings of spirit and shows a good balance between spiritual and earthly love.

Understanding and balanced friendships are developing here. Together, these two can achieve their plans. The 2 of Cups represents good partnerships, cooperation with each other, and the kind of sharing that can lead to bigger and better things. Here you'll find harmony and a sharing of good ideas between you. Kindness and thoughtfulness also take place, bringing out the best in both of you. Sometimes the 2 of Cups predicts a letter, gift, or happy event on the horizon. This is a card about the best of relationships.

Reversed imagery and meanings: When the 2 of Cups is reversed, the couple still has the desire to connect and understand one another, but the water is running out and the lion has no power to give help or protection. Upside down, you no longer have any balance, and disagreements or misunderstandings with a good friend or loved one may occur.

The 2 of Cups reversed represents that the problem can be solved, but someone has to make the first move. Perhaps one of you is being stubborn or unwilling to give assistance. Emotions can run away with you when this card turns over, so try to stay balanced and aware that the need for communication is more important now than ever before.

This card can indicate a loss of balance in a close relationship, so you should try not to be possessive or jealous. What is needed is understanding or a new perspective to get things back on an even keel. Sometimes this card comes up for people who are at the point of breaking off a relationship or who are involved in a passionate situation that needs to be kept in check.

3 of Cups: Emotional Joy

3 of Cups.

Upright imagery and meanings: In the 3 of Cups, three young maidens hold high their cups full of promise and celebration. Fruitful garlands and vines lie at their feet. Perhaps they offer us a look into the pleasure good friends and family bring us or a celebration of harvest time; fruition with success is worth celebrating, after all.

This card represents the happy conclusion of an undertaking and the success and recognition that follow. "Party time!" the girls seem to be saying. Their work has been done and the harvest has been brought in, so now they're ready to celebrate the bounty of their labors.

There's plenty to go around when the 3 of Cups appears: Good food, good friends, and the happiness to enjoy the good things in life are all present. This card can also indicate talent in the arts, music, design, beauty, or the hospitality business. In any event, you have that good combination of friends and family and can look forward to great things coming into your life.

Reversed imagery and meanings: The 3 of Cups reversed shows the maidens tired or uninterested in what's around them. In this position, the 3 of Cups reflects that over-indulgence or overdoing a good time can lead to arguments or poor decisions. Sorrow or pain can come from the 3 of Cups reversed, especially because gossip, or talking without thinking about what you're saying, can be shown here.

The 3 of Cups reversed suggests that it's time to take command of yourself and make new plans. You might need to apologize to friends, but it can all be worked out. Meanwhile, you recognize your excesses and bring them under control. It's important to try to communicate your feelings with the someone you're asking about in the reading, too.

4 of Cups: Boredom and Discontent

4 of Cups.

Upright imagery and meanings: Here we see a young man sitting under the ol' apple tree, being offered a fourth cup, which is coming toward him out of the blue. We recognize the three cups on the ground from before, but now an added cup gives us a different feeling. The man is being offered a fourth cup—and yet he refuses them all! He's so busy pondering the three cups, he wonders if he should go into *anything* that could bring out his emotions.

This guy looks a little leery; his arms and legs are crossed as if he were protecting himself (remember Body Language 101?). This card represents a person or situation that's detached from the world. For you, it could mean discontent or boredom as you reevaluate your life.

You might feel as if you don't care what happens when this card appears. Perhaps you lack motivation or feel that others don't care right now. You're feeling introverted and looking for a spiritual level to attach to. You might feel as if no one understands you, and that's because you have inner work to do.

Reversed imagery and meanings: The 4 of Cups reversed allows you to come out of your contemplation and go in a new direction. You're once again motivated to try something new, including new love or a new focus on something that truly moves you. You'll have a great desire to accomplish new work, new goals, and new ambitions.

Now's the time to take emotional action and start to re-create your goals and dreams. It might appear as if nothing's happening, but be prepared for an exciting change of events when the 4 of Cups reversed appears. Movement is in the right direction, and activity will be renewed with the hope of a good cycle starting.

5 of Cups: An Emotional Loss

5 of Cups.

Upright imagery and meanings: The 5 of Cups shows a man in a dark cloak looking down at three cups that have tipped over and spilled the wine of life. He has such sorrow as he concentrates on those three cups that he doesn't even notice two upright cups behind him.

The 5 of Cups always represents a loss of some kind, usually of something or someone you've been attached to. When this happens, you can find it difficult to explain how you feel inside; you're experiencing grief, loss, or heartache, and it's hard to express those painful emotions.

The 5 of Cups knows that sorrow takes a while to heal. It's okay to cry or grieve over a loss, and sometimes it's good to get emotions out and release pent-up feelings of sadness. The bridge in the distance reminds us that this loss will pass in the time ahead, and the two upright cups behind the man show that tomorrow will bring a renewed interest in love, as hard as that may be to believe right now. For now, though, you're engrossed in your loss, whether it's the end of a relationship, someone who's left, or disillusionment, regrets, and broken dreams. Not all matters of the heart are happy ones, after all.

Reversed imagery and meanings: When this 5 card is reversed, it brings a positive message, as do all Minor Arcana reversed 5 cards in the Tarot. The 5 of Cups reversed indicates the reversal of negative energy. Loss is replaced by improvements. Hope and happiness return, and your energy is increasing daily.

You might make new friends when the 5 of Cups reversed appears, or old friends or acquaintances might call on you. It's time for the return of good memories, new hope, renewed confidence, and just getting back to your old self. You've summoned the courage to rise above your loss. Don't be afraid to develop new ideas or make new plans.

You've learned from your past; now you remember that tomorrow is a new day. This card can indicate a new job on the horizon or a change in plans that will turn out for the better. "All is not lost," says the 5 of Cups reversed. "So cheer up! New things will replace the old ones." The 5 of Cups reversed reminds us that as one chapter closes, another opens.

6 of Cups: A Blast from the Past

6 of Cups.

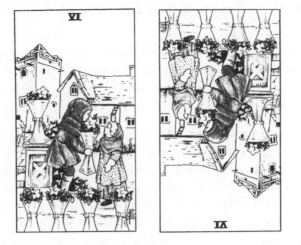

Upright imagery and meanings: The 6 of Cups is a good indication that friends and family have generated happy memories for you. A little boy is giving a cup of flowers to a little girl in a nice hometown setting. Nearby, five more cups hold flowers, which are, as we know instinctively, gifts of the heart. The cottages in the background can bring us back to good memories of our childhood, past, or hometown.

This card represents a meeting with someone from your past, such as a childhood friend or old love, or a reunion with family members. You will find the happiness and enjoyment that come from the past as well as good memories. If you're presented with an opportunity to grow into a new relationship or new job, it will have some connection to the past, too.

This card often comes up to refer to siblings and family values. It could mean a gift from an admirer or old friend, or that something from the past will resurface or be returned to you. At the same time, new people for whom you feel an affinity may enter your life. Maybe they'll be from your hometown or have graduated from the same high school or college as you. And if a gift or inheritance is represented by the 6 of Cups, it will be more than you expected!

Reversed imagery and meanings: The 6 of Cups reversed represents the past turned upside down. This translates to rewards being delayed, a memory of the past that's not happy, or news from the past that could be disruptive to you. Maybe you're clinging to outdated ideas, experiencing feelings of nostalgia, or living in the past instead of the present.

The 6 of Cups reversed can indicate that you wish the past would return, although sometimes people get this card to remind them to reflect on the past but not live in it. Perhaps you need to get out of a condition that's harmful or hurtful to your future—to put it in the past, in other words.

This card can represent a disappointment having to do with family or your expectations of family. Maybe you expected your family to be there for you and they weren't. It's time to let go of past ideas and obsolete conditions in your life when the 6 of Cups reversed appears. You can grow into a new future that will once again create new memories.

7 of Cups: Emotional Choices

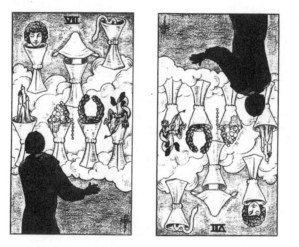

7 of Cups.

Upright imagery and meanings: The 7 of Cups shows a man trying to make a choice. Should he take the castle or the jewels? The wreath of victory or the red dragon? The woman or the ideal of himself? Too many choices! And then, in the center of the card, is a draped individual ready to be revealed. What's under that draped cup?

All these questions are part of the interpretation of the 7 of Cups. Maybe your imagination's working overtime and you're having difficulty making a decision. Chances are, you can't see the forest for the trees.

With your dissipated forces, you're meeting confusion at every juncture. Which way should you go? What should you do? Which do you choose? This card can indicate a selfish indulgence in dreams instead of action, or being stuck in a condition due to wishful thinking, daydreaming, or choosing illusion over reality.

Reversed imagery and meanings: When the 7 of Cups is reversed, a decision will finally be made. The man can choose his direction through good use of his will and determination. Now that he's made up his mind and chosen one direction to go, he's on the right track and will continue on this course.

When the 7 of Cups is reversed, it always means you've made a choice you'll follow through on. You'll select a project that you care about and have the commitment to see it to its end. Don't give up your dreams, because your plan is starting to work when this card appears. The choice you made was right for you. Persist with that choice, and you'll soon be reaping what you sowed.

8 of Cups: Leaving an Attachment

8 of Cups.

Upright imagery and meanings: The 8 of Cups focuses on the spiritual side of the heart. Here we see a man with a staff walking toward barren mountains. He's walking away from what was once near and dear to him, because now he has a need for spiritual insight.

When the 8 of Cups appears, you're totally dissatisfied with your present mode of life and want something more. Is the grass greener on the other side of the mountain or does it just seem that way? You might abandon your present daily routine in order to find out.

Note that in this card, the man has stacked his cups neatly before moving on. He appears to be finished with those past concerns and worries of the material world. Now he seeks something different, and even though he's not sure what he'll find on the other side of those mountains, he's setting off to seek it.

Reversed imagery and meanings: When the 8 of Cups is reversed, the man turns back around to the material world and searches for pleasure and success of a material nature, with joy and feasting on the horizon. With a flip of the card, he's back in the physical world, which isn't always a bad place to be.

When this card appears reversed, you have renewed interest in people and connections to the earthly plane. This can mean that a new love interest is in view, whether a person or a condition. You'll get your passion for the physical world back again with the 8 of Cups reversed. It comes up for people wanting to enjoy life, whether through friends, travels, or new adventures. It indicates a need for love, passion, and adventure, all of which add up to bliss, a time for reentering the world after a period of retreat.

In the Cards

Why do we climb mountains? Why do we search the world (or the universe) for new adventures or new land? The 8 of Cups represents a spiritual quest, a search for something you can't see but can only feel. When this card appears, your higher self will proceed with an inner search. It's time to get in touch with your own heart.

9 of Cups: A Wish Come True

9 of Cups.

Upright imagery and meanings: The wish card! Naturally, a lot of Arlene's students want this card in every spread they have! The well-satisfied man sits content, with his nine cups on the arched shelf behind him. As if he's rubbed a magic lantern, he will get his wish!

This card assures that your dreams will come true and your future will be secure. "Your wish is my command," says the genie. "What you desire will come to you!" You'll have much happiness in attaining your wish, whether it's a new car, a new relationship, a new job, extra money, or simply happiness coming your way. Other cards in the reading will tell you how and when the wish might take place. It's nice to have those wishes for luxury and the sensual pleasures in life to come true.

Reversed imagery and meanings: The wish card reversed is reason for a pause. What do you mean it won't happen the way I want or not happen today?! Most people who get readings want to have a positive outcome with every question they ask, but the wish card reversed indicates that the wish won't be fulfilled as asked or that the wish won't be fulfilled at this time.

> **In the Cards**
>
> The Gypsies of Europe called the 9 of Cups the wish card, and you can depend on a "Yes!" answer when this card appears. When the upright 9 of Cups shows in your spread, you will get your wish. It's like a genie!

Sometimes the 9 of Cups reversed can represent a lack of money or resources, overindulgence, or overdoing a good thing. Are you pushing for this wish to happen? Are you anxious about not getting what you want? Are you trying too hard to have it happen *now?* Your wish can come another day, but for today, you'll just have to wait.

10 of Cups: Happily Ever After

10 of Cups.

Upright imagery and meanings: This is the ultimate that the suit of Cups can bring. It's the happily-ever-after card, where a young couple stretches out their arms in happiness and gratitude for home, love, and family ties, which are joyful and happy. Their modest home is in the background, and two children are playing next to them.

When the 10 of Cups appears in your spread, you're experiencing the happiness you've always wanted. You've realized your personal hopes, dreams, and desires; have a happy family life; and enjoy true friendships.

Here's the lasting happiness inspired from above. This can be an indication of a marriage, the start of a family, or a family reunion, celebration, or anniversary. With the 10 of Cups, things happen in a way that makes all of us shed tears of joy. This card might also predict buying a new home, bringing home a new baby, or moving into a cycle of your life where everything just flows like magic. With the 10 of Cups, you really do live happily ever after!

Reversed imagery and meanings: When the 10 of Cups is reversed, the desire for family contentment still persists, but it hasn't completely arrived yet. The present situation might be bothersome: Perhaps the house deal isn't going through correctly, the children are turning against their parents, the wedding's being put off, or the new job's being put on hold.

Some delays and difficult times are ahead before anything goes well. Patience is definitely needed, because your wonderful venture is not going to happen right now. Perhaps a family disagreement is causing problems or your reunions are unhappy ones. This card can indicate the loss of a friendship or fighting among siblings or relatives.

There could be a loss of reputation or damage done to the home or family. This card sometimes comes up for physical damage done to the home because of flooding, bad weather conditions, or what those insurance policies call "acts of God." It can also relate to thoughtless or painful actions from those close to you.

It's important to remember with the 10 of Cups reversed, as with any card with a negative message, that time will bring healing. And as with all the Minor Arcana cards, this is a Free Will card that you can turn upright with effort and determination.

The Least You Need to Know

- Cups are connected to the element of water and represent your emotional life and creativity.

- Royal Cups explore the nature of your heart and soul.

- Everyday Cups indicate the ways you interact emotionally with others.

- You control your emotional nature.

Swords: Action, Power, Obstacles

In This Chapter

- Swords represent conflict, obstacles, and aggression
- Royal Swords: logic and thoughtful attention to all sides of issues
- Everyday Swords: struggles and difficulties

Swords represent strife and aggression as well as the process of developing courage and mental strength. These are the cards of everyday conflict and problems, the obstacles you encounter, and the way you use your mind to deal with those obstacles. No life is entirely a primrose path, and Swords are the first to remind us of that!

In medieval times, the way someone held his sword next to him would tell other tribes what his tribe was thinking. If the sword pointed up, it meant victory; pointed down, it meant retreat or submission. If it was held to the side of the body facing downward, the tribe was ready to speak or negotiate, while pointed down with both hands on the sword meant the tribe was ready to listen or debate with an open mind. And if the sword was held across the front of the body horizontally, it meant the tribe was prepared to hand over a victory or power to another.

The Royal Court

Royal Swords are logical, analytical folk, well educated, reasonable, and always looking at issues from a balanced perspective. This is the suit where the term "Royal Court" can be taken quite literally to mean those who sit in judgment. Like the astrological signs that share the element of air—Gemini, Libra, and Aquarius—the Royal Swords attack problems with logic and their fine-honed minds. For this reason, Royal Swords often represent people who deal with law and life's legalities. Royal Swords bring messages about how to deal with the problems facing you. The message might use a rational analysis to get to the core of the issue; this is the way the King of Swords approaches things. The Swords might be saying that you should look at the issue from every side, which is the message the Page of Swords is quick to remind you of. But no matter what, when Royal Swords talk, people should listen.

King of Swords: Logical and Balanced Counsel

King of Swords.

Astrological sign: Libra

Upright imagery and meanings: Behind the King of Swords, who holds a sword in his hand, are storm clouds, and cypress trees are also present, as we'll see in all the Royal Sword cards. The air movement and the clouds represent some turbulence and stormy weather. This is a stern king who sits on a throne decorated with butterflies and sylphs, and he's looking right at you, as if he's studying or analyzing you, making you feel rather uncomfortable.

The King of Swords is well educated, understands the human mind, and deals well with logic and reason. He has the right authority for his ability to counsel, and he can give good, logical advice. He can also represent a judge in government or law, because, like the astrological sign Libra, he balances both sides of an issue before coming to a conclusion.

The King of Swords has the power to command because he always knows what's at the crux of a situation. Good counsel and good advice help him come to a fair and rational decision. He's just and honorable in all that he does, making him a firm friend. And he desires fairness is all his dealings.

The King of Swords has a good memory and can be sharp as a tack when it comes to statistics, analysis, and recall of an event. He's direct in all that he does, but because he's upright, he's also flexible—as long as the argument's logical.

In the Cards

The King of Swords can appear cautious, and that's because he needs time to come to a conclusion. He's a good debater and a master of intellectual pursuits. As a father he can appear stern, serious, and thoughtful—the better to hone his children's mental abilities.

Reversed imagery and meanings: This King isn't too happy when he's reversed. His sword is pointed down, as if he's fought too many battles or because someone else has won the battle. Upside down, the storm clouds have become dominant, and the wind has blown through and made the King of Swords retreat from his throne.

He certainly has a bad attitude now. He feels mentally exhausted, unable to handle the stress of the situation. Possibly some bad news has arrived that he's not handling well, or he can't find the balance that's so important to him. He's critical, cool, aloof, and obstinate, and he can be cruel, especially in his words.

The King of Swords reversed won't be sensitive to the needs of others. He's preoccupied with his own thoughts and ideas and can become obsessed with his own intentions and actions. Because of his lack of concern for others and his lack of diplomacy now, he can upset others. And because he can't see both sides clearly, he can be severe in his judgment, make unfair assessments, and just be downright opinionated about everything.

Queen of Swords: Analytical Thinker and Advisor

Queen of Swords.

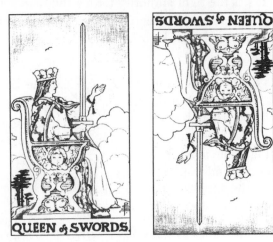

Astrological sign: Aquarius

Upright imagery and meanings: The Queen of Swords is seated on a high throne that looks out into a clouded sky. She's resting her sword on her throne and holds out her hand, maybe to call our attention to something. Note, as in the King of Swords, the presence of the cypress trees, the sky with clouds, and the throne of butterflies: All of these focus our attention on our thoughts and our mental state. In this card, a bird hovers above, symbolizing messages coming through.

The Queen's upright sword represents spirit penetrating matter and informing us with knowledge. Like the King of Swords, this Queen can be an excellent teacher, lawyer, or counselor. She has a sharp mind, is a keen observer of people, and is a good listener who will analyze all conditions with her sound logic and reasoning.

The Queen of Swords is a good public speaker and organizer. She's got great leader-ship qualities and can handle a crowd quite well. She's also thoughtful and able to keep her emotions in check. Like the astrological sign Aquarius, she's a cool customer who favors logic and common sense.

This card indicates a woman of strong character, but also one who's seen many hard-ships. Because of her character, she bears her sorrow well; she's adept at handling loss, too, and knows how to deal with the most difficult of human conditions. And with her clear and direct way of speaking and addressing issues, the Queen of Swords is a good psychologist.

Reversed imagery and meanings: The Queen has lost her sword! She won't like that; it indicates she's been through some kind of loss. Upside down, she can barely keep her calm exterior and is easily angered, unable to discipline herself as she could when she was upright.

This reversed Queen still has keen observations but can use them in a narrow-minded way. She's not so open to listening but will instead tell others what to do. Often when she's reversed, she'll be misunderstood, which is why she'll have difficulty with others. But she can also cause her own downfall by being too judgmental or dogmatic.

The Queen of Swords reversed is, as in her upright position, both strong and stern, but she needs to use more self-control when she's reversed. Her perception of a situation will now be colored by her one-sided view, and she might have a tendency to gossip and embellish matters to force others to share her opinion.

Knight of Swords: A Heads-Up Reminder

Knight of Swords.

Astrological sign: Gemini

Upright imagery and meanings: The young Knight of Swords is off on a journey on his beautiful thoroughbred racehorse. With his speed, this Knight brings messages of caution and the need to stay alert. When he comes up in your reading, he's telling you to pay attention to coming events. This Knight can also represent a person or event coming into your life. Either way, he cuts to the chase and tells the truth—even if the truth hurts!

The Knight of Swords has a great need to inform us of something important. Like the astrological sign Gemini, he represents the urgency to get things moving in your life—*now!* He doesn't dillydally along; he's a mover and a shaker. Although this Knight is courteous and kind and has good intentions, he's also quick witted and sharp. Because he expects the same of others, he can seem a little pushy at times. Still, his focus never wavers.

This is a courageous, skillful Knight, who with his good mind can be a helpful advisor. He'll always defend the underdog and is concerned with getting the truth of the matter out in the open. His desire to warn us makes us alert and ready for action. "Forewarned is forearmed," says the Knight of Swords.

Reversed imagery and meanings: Reversed, the Knight of Swords' mighty horse is upside down and can no longer move in the direction he was going. This can mean delays, apprehension, conflicts, or battles yet to be won. There might be difficulty maintaining stamina, strength, or mental attitude, and he's not able to cope with conditions because he's just mentally worn out. This Knight may also be unable to help or warn others of an impending trauma.

Sometimes the Knight of Swords reversed can be argumentative or a troublemaker, always ready to start a fight or a war—you know the type. This can also be someone who's opposed to your thoughts and actions right now.

This card reversed signals constant delays and struggles that can seem never-ending. If a young man is around you, make sure you understand his lack of concern for others, and try to steer clear of this guy when he's reversed. Something's wrong around him and he might not be saying what; because he can't carry his sword well, he might not be communicating very well either. This card can also represent dishonesty and deception, so in any event, caution is advised.

Page of Swords: Messenger of Vigilance

Page of Swords.

Upright imagery and meanings: This Page holds his sword with both hands, ever vigilant and intent on the message he's carrying. If this is a young person, he or she is very intelligent, a quick thinker able to handle any emergency well.

The Page of Swords is a messenger who urges us to look deeper into the meaning of a situation. "Pay attention!" he keeps saying. "Take a closer look. There's more to this than meets the eye!"

The Page of Swords has the qualities of grace, dexterity, and inquisitiveness. He has a desire to communicate and help others by providing added information. At the same time, there could be a delay in your plans or some disappointing news. Courage might be needed to deal with the problem at hand.

> **Wheel of Fortune**
>
> Sometimes the Page of Swords upright means spying or receiving information through a third party. This can be the card of secret agents and secret information or of hiring a private detective!

Reversed imagery and meanings: When the Page of Swords is reversed, he's got a lot to do with information that will reveal the whole truth and nothing but the truth. This card is actually better reversed than it is upright; now the Page of Swords shows unpredictable behavior or sudden events, or those with a strange twist coming into your life. But whatever these changes are, they usually turn out for the best.

Remember, all changes the Page ushers in eventually turn out for the better, like the proverbial silver lining around the dark cloud. If the Page of Swords reversed represents a young person or dealing with teenagers, it can suggest that they'll be unpredictable, but you will be able to get to the source of the frustration and talk about it. Great communication comes with the Page of Swords whether he's upright or reversed, because truth eventually comes out. The desire to speak that comes with this card is too great to be kept silent.

Everyday Swords

Life can't always come up Cups and Wands, and everyday Swords are the cards that help us face and deal with some of life's more difficult aspects by reminding us to focus on what the element air represents—mind over matter. It's important to remember that the force of Swords can be used for good as well as for harm, and with this positive aspect, you can force difficult situations to resolve themselves. Remember, too, that like all Minor Arcana cards, everyday Swords are Free Will cards. How you use their force is up to you.

Ace of Swords: New Ideas, New Direction

Ace of Swords.

Upright imagery and meanings: The Ace of Swords is double-edged and can cut both ways: constructively, to cut away the dead wood, or destructively, to harm or force a situation. This card shows a Hand coming out of the clouds (which you should by now recognize from the other Aces we've seen) firmly holding an upright sword encircled by a crown with the olive branch of peace and the palm of victory. Six *yods*—the life force or drops of light from heaven—protect the sword.

Card Catalog

Yods are actually representations of the Hebrew letter *yod*. This letter represents the name of God and is also symbolic of the life force, or the light from heaven that protects us all.

Like all Aces, the Ace of Swords signals a beginning and resonates to the number 1, in this case the card signifies an undertaking that will prove successful. Forward thinking and focused action assure that victory is near and that conquest and success for the goal are at hand. This card can signify the birth of a child who could become a courageous leader or of people who champion the underdog. The Ace of Swords assures that new ideas and swift action will win the day.

When this card appears in your spread, you feel powerful and in control. The situation you're in might have risen out of a more difficult one, but now you hold the cards, so to speak. Because Swords represent the element air, you've got focus and logic on your side, as well as the strength to see your project through difficulties to its conclusion.

Reversed imagery and meanings: The reversed Ace of Swords has a negative focus: It cuts to harm or inflict pain. Remember, the Sword both penetrates matter and informs it, so this Sword reversed is too forceful and can hurt others. Beware of trying to use too much force to gain an end. Do your work gently and try not to push.

The Ace of Swords reversed reminds you not to apply pressure to the situation because that will just make it worse. You can attract opposition at this time, so you should be cautious and diplomatic. Try to avoid arguments by using the good common sense and reasoning ability the air element represents.

2 of Swords: Stalemate, Indecision

2 of Swords.

Upright imagery and meanings: In the 2 of Swords, we find a blindfolded young woman sitting on a bench holding two large swords. Because she's blindfolded, she can't see her way through these difficult times; in fact, chances are she doesn't want to see what's right in front of her. In addition, she's turned her back on the water (her feelings) and, therefore, can't see or sense anything to help her out of the stalemate she's in. The jagged rocks and new moon symbolize the instability around her.

Like all cards resonating to the number 2, this card shows the need for a well-balanced life. The woman is at a point of indecision: Which way should she turn? Which way should you turn in your life? When you get this card, not only will it be hard to make a decision, but it will be difficult to even think of acting on it. This card can also indicate a temporary truce, stalled negotiations, or inadequate information.

You probably feel completely on hold, delayed, and confused about your direction when this card comes up. The 2 of Swords suggests a need for guidance and direction, but note that the woman can still hold those swords upright! She can sit in contemplation instead of action for now—and that might be the best course of (in)action when this card appears.

Reversed imagery and meanings: The reversed 2 of Swords indicates that a decision has been made. The woman will now take action and things will occur quickly. When you get this card in a spread, you'll be free to make your own decisions with the faith that action is now taking place.

This card indicates release and forward movement in your affairs. The rocks are still in the water; therefore, you need to deal with the right people and be careful not to share any confidences, but you should follow through and keep to your own path. What the 2 of Swords has reversed and what it doesn't have upright now is confidence—the confidence to proceed toward your goal.

3 of Swords: Heartache and Disappointments

3 of Swords.

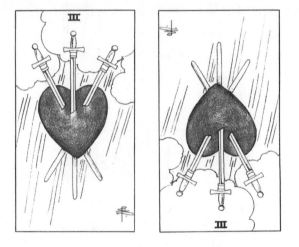

Upright imagery and meanings: The 3 of Swords' symbol of a red heart pierced by three swords is a universal symbol of loss of a loved one, grief, or sorrow in life. Rain clouds fill the air and a storm has developed. When this card appears, sorrow is evident, and it's the other cards around it that will tell us in more detail where the sorrow comes from.

This card indicates that an argument can lead to a separation or that a quarrel can lead to the breakup of a friendship or partnership. Pain and sorrow are expressed when this card appears, and disorder or upheaval may cause distress. Due to some kind of misfortune, loved ones might be separated by war or political strife. The 3 of Swords indicates that you need to express the sorrow you're feeling in your heart.

Still, the sorrow indicated in this card also signals the end of the stalemate of the 2 of Swords. So although the 3 of Swords indicates pain and sadness, the tension of not knowing has been released.

Reversed imagery and meanings: When the 3 of Swords is reversed, its intensity has lessened. The situation isn't as severe as when this card is in the upright position. You might be dissatisfied with the present outcome or situation, and sadness might result, but when the 3 of Swords is reversed, it will be of a passing nature.

The 3 of Swords reversed means that you'll work through this difficult time more quickly than you thought you would. An apology might be in the works or a peacemaker will be at hand. As when the 3 of Swords is upright, its surrounding cards will tell us where the sadness is coming from, as well as whether the sorrow is in the past or future.

4 of Swords: Rest and Recuperation

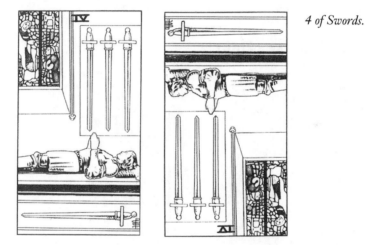

4 of Swords.

Upright imagery and meanings: This can be a frightening card to those unfamiliar with the Tarot's imagery. "Am I going to die?" more than one Querent has asked. In this card, a knight is resting upon a tomb, but he's resting after war and strife. This is not a card of death, but of convalescence and repose. The three swords we saw in the previous card hang over him, while the fourth rests alongside him.

This card actually means that the knight is now at peace with all that's happened. He's finished his work and can rest and take time out to think about his future. What shall he do now? Where shall he go? What if he has to fight the same battle again? The 4 of Swords represents a break in his life, a rest to contemplate and evaluate what he's accomplished.

Sometimes this card represents someone on vacation or on a retreat. It can mean convalescence after surgery or coming home from the hospital and resting comfortably there. The 4 of Swords represents a time to renew your energies, both physical and mental. We authors are both quite pleased when this card comes up for us, because it indicates a calming period. Enjoy the peace and quiet before the next storm rolls in, says the 4 of Swords.

Reversed imagery and meanings: The reversed 4 of Swords signals that the knight's now ready to get back into action. The three swords come alive off the wall, so the knight will get up from his tomb and focus on future plans with renewed energy.

This card suggests that good opportunities lie ahead, but you should be thoughtful in how you handle them. Sometimes it can indicate political upheaval or unrest in the work force, such as labor problems, employee discontent, or unions or political parties that want to take action to change existing laws or practices. This card suggests upheaval, in both its positive and negative aspects.

5 of Swords: Spoiling for a Fight

5 of Swords.

Upright imagery and meanings: The young men in the 5 of Swords are just spoiling for a fight and have difficulty even dealing with each other. Storm clouds are gathering and the wind howls as one rebel looks at the others, whose swords he has captured.

This card shows a lack of sensitivity or concern for others. The young man's tenacious grip on the sword indicates both selfishness and the breakup or severing of ties. This card can represent an unfair application of power, degradation, or worse—disgrace.

Legal complications often come up with this card, and the cards surrounding this one tell exactly how things will turn out. The 5 of Swords can represent taking what's not really yours, stealing away energy, power, or, literally, the swords of the other men. It can represent slyness and cunning or the ability to coerce others out of something.

The 5 of Swords can also represent deceptive actions or manipulating either people or a situation to suit one's own needs. It can also indicate developing a bad reputation, an unethical victory, or just plain destructive behavior.

Reversed imagery and meanings: The 5 of Swords reversed isn't as difficult as it is upright. The men are on more equal footing, so no deception is going on here. Instead, all three know exactly what each is thinking or planning.

This card can indicate sneaky behavior or a desire to create conflict. When it appears upside down, you're aware of the difficult lawsuit ahead of you or of a certain situation that can cause all kinds of emotional problems. A chance of loss still exists, but to a lesser degree—small claims court, say. Or perhaps you win, but it's not the victory you wanted.

Gossip comes up with the 5 of Swords reversed. When you hear about it, you try to clear it up and get to the truth of the matter. This isn't the easiest card to have, so when it comes up, it's important to study the surrounding cards to accurately describe the question's outcome.

6 of Swords: Leaving Sorrows Behind

6 of Swords.

Upright imagery and meanings: The picture in this card shows a ferryman rowing a sorrowful woman and child to the farther shore. When we focus on the rough water on the right side of the boat and the calm water on the left side, though, we see that they're moving away from difficulty.

The 6 of Swords indicates that a difficult cycle is now starting to come to an end. You can set your vision on the future, which is certainly brighter than the recent past.

This card can also represent a journey taken over water or a trip away from a sad condition.

Once you leave the old conditions behind, harmony will once again prevail. The woman and child in this card are recovering from problems, and their family might have had much loss. Now, though, the healing process will begin. This can indicate that an unpleasant work situation or a family difficulty or sorrow will give way to peace once more.

This journey to tranquility can be done in the mind. No matter how it comes about, though, you'll journey to a higher state of consciousness and be at peace with yourself on the opposite shore.

Reversed imagery and meanings: In the 6 of Swords reversed, the boat is no longer afloat and the people have had to abandon ship. This indicates that the journey to a better environment has been postponed. You'll feel as if you're stuck in a negative situation with no way out.

Nothing will be accomplished at this time, and you'll need to wait for a better opportunity. You might need to go within yourself to find an answer or to rethink a situation. Plans will be kept on the shelf, and it's advisable to shift to a different frame of mind in order to proceed.

The freedom to do what you want might be postponed. A legal issue could be holding up your life, or a loss or grief might be slowing you down, creating stagnation at the present time. The 6 of Swords reversed indicates delay.

7 of Swords: Sneaky!

7 of Swords.

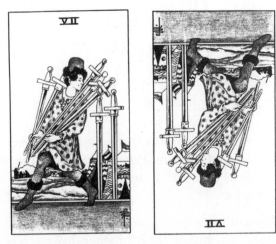

Upright imagery and meanings: This is a pretty literal card! It shows a man sneaking away with five of the seven swords, unseen by those in the encampment behind him. Two swords remain in the ground, left behind as evidence that something has been taken.

When the 7 of Swords appears, things might not work out the way you've planned. It's possible that someone is being deceptive or stealing away with something that's important to you. Unreliability can be indicated or that perhaps someone's not telling you the truth or is hiding it from you.

Reversed imagery and meanings: This card is actually good reversed. The swords will be returned or the person who's been keeping a secret will reveal the deception. You'll find out what's really been going on now.

An apology might be forthcoming, and the people involved will accept it. "Sorry for causing so much trouble. It was an innocent mistake—honest!" Good advice and counsel will be given if you're involved in a lawsuit or in need of legal advice. A thief will return what was stolen, or what was lost will be found. In short, the truth will come out. The other cards around the 7 of Swords can help you interpret it more specifically.

CAUTION

Fools Rush In

The 7 of Swords isn't a traumatic card, but rather one of the mind. It represents an attitude, and a sneaky one at that. This card is kind of like, "Don't tell Mom, but …" Flight away from a dishonorable act is being taken when this card appears. So if *you're* not sneaking around, maybe you need to take a good look around you and see who is!

8 of Swords: Fear, Fear, and More Fear

8 of Swords.

Upright imagery and meanings: A woman stands alone in a marshy place with eight swords surrounding her—but notice that they don't pierce her. The woman is bound and blindfolded, and a castle in the distance may be either home or a place of future refuge.

The 8 of Swords reminds us that our fears can certainly render us helpless and put us in the very position in which the woman in the card finds herself. This can be the fear of moving out of a situation or of leaving something because we don't know what will replace it. The bondage of fear is a strong one, and when it's got you in its claws, you don't feel secure with anything new.

The 8 of Swords represents restricted action because of indecision and an inability to cope with the changes going on around you. Sometimes this card makes you feel like you've created your own prison or that your fears have kept you from attaining your personal goals. It can also represent deep guilt, even when that guilt is unfounded.

The woman could be too weak to fight for her rights, or continuous worry might be causing her still more stress, initiating a vicious cycle of self-imposed restrictions. Unable to think clearly, the woman needs good, sensible advice.

Wheel of Fortune

Like all the Tarot cards, the 8 of Swords has its literal meanings, and sometimes it can actually mean someone you know is in prison. Remember, too, that fear or guilt can keep you from accomplishing some wonderful ideas, putting you in a prison of your own devising.

Reversed imagery and meanings: When the 8 of Swords is reversed, the woman can let go of those swords that surround her and relax from her fears. She's now able to see through her difficulties, make a decision, and feel in control again.

New beginnings are now possible. Hope and inspiration have returned, and you're free from the restrictions brought on by your own fears. The pressures that were once weighing on you are now leaving you. The 8 of Swords reversed allows you some breathing room.

9 of Swords: Despair and Anxiety

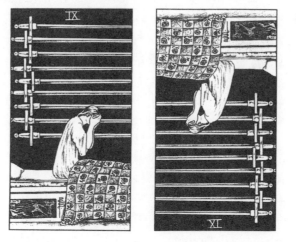

9 of Swords.

Upright imagery and meanings: Of all the Sword cards, the 9 of Swords is the most difficult. The woman crying in her bed represents the loss of hope, bad dreams, depression, desperation, and nightmares. Despair and anxiety are causing misery, pain, and emotional distress, and the woman can't seem to get out of bed, as if too much trauma has occurred. Maybe she needs medical or legal help, but in any event, it's clear that truly unfortunate conditions and sad circumstances surround her.

When the 9 of Swords appears, analyze the cards around it to see if the other cards reflect more of the same or a turnaround for the better. Each card in a spread either magnifies the turmoil or decreases it. Sadness, loss of a loved one, or just plain depression are in this card—but whether it's coming or going depends on the surrounding cards.

Reversed imagery and meanings: In its reversed meaning, the 9 of Swords shows the woman getting through the traumatic events or conditions in her life. Time will bring healing. Tomorrow is a new day.

Patience and prayer can help you on the long journey. This card can indicate that the goodness of a loved one is coming or that a life-threatening surgery was a great success. The dark cloud of trauma will pass, and you'll have developed strength of character because of it, along with the awareness that you can surmount a major tragedy.

In the Cards

For obvious reasons, the 9 of Swords is called "the Nightmare Card." When it appears in a reading, the Querent is often not surprised and tells the reader exactly what the nightmare is. Like dreams, nightmares can represent many things: fears, worries, or difficult times.

10 of Swords: The End of a Cycle, Karmic Release

10 of Swords.

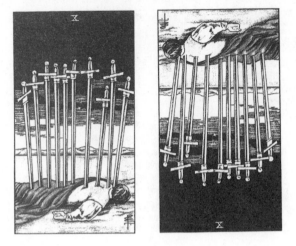

Upright imagery and meanings: The 10 of Swords shows a graphic picture of a man lying in a desolate wasteland with 10 swords piercing his back. He represents what war, strife, and major trauma can do to all of us: break us down so that we give up our will and fortitude.

This card represents the end of a cycle. This could be getting a divorce or quitting a job, but the final conclusion is at hand because no life is left in the situation. The conditions are obsolete and could lead to sudden misfortune if they don't reach their natural conclusion.

This card can indicate a deep sense of loss, which could be about a legal, work, or social situation. This card signals the end of a karmic cycle and the end of a lifestyle. But past obligations are now concluded so the old lifestyle comes to a close and the karmic debt is completed.

Reversed imagery and meanings: The reversed 10 of Swords indicates that the cycle of change has finished. Now we can see the sunrise in the background of this card, the light at the end of the tunnel.

The 10 of Swords reversed indicates a steady improvement in health and that any losses are now in your past. If you went through a divorce, for example, it's now final and you're ready to move on. Usually, by the time you get this card, you no longer have deep feelings about the loss. It was something important that you experienced, but you've detached yourself from it emotionally; the trauma is now truly in your past. This card comes up a lot when people have gone into rehab and are ready to come out, start clean, and renew their lives. New horizons and a positive cycle will begin when you receive the 10 of Swords reversed, because you've been released from a long and difficult struggle.

The Least You Need to Know

◆ Like the element air and the astrological signs Gemini, Libra, and Aquarius, Swords represent mental activity, often leading to conflict, obstacles, and aggression.

◆ Royal Swords represent a logical and balanced approach to issues.

◆ Everyday Swords indicate daily struggles and difficulties.

◆ The way you wield the power of Swords is in your hands. You have the strength to overcome your obstacles!

Chapter 16

Pentacles: Possessions, Wealth, Security

In This Chapter

- Pentacles explore your material and financial worlds
- Royal Pentacles: matters of money and success
- Everyday Pentacles: your path to financial success

Pentacles are the suit of wealth, possessions, and security. They are the cards we look to for our security in the material world. Here's where you'll find the things you value: your money, your investments, your home, and the things in it. As you look at your deck of cards, you'll notice all the yellow; this is the color of success and optimism, the color of the sun.

The Royal Court

The Royal Pentacles have the qualities required for material comfort and security. Here's where we'll find the steadfast prosperity of the King of Pentacles, the Earth Mother Queen, the hardworking Knight, and the studious Page who brings the good news we've been waiting for. Like the earth signs of astrology, Taurus, Virgo, and Capricorn, Pentacles represent the rewards of hard work.

King of Pentacles: Steadfast, Prosperous, Benevolent

King of Pentacles.

Astrological sign: Taurus

Upright imagery and meanings: This is a king of regal robes embroidered with bunches of grapes and vine leaves. Bulls' heads—which represent the astrological sign Taurus—are on the back and arms of his throne, and his home and vineyard are behind him. In his lap, he holds a pentacle and a scepter, which show his power.

The King of Pentacles has an easygoing exterior and is friendly, kind, generous, thoughtful, and industrious. He can represent a father with a kind disposition, a businessman of prosperity, or a reliable married man with his main focus on the security of his family. This king has a tremendous ability to make decisions about financial issues, and like the astrological sign Taurus, he's logical, thoughtful, methodical, and responsible. He's also very solid and steady with everyone he meets.

The King of Pentacles truly believes everyone can have security on the material plane, and he wants his family and friends to attain material success to ensure their future security. He's also accomplished at math, science, and business, and so deals well with investments, banking, and real estate. If you ever need any financial advice, this is your king!

Fools Rush In

Though slow to anger, the King of Pentacles reversed can react quite harshly if threatened. He reminds us of a bull in the field—make sure you don't wave a red flag at him!

Reversed imagery and meanings: The King of Pentacles reversed will lose the pentacle he holds and his scepter will fall away. He still desires financial security and prosperity, but upside down, he has an ulterior motive: He doesn't want to work too hard for it!

The reversed King of Pentacles wants all the good things in life but isn't able or willing to do what it takes to get them. He's stubborn, materialistic, slow to move on things, unaware of his spending habits, and makes unwise choices about money matters. This card might come up for a person who is easy to bribe or to coerce, or for a situation where deceptions about money or finances are evident.

Queen of Pentacles: Fertility and Abundance

Queen of Pentacles.

Astrological sign: Virgo

Upright imagery and meanings: This Queen holds a pentacle in her lap as she sits on a beautiful throne covered with symbols of nature and animals. A bower of roses is above her, and a cupid and some goats form part of the throne's arm. This scene of abundance is in the midst of a fertile field, and indeed, the Queen of Pentacles is the queen of fertility and abundance.

This Queen is a creative woman who knows how to raise a family and take care of the financial conditions in life. She's good at business careers and at taking care of children and gardens; she is not afraid of hard work. The Queen of Pentacles is a productive individual and enjoys seeing things or people grow. She's charitable and generous with what she has and wants to share it with others.

Like the astrological sign Virgo, the Queen of Pentacles has a quiet personality, is responsive to others, is easygoing, and is the Earth Mother type. Because she's responsible, she always fulfills her duties well.

Reversed imagery and meanings: When reversed, the Queen of Pentacles has a lot of insecurity about finances and her ability to make ends meet. She can appear moody and melancholy because she's having a hard time with the material world.

The Queen of Pentacles reversed can become too dependent on others for her well-being, or she might neglect her duties or responsibilities because of insecurity or fear. She can also show a mistrust of others and is suspicious by nature.

Fear of failing makes the Queen of Pentacles quite vulnerable to changeable moods. She can appear needy and can manipulate funds to acquire things other than life's basic needs. She's seen some hard financial times in her life—and she might well see more.

Knight of Pentacles: Steadfast Growth

Knight of Pentacles.

Astrological sign: Capricorn

Upright imagery and meanings: The Knight of Pentacles holds a pentacle out to us to show us the way to prosperity. His horse is a dark draft horse that plods along the fields of life, cultivating and developing new horizons. This young Knight is thorough and will take his time and do a good job. Trustworthy and honest, he'll get the job done the way you'd like, too.

The Knight of Pentacles has an easygoing nature, is compassionate, loves animals, enjoys children, and loves the gifts he can give others. Like his astrological counterpart Capricorn, his focus is one of helping others get ahead, and he can represent a future event such as a sale, a business deal, or an investment in something solid and stable.

Solid and stable himself, the Knight of Pentacles can bring good news concerning a pay increase, a new job offer, an investment that will increase in value, or a loan that's been approved. He could be a good broker, financial investor, veterinarian, or farmer.

Reversed imagery and meanings: The reversed Knight of Pentacles can be irresponsible, largely because he's scattered and can't focus on the job at hand. He can't follow through on things and is slow and laborious in his actions. In fact, his upside-down horse means progress is impeded.

When the Knight of Pentacles appears reversed, money, new work, and important matters in his life are at a standstill. He needs lots of encouragement to get through this difficult time. He seems to want to avoid any confrontation and is moody and withdrawn, wishing to be far from the crowds.

The Knight of Pentacles reversed could be called the loner of the Tarot, or worse, the malcontent. He's probably received his share of hard knocks and can't seem to get his life going on track the way he'd like. He neglects his duties and is unable to follow through on the commitments he originally made.

Page of Pentacles: Practice and Perseverance

Page of Pentacles.

Upright imagery and meanings: The Page of Pentacles brings to the forefront the need to study the pentacle before him. He loves to study and learn practical things and is diligent about his life. The messenger of the Pentacle suit, the Page brings to us hope and the promise of good luck in the material world.

The Page of Pentacles can be a young, persevering scholar, generous and kind with everyone he meets. He's enthusiastic about education, progress, and the material rewards that come with both. Careful and cautious, he studies everything before he makes a decision.

Reversed imagery and meanings: The Page of Pentacles reversed comes up a lot when delays prevent you from receiving good messages about finances, job offers, or scholarships.

> **Wheel of Fortune**
>
> What a guy! The Page of Pentacles' messages include things like "You got the job!" "You got a raise!" "You got the grant for college!" or "You won something for your efforts!" We hope he'll show up in your spreads often.

This Page reversed is someone who can't follow through on directions. He'll be the one to follow his young peer group, refusing to listen to good, logical counsel from adults. Rebelliousness and frustration are hallmarks of this Page reversed.

When his card is upside down, the Page of Pentacles is quiet and moody and can withdraw from or sabotage events. He has a love of luxury and material goods, but not much desire to work for them. We could call him lazy because of his procrastination and lack of motivation.

Everyday Pentacles

We all want to know if money's coming—and what to do with it when we've got it. Everyday Pentacles are the cards of your material resources: how you work to earn your money, whether you should take that gamble or play it safe, and how your efforts will pay off over time. Here is also where you'll find the comfort of your home and the security of your family. Like the element earth, Pentacles are concerned with hard work and the rewards that come with it.

Ace of Pentacles: Financial Reward Is on the Way

Ace of Pentacles.

Upright imagery and meanings: The Ace of Pentacles' Hand coming out of the clouds offers you a shiny, bright pentacle, while below it is a well-tended garden with an archway entrance. Monetary reward and the bounty of the earth are both hallmarks we'll see in all the Pentacles.

This card heralds the beginning of prosperity, wealth, and new business. You'll find it come up when you're seeking a new direction in your career and also when you're curious about matters concerning money, investments, and loans. A gift of money or material goods could be coming when this card appears in your spread.

A good foundation is developing when the Ace of Pentacles appears in a spread. You're slowly making headway with your finances, and extra money and/or an inheritance could help. The Ace of Pentacles can also signal awards, as it represents a gift given, not necessarily just money or something of material worth.

Reversed imagery and meanings: The Ace of Pentacles reversed represents a lack of prosperity. You've taken the wrong road for the new beginning, or the new beginning might not be prosperous. When this card appears, you need to look at what you're lacking before jumping into this new venture. Are you really prepared? Are you sure this is the right way to go with your money?

You might have a false sense of security, and great plans you had might not materialize. Take caution against greed or being preoccupied with money at the cost of the heart: Comfortable material conditions might not be what you need right now. Take a closer look at your checkbook and make sure everything is in order. Have you overextended yourself financially? The Ace of Pentacles reversed advises you to examine your financial management before you make your next purchase or investment.

2 of Pentacles: Juggling Resources

2 of Pentacles.

Upright imagery and meanings: In the 2 of Pentacles, we find a juggler balancing two pentacles with the ribbon of life connecting them. This juggler is literally juggling funds, trying to balance his decisions about money matters. Fortunately, he's lighthearted about this; he knows he can handle the situation at hand.

The 2 of Pentacles indicates the ability to handle several projects at once. You're able to maintain balance in the midst of change and decision-making. New projects might be difficult to get started, but you have the stamina and strength to get through them. It's important that harmony is maintained and that you don't let disturbing news set you back. Helpful advice is on its way.

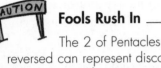

Fools Rush In

The 2 of Pentacles reversed can represent discouraging news or indicate negative information that could bring your venture to a grinding halt. It can also indicate too much money being spent on small things or frivolous goods. It could be time to double-check your numbers.

Reversed imagery and meanings: The ships in the background of this card reversed show that the ideas and conditions around you are having a hard time staying afloat. The juggler now has too many irons in the fire and can't handle everything at once.

When the 2 of Pentacles appears reversed, disorganization might be causing difficulty, and you should think ahead to prevent total failure of your plans. Although they might not be hard to handle one at a time, right now you're handling more than necessary and need to let go of one of those pentacles.

3 of Pentacles: Reward for a Job Well Done

3 of Pentacles.

Upright imagery and meanings: In the 3 of Pentacles, we see a man receiving approval from a nun and a monk. He's finishing a masonry piece in the church, and his skill and ability will be rewarded.

This card promises recognition of your skill and ability. For example, your boss will approve of your work and a pay raise might be in the works because of it. It could indicate a good review at work or acceptance for your education and talents.

Congratulations are due to you. Material gain and success are yours through your hard work and effort. The 3 of Pentacles can also represent being accepted in a group, club, or other organization.

Reversed imagery and meanings: When this card is reversed, the rewards are not coming and approval of your work and skill is delayed. The tools have fallen away from the man on the bench so he can't do his work the way he had intended.

Sometimes the 3 of Pentacles comes up reversed to mean you can't do a good job at work because you lack the proper goods or equipment. This card can also represent union or contract disagreements. If that's the case, negotiations are possible, but they might not have the outcome you desire. This card can also indicate mediocre work or that workplace conditions are not safe.

4 of Pentacles: A Firm Foundation

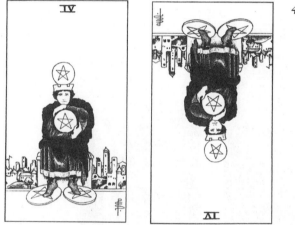

4 of Pentacles.

Upright imagery and meanings: In the 4 of Pentacles, we find a man holding tightly to the gold he's worked so hard for, and in the background we can see the city where he lives and works. This card expresses both the solidity and sound foundation of the number four and the security pentacles can bring.

The 4 of Pentacles indicates good judgment in business matters as well as many talents that could bring you and your family prosperity. The man in this card has a love of earthly possessions and feels comfortable when he has all his material goods around him. In firm command of his money and possessions, he'll work very hard to gain even more in the future.

This man has a strong attachment to the money and possessions he's worked so hard for and earned over time. Sometimes this card comes up when you're a little too tight with your money or if you have a somewhat ungenerous character. Often, this comes from the reality that it took a long time to get your money, so you're not likely to give it out so quickly. It can also indicate conservative spending habits.

Reversed imagery and meanings: Upside down, the man's no longer in control of the four pentacles he's trying to hold and balance, so one of these pentacles will fall away from him. The reversed 4 of Pentacles shows a person letting go of money or having to spend more than anticipated, as well as the chance of losing some money or earthly possessions.

This card reversed can indicate problems or an opposition in maintaining financial security at this time. The paycheck you thought was coming might be delayed, or the extra money you were anticipating doesn't arrive in time for you to pay off something. In business matters, you might be facing opposition or an extra cost you hadn't counted on. It could indicate that you might be overextending yourself financially and need to be cautious not to go overboard.

5 of Pentacles: Trying Times

5 of Pentacles.

Upright imagery and meanings: The frightening picture on the 5 of Pentacles shows two homeless people out in the snow in front of a church window. But are they willing to go in from the cold? Or do they even see they're being offered help? Maybe they'd rather take care of themselves? These are just some of the questions that come up when we study this card.

The 5 of Pentacles upright describes a condition of some kind of impoverishment. Is it spiritual loss? Financial loss? Or is it just that you don't feel connected to your community? Do you feel lost or abandoned? All these descriptions can be found in the 5 of Pentacles upright.

It's possible you've neglected your health or spiritual needs and feel at a loss as to how to handle those areas of your life. Sometimes, depending on what question you asked, it can mean loss of a job or unemployment, but this depends on the other cards around it. Clearly, though, this is a card of feeling left out in the cold.

Reversed imagery and meanings: The 5 of Pentacles is better in its reversed position. This indicates a reversal of bad luck, and you may now find new work, ending your unemployed days. You might feel that your courage has come back to you and that you're able to get back into the action of your community or home life.

When the 5 of Pentacles appears reversed, you've accepted the conditions of loss and have moved on to a higher level of understanding. You've developed compassion for those homeless folks and understand that life has its highs and lows. You have a new interest in spiritual matters and feel more hopeful with the 5 of Pentacles in this position. Courage and hope return to you now.

6 of Pentacles: A Bonus!

6 of Pentacles.

Upright imagery and meanings: Here we see the two people being offered help and extra money. The man handing out the pentacles or gold is distributing a bonus or gift, sharing what he has with the two people. The 6 of Pentacles represents sharing alms. Gifts are given and monies are shared with everyone involved.

This card is a good one. It can indicate a happy union with fellow employees, a raise in pay, a possible promotion, or profit-sharing opportunities. "You will receive what is rightfully yours," it says. This card can also indicate an inheritance coming to you.

Reversed imagery and meanings: When the 6 of Pentacles comes up reversed, the man handing out money is upside down and the scales are no longer balanced. This card indicates that the gifts may be small, that the bonus is not as large as hoped for, or that a gift is coming, but with strings attached.

In the Cards

The 6 of Pentacles represents charity, philanthropy, and the sharing of wealth. What you do will come back threefold, the ancient wisdom goes, and in this case, it's a happy return of fortune!

The distribution of an estate or bonus could be handled unfairly when the 6 of Pentacles reversed comes up. Business practices might be unfair or unethical, or your present prosperity might be threatened in some way. It's possible you're not being recognized for all the hard work and time you put into a situation. The card reversed may indicate a 401(k) plan that is not being managed very profitably or that your investments have lost value.

7 of Pentacles: Reaping What You Sow

7 of Pentacles.

Upright imagery and meanings: The 7 of Pentacles shows a farmer leaning on his hoe, contemplating how much his crop will bring this year. This card suggests that you've put your time and labor into something and will now reap the rewards.

This can mean the investment you made will have a good return, or that the garden you planted will reap a harvest plentiful enough to feed your family. The 7 of Pentacles indicates all your hard work and effort will pay off and you'll make a good profit for your time and work.

This card doesn't predict wealth, but rather good, solid accomplishments in your investments and workplace, as well as satisfactory rewards. Notice that one pentacle is not yet in the pile; a few finishing touches are still needed to bring your project to completion. With the 7 of Pentacles, though, good work and satisfaction are guaranteed.

Reversed imagery and meanings: The 7 of Pentacles reversed shows the farmer upside down. Reversed, his hoe will slip away from him and the pentacles will fall away as well. Hard work and a good amount of labor have been put into this venture, but little or no profit is gained. This card can indicate that your crop failed because of bad weather or that your investment showed no profit because of low economic times. Perhaps you didn't get a bonus because of circumstances beyond your control.

Poor speculation might be indicated when the 7 of Pentacles appears reversed, and in fact this card comes up a lot when people are gambling on what they mistakenly think is a sure thing. Be cautious with your money when this card shows up; it could be warning you that an investment won't pay off as you hoped.

> **Wheel of Fortune**
>
> If the 7 of Pentacles comes up reversed when you've asked about whether you should invest or not, it's best not to take any chances: Money is slipping away in this card!

8 of Pentacles: The Master Artisan

8 of Pentacles.

Upright imagery and meanings: The 8 of Pentacles shows an artisan/craftsperson who's worked hard on the previous seven pentacles and is now focused on an eighth one. He's hammering away, producing more with his talent. He's good at what he does and is skillful in the process. Quick and sharp, he can produce his wares at an amazing speed (kind of like us, if we do say so ourselves!).

Here you have the ability to move ahead quickly because your talents and capabilities are well rounded. Your past expertise has culminated as profit and recognition. The 8 of Pentacles predicts that you'll do well in your career or job, or that you'll profit because of your keen awareness of the need to continue and to further develop the skills you have. You can only get better at what you do by continuing to practice your craft. Practice makes perfect. That's the 8 of Pentacles.

Reversed imagery and meanings: When the 8 of Pentacles is reversed, a slowdown in production is evident. Now the artisan has trouble finding his tools and can't produce as quickly as he would like. Less than perfect work or a mediocre workplace adds up to slower or delayed production and, therefore, a loss in attaining the desired results of good and steady profit.

When this card appears, work conditions can lead employees into a labor dispute with the company, or employees might not be happy with the results of a contract. Investments will show little or no profit this year, and it's possible you should be thinking about either finding a different place of work or training for a new career. Now's the time to think about how you spend your time and what you can do to change this nonproductive situation.

9 of Pentacles: The Fruits of Your Labors

9 of Pentacles.

Upright imagery and meanings: Here we find a woman looking very calm and peaceful in her garden with rich surroundings. She's reached a secure position in her life and can spend time with family and friends or by herself. She's content in all she does.

The 9 of Pentacles indicates self-sufficiency, independence, and self-mastery of your financial/material world. When this card comes up for anyone who's working toward any type of financial independence, it assures success in those ventures.

Your past investments are coming to sound fruition with the 9 of Pentacles, and you've mastered the road to prosperity. Now you're able to share what you have with others and still have enough for yourself.

The 9 of Pentacles also represents a strong connection to the environment. It can mean a lover of wildlife and wide open spaces, someone who appreciates the beauty of Mother Earth. The woman in this card has her feet planted firmly on the ground, so if a problem ever occurs (especially if it's of a financial nature), she can handle it with sound judgment. This is a card of personal security.

Reversed imagery and meanings: The 9 of Pentacles reversed shows the woman's security slipping away. The bird will fly away, the garden hasn't been tended, and the pentacles will lose their luster. Upside down, the woman is no longer secure about her present situation.

This card could suggest that you're upset with your present home environment. Maybe money's not available for what you want to do or your growth is restricted in some way. It's possible that low income is causing concern or that a business deal or investment is causing you anxiety. Whatever the case, you're not happy with your present financial condition.

You might be afraid of losing all you've worked for when the 9 of Pentacles comes up reversed. As with all cards, the cards around this one will tell how well or poorly it all will go. Perhaps you've been depending too much on others during a rough time or you're suffering from an inadequate sum of money. The freedom to do what you want just hasn't come, so move with caution on any speculation and don't let others take advantage of you.

> **Wheel of Fortune**
>
> It's wise not to be too generous when the 9 of Pentacles shows up reversed. You might need that money for yourself in the near future! Generosity is wonderful, but not at the cost of your own personal security.

10 of Pentacles: Success over a Lifetime—Generations Even!

10 of Pentacles.

Upright imagery and meanings: If we could wish for any of the Pentacle cards to show up in a reading, this would be the one! The 10 of Pentacles represents all the wonderful conditions and material things we can accomplish in this lifetime.

This card shows a stable family with the riches we all dream of. This family has worked hard for long periods of time, maybe even generations, to accomplish this type of security: The grandparents, parents, and children represent several generations of acquiring this financial stability.

This card often comes up when the purchase of a large item, such as a house or car, is in your future. You have the money or the financing to be able to attain your dream with the 10 of Pentacles. If it seems out of your reach, your family might be able to help or a bank loan is on the horizon.

In the Cards

The 10 of Pentacles also comes for large corporations that have done well and are able to employ many people. A corporation is solid financially if the 10 of Pentacles shows up in its cards.

Everything is simply wonderful in the world now. Not only do you have money, you have security as well. Your wise investments will last a long time, providing a strong, stable foundation for yourself as well as future generations. Great wealth or great security—we'll take both!

Reversed imagery and meanings: The 10 of Pentacles reversed shows an inharmonious family. This card can signal family fights and feuds over an inheritance, estate, or stocks in a corporation. Whatever it is, the established wealth is now in question.

Did the group jeopardize its company? Its investments? Did it take too many chances that are now proving unstable? Values go up and values go down—that's the story on this card.

Sometimes the 10 of Pentacles reversed represents family misfortune, poor investing, or the squandering of finances. Corporations might have a hard time making ends meet when the 10 of Pentacles reversed shows up, and the investors/shareholders might be up in arms about their stock prices going down. Volatile and/or down-market trends certainly can be represented by the 10 of Pentacles reversed. This card can also suggest that something you own or have invested in has lost its original value.

This card can indicate financial loss due to either weak economic conditions or because of poor business management. As always, what it is depends on the other cards that appear around this one. Sometimes when the 10 of Pentacles is reversed, financial loss can lead to a legal battle or one connected to a will, pension, or investment property.

The Least You Need to Know

- Like the element earth and the astrological signs associated with it—Taurus, Virgo, and Capricorn—Pentacles represent your material and financial world.

- Royal Pentacles are your financial advisors.

- Everyday Pentacles show you the path to financial success.

- You hold the cards when it comes to Pentacles. You can create your own wealth—both financial and spiritual!

Part 5

Tarot Readings Any Fool Can Do

Getting the cards to tell a story involves a Tarot reading, which, in turn, requires a reader, a Querent (or questioner), a question, and a spread. Quite possibly, there are as many Tarot spreads as there are Tarot readers. To help you decide which spread works best for you in a given situation, we'll provide you with lots of choices and samples to choose from. Happy reading!

Chapter 17

Getting or Giving a Good Tarot Reading

In This Chapter

◆ Choosing your Tarot reader

◆ Tarot online!

◆ What should you ask?

◆ Some common spreads

◆ Reading someone else's cards

Now that you've gotten to know the cards, it's time to take advantage of what they can do for you. A Tarot reading brings together a Tarot reader and a Querent, who is a seeker with a question. The reader uses a Tarot spread, or card layout, to explore the Querent's question.

There are as many Tarot spreads as there are Tarot readers, and as you get to know the cards better and better, you might develop some spreads of your own as well. But first, let's talk about the things (and people) involved in a good reading.

Getting a Good Reading

The first essential for a good reading is that the Querent must feel comfortable with the idea of having a reading. You've got to want to have a reading, be willing to talk with others who've had readings, and be ready to trust both the reader's instincts and your own.

When we Tarot readers know it's your "first time," we like to make sure the reading is a good one as well as an introduction to what the Tarot (or any metaphysical tool) is. And we don't want to overwhelm you. When you're a first-timer, we think it's nice to do a reading that gives a basic overview of your life now—in other words, beginning in the present tense. Then we like to move on to either future conditions or things that could possibly happen.

After we've gone over the present and future, we like to talk a little about the past, which helps you know we're good at what we do. "Hey," you might say. "How'd you know that?" "Hey," we'll answer. "It's in the cards."

A good reading leaves you both enlightened and personally empowered. You come away feeling that things you are already know about have been validated, while at the same time, you've become aware of future possibilities and conditions. A good reading should make you feel "whole," or complete at some level.

> **Wheel of Fortune**
>
> If you've never had a reading of any kind, you're not alone. Arlene is often surprised by the number of people who come to her who've never had a reading before. About half say they haven't had even a palm reading at a carnival or a psychic reading at a psychic fair. Talk about spinning the Wheel of Fortune!

> **Fools Rush In**
>
> First-timers usually want to get some help making decisions and improving their life path. After all, who wants to know the negative stuff? Querents quickly learn to stay away from readers who seem to have too much "doom and gloom." They might be first-timers, but they're no fools.

How to Choose a Tarot Reader

Most people find their Tarot readers through word of mouth, from the recommendation of a close friend or family member. Because a Tarot reader can and will get to the heart of what's going on around you, most people are understandably a little cautious about whom they trust, so they turn to those they *do* trust to find the right reader for them.

Although collectively we as people might seem interested in the gory details provided by the mass media, when we consult someone privately about the future, what we really want to know is the truth—and how to handle that truth. When it comes to a Tarot reader, we want someone who will help us make progress in our lives.

So ask around. Check out the bulletin boards in your local metaphysical bookstore, and then ask the people working there about the readers who've posted their notices. Tarot's an instinctive art, and you'll instinctively know when you've found the right Tarot reader.

What About 900 Numbers?

Those who've called 900 numbers have had mixed results, and, like any reading, that depends on who the reader is. With 900 numbers, there might be the additional factor of the reader being pressed for time, because he or she has to do so many readings an hour. You might hear the rush in the reader's voice immediately, and if that's the case, you can just say, "Sorry, no thanks."

But we've also heard that readers get paid based on how long they keep Querents on the line. If a 900 number reader seems to be playing on your fears, hang up fast—he's in it for the money, not your best interests.

We recommend that for an in-depth reading you go to someone who can sit down with you for a good hour or so and "pick up your vibes."

Can You Get a Good Reading Online?

We think it's always nicer if the reader and Querent can be in the same room, but when necessary, online readings can be just as enlightening and helpful. The energy of your question will come through whether you cut the cards yourself, or whether you click for a computer-dealt spread. The quality of the reading, though, really depends on who interprets the cards for you.

As with all Tarot readings, when it comes to those on the Internet, it's a matter of who is reading the cards. The Tarot is unique in that it needs a *person* to interpret the cards. That person can be someone who knows little about the Tarot, because the pictures themselves can give a good, straightforward answer to a question using the language of universal symbols. But the best online reading, like any reading, will include both a Tarot reader and a Querent. Ideally, you've done your research to choose an online Tarot reader with a true gift and ability for reading the cards, or you are visiting a site where you can do your own card interpretations from spreads you generate at a click for free.

The Internet has become a new frontier for metaphysics as well as so many other areas of human existence and communication. Knowing full well that nothing can replace an up-front and personal reading with a "live" reader, we move into the new century with an online, do-it-yourself Tarot application. It's fun and enlightening, and it will help in a pinch when you can't make it across town to your favorite reader.

In the Cards

Several online Tarot applications can be found on the Internet, each with its own specialty. Of course, our favorite is Arlene's website: www.mellinetti.com.

In the Cards

In our newer, faster, twenty-first-century cyberspace world, a software program can actually "shuffle" Tarot cards. You decide when the shuffling stops with a push of a key, and the cards that come up are the cards for your reading. Arlene's tried this, and it's not too bad, although we still think a person-to-person reading is best.

You begin an online reading by typing your question in a space provided and then concentrating in front of your computer screen. Remember, you have to concentrate on what you really want to know. Think, type, and concentrate. Then, when you're ready, hit the "Go!" button, and the cybershuffling begins. As the cards come up onscreen, you can read the text next to each card as you select it.

For an example of how an online reading can work, we'll look at the cards for a question from Michael, who used Arlene's online Tarot application at her website: "Should I purchase the home I looked at in Seattle?" This is a simple yes or no question, so Michael selected a Three-Card Spread.

As Michael concentrated, the program shuffled, and then he hit Go. Up came Justice R, the 6 of Cups, and the Chariot R.

Michael's online Three-Card Spread.

Michael called Arlene so she could look at the three cards, too. Arlene took one look and said, "Well, nope!"

First of all, the two Major Arcana reversed indicate that too many negative lessons would be learned if Michael were to buy this house. In fact, the 6 of Cups points to why Michael had fallen in love with this house in the first place: It made him homesick for a home he'd had in Dallas. But love or not, these cards suggest that this Seattle house was either overpriced for him or that there might be legal complications with Justice reversed.

Later that week, Michael went to his bank and found out that not only was he not yet qualified for the type of loan required for that purchase, but that the home had a 10-year-old lien against it!

For Michael, the online Three-Card Spread generated by the Tarot application on Arlene's website showed far more than the "essence" of the conditions surrounding his question—it showed precisely what the problems were! And all Michael had to do was think, type, and concentrate. If you can you imagine this, you're ready for an online reading of your own.

Ultimately, the Tarot reader and the Querent will determine whether a reading is accurate or not. The only thing that's really different with an Internet reading is the method of sending the answers, and how they're sent. Whether by fax, e-mail, or mental telepathy, a good message gets where it's going! And whether by personal reader, telephone, or cyberspace, the Tarot can provide answers to guide us through those quick-fix decisions.

Whether You're Getting or Giving, Keep an Open Mind

One of the most important things to remember during a Tarot reading—whether you're getting it or giving it—is that you need to relax and keep your thoughts and heart open during the reading. When you're relaxed, you're helping the reader get and give more information rather than blocking her ability to "pick up" what's going on with you.

Your thoughts are powerful things; they can get in the way of your reading. Zen practice calls this "monkey mind": the mind that chatters on and on when you really need to focus on something.

Sometimes, when Arlene knows her client, she'll actually stop the reading and say, "Hey, knock it off! Stop thinking that way and listen for a minute, would ya!" (Needless to say, this might not be effective or appropriate with new clients.)

Before you even shuffle the deck, you need to concentrate on what you want to know now. Don't worry about the small details of life. Think about the big picture, and leave the small stuff for later in the reading. Stay open and the reader will be able to help you even more.

Is There a Specific Question to Answer?

Many times a student or client is surprised by the fact that he can ask a specific question. Many think they can only ask a general question such as, "How are things at work?"

Instead, you can—and should—ask more specific questions. Here are some examples:

◆ "How will I get along with my boss in the next six months?" (Notice that we put a time frame in the question.)

◆ "Will the person I'm dating suggest we make a special romantic trip to discuss our future on the anniversary of the day we first met?"

◆ "Is this a good time for me to take that art class I've been considering?"

◆ "Can I pay off my VISA card within the next three to six months?"

You can ask any type of question, but make sure you want to know the answer. If you don't want to hear that you need to start saving money, maybe you'd better ask about your love life instead.

As for including a time frame in the question, when a reading says you'll get a new job, wouldn't you like to know when or where, or even what? The cards can answer those questions—if you phrase your question right.

Wheel of Fortune

Be sure to phrase your question so that you get the answer in the form you want. Many people ask when their next romance will come along. When the cards say soon, the next person who comes along might indeed be romantic, but might not be the Mr. or Ms. Right they want. Be as specific as you can, and you'll get the answer you're looking for.

Understanding Tarot Spreads

Many different kinds of Tarot spreads exist, each specific to the type of reading you want to do:

◆ If you just want to know a little bit about something, use a Three-Card Spread.

◆ If you want an overall picture of the events in your life, use the Horoscope Spread.

◆ If you just want a yes or no answer, use the Wish Spread.

◆ A more universal spread is the Celtic Cross Spread, which many readers use as a general, all-purpose spread. We use it often in this book as well.

You can also make up your own spreads. Some people like the Three-Card Spread, while others prefer to use a Four-Card Spread. Whatever feels right to you is fine.

The Most Commonly Used Spread

The Celtic, or Keltic, Cross Spread is the most commonly used spread. Ten cards are laid out in the form of a cross and a staff. The cross represents the earth plane, and the staff represents a connection to heaven—in other words, heaven and earth in communion.

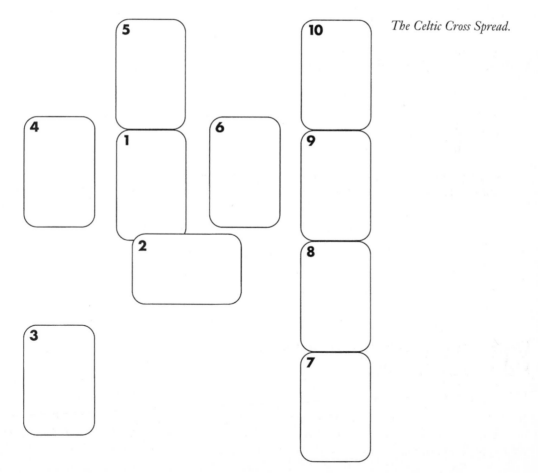

The Celtic Cross Spread.

This spread can be used for any question when you want to know not just an outcome in the mundane sense, but also the spiritual applications. A Celtic Cross Spread covers the following factors related to a question:

- The question's background

- How you yourself are feeling about the question

- How others feel about the question

- How the question can be affected by others

- What kind of Free Will and karma are present

- The question's ultimate outcome

The Celtic Cross Spread was created so you can see all of a question's ins and outs. Now you know why it's the tried-and-true favorite spread most Tarot readers use.

Shuffling and Dealing the Cards

Shuffling the deck is one of the most important aspects of the reading. How the deck is shuffled helps put the energy of the Querent into the reading. The Querent should always be the one to shuffle the deck and should do so as many times as he wants. Whether it's 5 times or 10, the Querent should feel comfortable with his shuffling.

Having the Querent do the shuffling accomplishes two things: First, it gets him to concentrate on the deck, and second, it focuses his energy and subconscious thoughts on the Tarot. Readings shuffled by the Querent tend to be more accurate because the reader gets the feel of that person very quickly and accurately.

Separating the deck into three stacks is equally important, and the Querent should do this as well. According to ancient wisdom, this separating is considered "blessing the deck." As the deck is cut into three piles, the Querent is giving permission to be read with good blessings from above. We think a little ancient wisdom, not to mention a blessing, never hurt anyone.

Pick a Card, Any Card ...

For certain spreads, such as the Horoscope Spread (which we'll show you in Chapter 19), we like to have the Querent pick out a court card (Kings, Queens, Knights, or Pages) that she feels represents herself. But how do Querents know which court card represents them?

The answer is to ask the Querent to pick a card that feels like herself. To do this, have her separate the Royal Court cards from the rest of the deck and then lay them out by suit: Wands, Cups, Swords, and Pentacles. As the Querent looks at the cards, she should consider the following:

♦ Which one of the suits do you gravitate toward?

♦ After you've picked a suit, which one of the court cards in that suit do you think represents you?

In many Tarot books, you can find physical descriptions of each of the suits. Wands represent light- or reddish-haired people, with light or ruddy complexions and blue or hazel eyes. Cups are considered fair types, with sandy-colored hair and blue or green eyes. Swords represent brown-haired people with brown or hazel eyes and medium to fair complexions. And Pentacles are people with dark or even black hair and brown or black eyes.

But what if a Querent picks a card that doesn't "look" like her? Not to worry—the card is an emotional representation, not a physical one. That's why we stuck all those descriptions in one little paragraph; we think they're too limiting.

At the same time, though, Royal Court cards can represent people in a reading. If a Querent's asked a question that involves someone in his future, we can sometimes tell what that person looks like (in general) before he or she even shows up.

The Querent has to ask a specific question to get a specific answer like this. For example, he might ask the Tarot, "Show me what my next relationship looks like" or "Give me a physical description of the person who's coming into my life." If a court card appears in the spread, it will be that person!

Fools Rush In

If there's a Doubting Thomas in the room, the reading will be adversely affected. The cards pick up that negative energy and might turn it into a garbled or nonsense reading, which is, of course, what the person was expecting. The same goes for people who laugh at the cards; their negative energy is what the cards pick up, and they in turn will laugh at them.

When You're Reading Someone Else's Cards

Atmosphere is important in a good reading. You don't have to light candles and talk softly, but both can add to the creation of a comfortable atmosphere for both reader and Querent. The Querent should feel comfortable in the room—and with you, the reader.

If you sense the Querent is feeling uncomfortable, it's up to you as the reader to voice it. "Are you feeling uncomfortable?" or "What can I do to make you feel more comfortable with this?" Offering tea or water can help put a person at ease, and sometimes just moving to a different room can help, too.

Staying Focused

Staying focused is important when you're doing a reading, and it's easy if your surroundings are quiet, comfortable, and relaxing. Take the time to create a space where you and the Querent feel relaxed so you can focus on the job at hand.

When everybody's comfortable, have the Querent shuffle the deck even before he asks the question. Then have him focus the question itself into the deck as he continues shuffling. He can do this by either thinking about the question or asking it aloud.

How the question is asked will also keep you, the reader, focused. Before the shuffling starts, you should ask the Querent, "What do you *really* want to know about this subject?" Gently insist that the Querent phrase the question to get precisely the answer he desires.

A Querent might answer, "I really want to know how I should handle my boss when she seems like she's not listening to me." Or he might say, "Is my girlfriend as committed to me as she says she is? I think she's seeing someone else."

A Querent can ask the Tarot for advice as well as just a plain yes or no answer. The Tarot can give as much information as a Querent's willing to ask for. You should encourage Querents to ask what they want to know, then have them shuffle the deck several times, and divide it into three stacks, as described a little earlier in this chapter.

A spread done according to this method will give information on what the Querent wants to know. "How should I handle my husband's temper?" "What can I do to communicate better with my child?" "What's the best way to approach this investment that everyone is so enthusiastic about?" Questions like this come up often, and if they're phrased right, the Querent will receive the advice she's seeking.

Let the Cards Do the Talking

The Tarot will communicate what the Querent *needs to know* about the question, but this might not always be what the Querent *wants* or *expects* to hear. Sometimes the cards confirm the Querent's suspicions, but just as often, they throw a surprise answer the Querent wasn't expecting or suggest an aspect the Querent hadn't considered before.

When you let the cards do the talking, the Tarot is a great tool for working with others on problem-solving. With its open perspective on the subject at hand, a Tarot spread reveals the truth about a given situation while saying it in a subtle way that allows the Querent to think about her life constructively.

You can think of the Tarot as a philosophical tool. Allow yourself and your Querent to muse over a layout of cards and meditate about what they say to you. Thinking about a spread in this way can force us to pause in our busy lives to actually think about an issue rather than just give it a quick, passing thought. Introspection allows us to become aware, once again, that we always have alternatives to choose from, no matter what the circumstances.

Creating a Positive Context

No matter which cards come up, it's your responsibility as a reader to put them in a positive context. If a reading seems filled with "negative" cards, you should spend time with the Querent exploring what those cards might be trying to tell him.

Remember, Minor Arcana cards in particular are Free Will cards, but the Querent always has the power to turn any reversed card upright, including the Major Arcana. Reversed cards in a Tarot reading can signal that the Querent, or someone near the Querent, is standing in his or her way, blocking the energy required to get something done. By understanding the energy of a reversed card the Querent receives in a reading, the Querent learns how to turn that energy in a positive direction by making good life decisions. The Querent's next reading might show that reversed card in an upright position—a reversal of fortune, indeed!

You can create a positive context by asking the Querent questions about the cards. "Is this someone you know?" "Does this represent something that's already happened?"

In one reading we know of, the skeptical Querent became convinced of the reading's validity when the King of Swords reversed appeared. "That's my boss!" he said. "It looks as if he's trying to keep me where I am instead of promoting me, because he wants me to keep doing the work I do." The rest of the reading indicated that the Querent would soon be moving on to something new. He hadn't seen his boss in this negative way before, and this new point of view encouraged him to strike out on his own.

One More Time: Practice, Practice, Practice

We can't say it enough: practice, practice, practice. You can't play the violin if you don't practice every day, and you can't master the Tarot if you don't stay in touch with the cards on a daily basis.

This can be as simple as taking a card from the deck every day and just noting what the card is. Or you can select a different card from the deck each day and spend some time meditating on its meaning.

No matter how you choose to get to know your Tarot deck, the key word is *know*. By working with the cards on a daily basis, knowing the messages they've got to tell you will become second nature.

The Least You Need to Know

- ◆ Your Tarot reader should be someone you trust.
- ◆ You should phrase your questions as specifically as possible.
- ◆ Different spreads are used for different kinds of questions.
- ◆ Reading someone else's cards requires an open mind and a positive attitude.
- ◆ If you can't get to an in-person reading with your favorite Tarot reader or want a fun change, try an online reading.

Chapter 18

What's Your Question? Ask the Cards

In This Chapter

- ◆ The Three-Card Spread for a quick fix
- ◆ The Seven-Card Spread for higher knowledge
- ◆ The Celtic Cross: your cards on the table
- ◆ When the answer doesn't fit the question

In this chapter, we're going to look at three of the most common Tarot spreads: the Three-Card Spread for a quick answer, the Seven-Card Spread for "higher knowledge" about a question, and the classic 10-card Celtic Cross, which provides all the information you need to know about a question—and maybe some you wish you didn't!

Three Cards for a Quick Answer

Sometimes you just need to know something *now*. When this happens, a Three-Card Spread can give you a quick answer to your question. Just remember, it might not always be the answer you *want* to hear.

The Three-Card Spread.

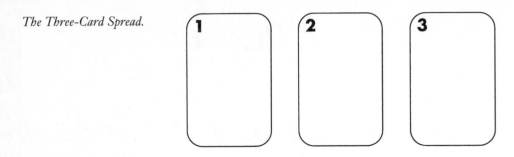

A Sample Reading

Background: With the dot-com implosion, Marie worried about her job. A Three-Card Spread provided a quick answer to her question.

Marie's Three-Card Spread: "Will I keep my job through 2003?"

What the Cards Mean

Marie's question: "Will I keep my job through 2003?"

Card 1: Ace of Cups. At the time Marie received her job offer in October 2001, it was done sincerely. This card indicates good luck with the company and the job environment for Marie's start on the job.

Card 2: Sun R. The Sun reversed indicates a clouded future. It's possible that the company is now uncertain about its financial future. Confusion exists about present conditions, and no one is happy.

Card 3: Hanged Man R. Marie might need to sacrifice one position for another. This card suggests that the position she has now will not be the same one she will have at the end of 2003. Because new job possibilities will come to her by that time, she shouldn't get too attached to her present position. Although this card indicates that Marie likely won't keep the job she has, the other cards indicate something else as well.

The two reversed Major Arcana cards show that although some troubles are destined to be brewing at Marie's workplace, they are not things she can control because—you guessed it—both of the reversed cards are Major Arcana. Marie's role will be to ride it out. In addition, we can find timing in this reading because Marie included a time (the end of 2003) in her question. By that time, Marie will have a new job!

> ### Wheel of Fortune
>
> When you do a reading similar to Marie's for yourself, be sure to include timing in the question. For instance, ask "Will my car sell within the next month?" If you ask "Will I sell my car?" you'll get a yes or a no, but you won't find out just how long that yes or no might take. The more specific you are, the more info you'll get in your answer.

Your Tarot Journal Worksheet: Do a Reading

Now it's time for you to try a Three-Card reading of your own. Go ahead—ask the cards a question.

 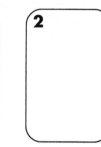 

Your Three-Card Spread.

Your Three-Card Spread Question:

_____

_____

Now shuffle the cards as you think about your question. When you're ready, place the cards as shown in the following spread figure and write them in the appropriate spaces.

Interpretation:

Card 1:

_____

_____

Card 2:

_____

_____

Card 3:

_____

_____

The Seven-Card Spread

The Seven-Card Spread is also used to get a yes or no answer, but it adds some extra spice to your answer. This spread was originally called the "Magic Seven" Spread because the last (seventh) card is the one that provides the question's resolution—and the number seven is the number of wisdom, higher knowledge, and introspection. So with a Seven-Card Spread, you get some higher wisdom thrown in to help you on your way. Lucky seven, yes?

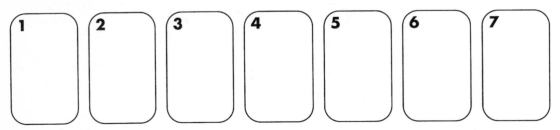

The Seven-Card Spread.

In the Cards

Numbers have all kinds of associations, both mystical and practical. In Chapter 23, you'll be taking a numerological look at the Tarot, but if you'd like to peek ahead now, we understand!

A Sample Seven-Card Spread

Background: Dennis is an adoptee who has been searching for his biological father since 1999. Although his adopted family provided him a solid and secure foundation, like many adoptees, both for personal and medical reasons, Dennis has a burning desire to know who his biological father is.

Dennis's question: "Will I find my biological father next year, and if so, how will it turn out?"

Dennis's Seven-Card Spread: Will I find my biological father next year, and if so, how will it turn out?

What the Cards Mean

Card 1: 3 of Pentacles. Dennis is seeking approval and recognition for his work trying to locate his father. He's been working on this for some time (since 1999), and although he has gotten some information about his birth mother from various legal documents, he hasn't found a great deal of documentation about his biological father.

Card 2: 2 of Swords. Until now, Dennis has been either kept back from information or has not been able to make a breakthrough in the systems he has used. In the recent past, not enough has been forthcoming, so he had to rely on his own logic and diligence. This card also reflects his meditation and contemplation about his reason for finding his biological father.

Card 3: 4 of Swords. This a card of repose and of connecting to your inner feelings and thoughts. "What shall Dennis do now?" the 4 of Swords asks. "There doesn't seem to be any type of action."

"Rest and renew your energies," the card answers. "Enjoy the peace and quiet before the next storm rolls in." Dennis should take this rest while he can, because later cards show action and movement!

Card 4: Knight of Pentacles R. Dennis's frustrations will continue a little longer, according to this card. Delays in attaining his goal and important matters still seem to be at a standstill, and as with the 4 of Swords in the third position, Dennis should rest and regroup his energy and resources. It's possible he'll need to go back to the drawing board or that he missed some valuable information in his previous research. If that's the case, the meditation and contemplation he's doing on this matter might help him see what he missed more clearly.

Card 5: The World. This is a great card to get for the near future. In Dennis's case, it relates to his need to seek outside help to achieve his goal. Travel might be involved or, at the least, communication with people beyond his local network. Still, organizations in his own community will help him in his quest. But most important to Dennis, he will succeed in his goal with help from outside.

Card 6: Ace of Wands. Here is the beginning of Dennis's renewed energy toward his goal. It looks as if something in the near future will rekindle his desire to find his biological father. This will result in renewed enthusiasm, courage, and stamina, which in turn will help him open new doors. Perhaps Dennis will get a new insight or an *aha!* and try a new approach. No matter what it is, whatever he felt was delayed or slow earlier will now take off. With the Ace of Wands, it's assured a new condition will enter Dennis's life, focusing him in an optimistic direction.

Fools Rush In

So you want to find out something that has been a secret or a mystery to you? And you want to know the answer *now?* Don't be surprised if the cards say "Cool your jets." In fact, if you listen closely to the cards' messages, you will find that they speak to you in good counsel. Yes, you might want the answer now, but the cards will gently remind you that all answers come in good time—not on your hurry-up time-table. Hang in there. It's your best and highest good that the cards are shooting for.

Card 7: Ace of Swords. This last card signals the beginning of a successful under-taking. "Victory is at hand," says the Ace of Swords, assuring Dennis that new ideas and concepts will result in swift action. With this card, movement toward his goal is so strong that it might appear to be coming out of the blue.

Dennis will have to be courageous and strong because the Sword can cut two ways—both for constructive ends, to cut away any deadwood or old hidden issues, and for destructive ends, to harm or force a situation. For this reason, Arlene advised him to be cautious in his approach to discovering his biological father. It is assured that he will find the answer he seeks, but how he handles the new information will be up to him.

Overall, Dennis's cards were positive, but they were clearly more focused on the business angle than the emotional one. The cards look positive for Dennis finding his biological father, so Arlene told him that if he remains patient and consistent, he will have the victory he has longed for. Dennis is a good, focused fellow who can handle adversity. His challenge will be to remain centered and solid while at the time flexible and supportive when he finds his biological father.

Your Tarot Journal Worksheet: Do a Reading

Now it's time for you to try a Seven-Card reading of your own. First, ask the cards a question.

Your Seven-Card Spread Question:

_____

_____

Now shuffle the cards as you think about this question. When you're ready, divide the cards into three stacks. Pick one of the stacks and deal the top seven cards, placing them as shown in the following figure. Write the cards down in the appropriate spaces, and then look up what the cards mean.

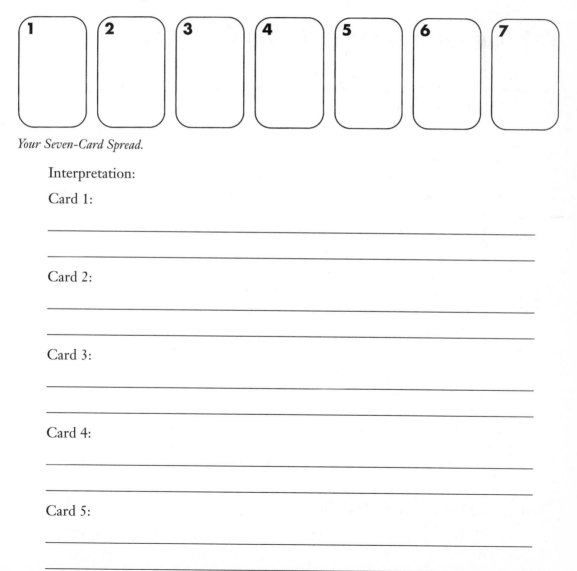

Your Seven-Card Spread.

Interpretation:

Card 1:

_____

_____

Card 2:

_____

_____

Card 3:

_____

_____

Card 4:

_____

_____

Card 5:

_____

_____

Card 6:

_____

_____

Card 7:

_____

_____

Put Your Cards on the Table: The Celtic Cross

The Celtic Cross Spread is far and away the most commonly used Tarot spread. The reasons for this are many, not the least of which is how much this spread can reveal about a particular situation.

The Celtic Cross Spread.

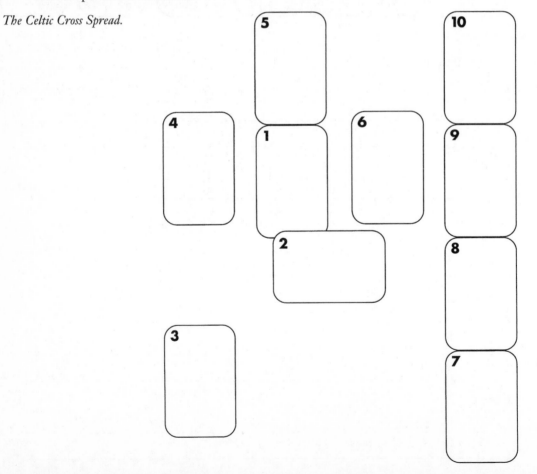

Let's look at the 10 cards in a Celtic Cross Spread one at a time:

Card 1: This card represents the Querent. It can either be dealt from the shuffled deck or selected by the Querent for that purpose. Many readers insist that this must always be a Royal Court card, but (and you know us by now) we think this is too limiting. What if you're feeling pretty 3 of Swords about the question? Or a bit like the Fool? Whether you're doing a reading for yourself or for someone else, if you decide to select this first card yourself, take the time to find the card that feels right for this particular question. You might find you go straight to a specific card you have in mind, or you might need to look more closely through the Tarot deck to find the card that has the right energy for you in this particular reading.

Card 2: This is the cover card. It is always upright and represents opposing or supporting forces. When it's a good card, it's supporting the Querent's energies—always good news. Yes, cards can be dealt reversed, but if that happens, the Querent will physically position card 2 upright for the reading. That's the ancient wisdom on the energies of card 2 in the Celtic Cross Spread.

Card 3: This card represents the Querent's energy and shows the foundation of the matter and where the question came from. In other words, this card answers the question of why you asked the question in the first place! When you look at the visual position of this card, you can see how it supports the rest of the reading and it stands for the basis of the question.

In the Cards

A Celtic, or Keltic, Cross represents everything there is to know about a question. Using the cross as its basis, it shows how a question (and its Querent) move through time.

Card 4: Here's your past experience regarding the question. This is the immediate background, and it is passing away or has already gone. We like to say, "So long, sucker!" especially when it's a negative card. Note its position next to the card representing the Querent and how it's part of the energy that surrounds him or her.

Card 5: Here's the energy around you now. This energy might manifest itself in the future, but it's Free Will energy, so its manifestation is up to you. Like the third, fourth, and sixth cards, this is part of the energy surrounding the Querent. In this position, it's the top of the matter, the possibility inherent in the situation.

Card 6: This is what's before you. Whatever the sixth card shows regarding the question will *always* happen in the future. The energies here are already at work but have not yet manifested themselves. They will. Its position here, to the right of the Querent, literally shows the future. The sixth and tenth cards in this spread also indicate timing.

Card 7: Here are your fears and hopes regarding the question. If you're afraid of others' opinions, you'll find it here. If you're hoping for their support, this card will show if it's available. Whether you recognize your fears or realize what your hopes are, they'll show up in the seventh Celtic Cross card.

Card 8: The eighth card shows how others feel about the matter you've asked about. These can be others directly involved, or they might be tangential others who don't know diddly. This card really depends on the question and how others may or may not affect its outcome.

Card 9: Here are the positive feelings about the question. You've got to get through whatever the ninth card represents to get to the tenth, and sometimes it won't feel quite so positive. If you've got to jump through hoops of fire, this is the card that will show you how high up those hoops are—and if you've got a net.

Card 10: This card represents the final outcome of the question. It will be modified and influenced by what the other nine cards have divined, but this is it, folks. Like the sixth card, the tenth card also indicates timing.

To us, a Celtic Cross is like a story about a question. What is its history? How did you get to where you are now? Where do you go from here? Who's involved? What's scary and what's not? When you want to know a question from every angle, a Celtic Cross is the spread to use.

A Sample Celtic Cross Spread

Background: Mary's career in business administration has been going well for 15 years, but she's getting tired of the routine and is ready for some new challenges. Her question for the cards focused on what's next for her.

What the Cards Mean

Mary's question: "What is the next ideal career I am meant to have?"

Card 1: The Querent: Ace of Swords. Mary is ready to start a new career. She knows a change at this point in her life might be represented by a double-edged sword, but she's tired of the same-old, same-old, and she's ready to take the risk this card implies.

Card 2: Crosses: 9 of Cups. Yes! The wish card! This card in this position indicates that Mary will get her wish! A new career is coming—one that Mary will truly identify with and care about.

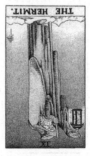

*Mary's Celtic Cross Spread:
"What is the next ideal
career I am meant to have?"*

Card 1	*Ace of Swords*
Card 2	*9 of Cups*
Card 3	*6 of Wands R*
Card 4	*4 of Swords*
Card 5	*10 of Swords R*
Card 6	*5 of Wands*
Card 7	*The Hermit R*
Card 8	*10 of Cups R*
Card 9	*8 of Cups R*
Card 10	*7 of Cups R*

Card 3: Foundation: 6 of Wands R. At the foundation of the reading, we find Mary's dissatisfaction with recent events. This could be her boredom with her routine as well as the fact that she has not received an expected promotion.

Card 4: Past: 4 of Swords. Mary has stayed where she is all these years because it's been secure. It's been a rewarding career, and the security is still there, so, with this card in this position, Arlene suggested she stay put for a little while and think about new careers, rather than take action immediately.

Card 5: What might or might not happen: 10 of Swords R. Mary has the power and insight to change and the courage to apply her past experiences to a new career direction. Her 15 years in the same position have shown her what she would like and what she wouldn't like in a new career.

Card 6: What will happen: 5 of Wands. More conflict will occur in the near future. It's possible Mary needs to stay where she is for the time being and wait things out, especially knowing that, with the 9 of Cups in the second position, something good is coming. Still, this card in this position suggests that Mary should continue to wait and see—at least for now.

Card 7: Fears or attitude toward the question: The Hermit R. Is Mary spending too much time dreaming about the perfect career? Our answer is no—you can never dream too much or aim too high. Our dreams can keep us alive, especially when we're feeling unchallenged, and that's what Mary is doing right now.

Card 8: Others: 10 of Cups R. Mary doesn't want to do what those in her family have traditionally done. She likes living in the city and enjoys the culture and surroundings offered in the Pacific Northwest. She shouldn't pay too much attention to what others think she should do or to the larger troubles of the world. It's important for her right now to focus on her new ideal.

Card 9: What you go through to get there: 8 of Cups R. New insight and hope are coming, and with them, renewed activity toward Mary's new career. We think the timing of this card could indicate that something will begin happening eight months from now: That's when Mary will be able to choose and connect to the career she wants.

Card 10: Ta da! Outcome: 7 of Cups R. Here's a plan! Mary shouldn't be hasty, but should instead focus on her goals. Because this tenth card is a Cup, it indicates that she should keep her goals heart-centered. Mary said she likes animals, and horses in particular, as well as working with children and the environment. Any of these may be related to her next career choice. Ultimately, Mary will find a position in which she can make people happy and enjoy life. We love happy endings!

Your Tarot Journal Worksheet: Do a Reading

Are you ready to try a Celtic Cross reading of your own? To begin, ask the cards a question.

Your Celtic Cross Question:

_____

_____

Next, pick out a card that you feel represents you at this moment. People most often pick Royal Court cards, but if you feel another card better represents you for this question, by all means use it. This is your number 1 card, sometimes called the significator.

Now shuffle the rest of the cards as you think about your question. When you're ready, place the remaining cards as shown in positions 2 through 10, and write them in the appropriate spaces. Then look up what the cards mean.

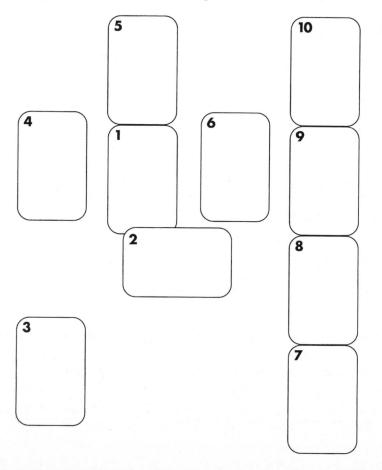

Your Celtic Cross Spread.

Interpretation:

Card 1:

_____

_____

Card 2:

_____

_____

Card 3:

_____

_____

Card 4:

_____

_____

Card 5:

_____

_____

Card 6:

_____

_____

Card 7:

_____

_____

Card 8:

_____

_____

Card 9:

_____

_____

Card 10:

_____

_____

What If the Answer Doesn't Seem to Fit the Question?

It happens—sometimes the answer doesn't fit the question at all. You asked about love and the cards talked about money. Or you asked about money and the cards talked about sex (things could be worse …). What gives? Why aren't the cards addressing the question?

This could be caused by a couple possible reasons:

♦ **You might have been thinking about another question when you were shuffling.** Maybe you were doing so subconsciously, but the cards know. The cards are going to answer the question closest to your heart—whether it's the question you voice or not.

♦ **The cards _are_ answering your question.** Maybe you asked about a relationship, but you've got to work to get there. Or the relationship you're in isn't the right one, no matter how much you want it to be. You and the reader should examine each card's meanings carefully to see just what the cards are trying to tell you. You might not want to hear it, but you might _need_ to.

With time, an answer will prove to be the right one, even if it doesn't seem to fit the question at the moment. Sometimes, at the time of the reading, situations haven't happened yet or we don't think they could ever happen. Six months later, the situation we thought wouldn't happen (or were a little foggy about) does happen.

For this reason, it's very important to either record the reading or write it down. You'll want to recall everything that was said. Most readings do take time to play out. Although the Tarot might be telling you things you already know, it might also be providing additional information about things to come. In fact, the events in readings can take from 2 to 10 months to actually happen!

Always remember that the cards only suggest, never order or preordain. A Tarot reading at its best reveals your own thoughts on a matter in a way you might not have been able to visualize. So enjoy the story; then consider its counsel carefully.

The Least You Need to Know

◆ A Three-Card Spread is a good way to get a quick answer to a question.

◆ A Seven-Card Spread adds divine wisdom to the mix.

◆ The Celtic Cross Spread, the most commonly used spread, takes a question from its roots to its outcome.

◆ With time, an answer will prove to be the right one—even when it doesn't seem to fit the question at the moment.

19

Past, Present, Future: Your Yearly Horoscope Revealed

In This Chapter

◆ The Horoscope Spread: your year in cards

◆ The Past/Present/Future Spread: the connection is in the cards

◆ Covering your Celtic: double your info

◆ A map to help you on your way

Now that you know how to phrase your question and the basic Tarot spreads, it's time to take a peek into the future. The three spreads in this chapter—the Horoscope method, the Past/Present/Future method, and a method we call covering your Celtic, which doubles the information you receive from a Celtic Cross Spread—give you three different methods of seeing things that have yet to occur.

Your Year in Cards: The Horoscope Spread

This method of reading the Tarot is called the Horoscope, or Zodiac, Spread. Your *horoscope*, or *birth chart*, is divided into 12 pie sections called *houses,* each for a specific area of your life. When you place a card in each house, the cards will show a general cycle of what will be happening in the Querent's life for the next 12 months.

Think of this spread as a yearly overview that shows both which cycle the Querent is currently in and a general glimpse of what's coming up for him. This type of spread is a good one for folks who want to know a little about something rather than specific details. This is the spread Arlene uses for anyone who tells her "There sure isn't much going on in my life right now. Can I see if something's coming—maybe something exciting or different?"

See how the 12 pie sections in the following figure are marked 1 through 12? If you know astrology, you know that this is what a horoscope looks like. Each of these 12 sections represents a specific area of your life.

Card Catalog

Your **horoscope,** or **birth chart,** is an astrological map for the moment of your birth. It is divided into 12 pie sections called **houses,** each for a specific area of your life.

The 12 houses of astrology.

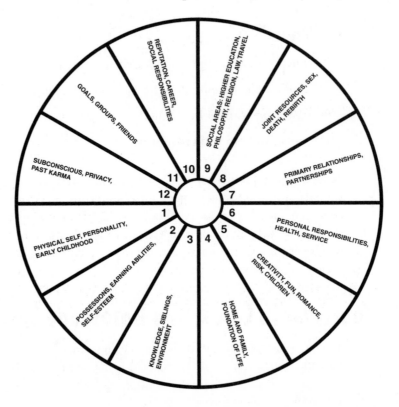

The zodiac. Find your birth date, and you'll find your astrological sign.

What's in Those Houses?

Each of the 12 houses represents a specific area of your life. You'll find everything from self-esteem to sex here.

As with any other reading, the cards will be shuffled as the Querent focuses her energy on the cards. The difference with this spread is that instead of thinking of a specific question, we look at a general overview of the life of the Querent for the next 12 months or less, so the Querent isn't thinking of a specific question. But if you're thinking, "*Aha!* Twelve months … 12 sections …," we say, "Verrry good."

Wheel of Fortune
When a client is being introduced to the Tarot, or when no burning question is asked, the Horoscope Spread is a great way to see how the Querent's year will go in general. Also, it's a good way for the reader to become acquainted with someone new to the Tarot. This spread gives the novice a good feeling for the Tarot, calmly and gradually showing what the Tarot can do and how helpful it can be, rather than hitting him with one prediction after another.

After the Querent shuffles, she divides the deck into three stacks. Then she selects one stack, whichever feels right (it's up to the Querent, as always). The reader will then use the top 12 cards, one for each month of the coming year, to lay out the spread.

The Horoscope Spread.

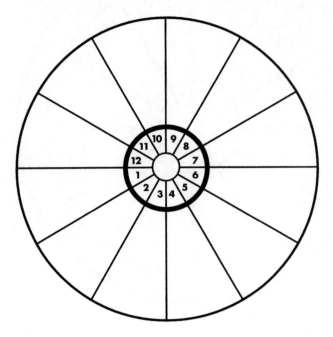

A Sample Horoscope Spread

Janice is 65 years old and has been in retail business management. She wants to add to her retirement savings while pursuing metaphysical work. For this reason, she wants to know if she will make enough money from doing psychic readings to supplement her Social Security.

Janice's Horoscope Spread: "How will my year be? Can I retire from one traditional career and start another in the field of metaphysics?"

What the Cards Mean

Card 1: Knight of Swords R. At the outset, this card suggests that Janice can't pursue her goal of being a metaphysical reader immediately. Too much conflict would occur among her various pursuits, which could cause a crisis.

Card 2: 9 of Wands. Janice is well prepared to be diversified when it comes to both work and money. She can run her home well and won't have to sell it if she doesn't want to. Janice expressed concern that she would need to sell her home if money became tight, so this card was a relief to her.

Card 3: Ace of Cups R. Janice has already started doing readings and is enjoying the work. She doesn't have many clients yet, which is likely why this Ace is reversed.

Card 4: 5 of Wands R. Janice is feeling stuck right now (hence the question). A lot of Wands up are up in the air right now, and she shouldn't force the issue, which would cause one or more of them to drop.

Card 5: 9 of Cups R. This card, too, indicates that Janice shouldn't make any big changes yet, no matter how impatient she is. It will likely take most of the year for her to get her Cups in order so she can move on to seeing her wishes come true.

Card 6: Ace of Swords R. Patience is advised here as well. In its reversed position, the Ace of Swords advises extreme caution and, in this case, patience as well.

Card 7: Star R. Yes, it's the Star, but because it's reversed, Janice needs to bide her time in order to make her dreams come true. Are you seeing a pattern here?

Card 8: Queen of Swords. Here's the first of the court cards that will arrive to help Janice achieve her goal. With her logical approach to all matters, the Queen of Swords will advise Janice whenever her emotions cloud an issue.

Card 9: Lovers. Janice has a choice here among a number of things she loves: She loves her current career, but she also wants to pursue a metaphysical one. When she gets to this card, she *will* make the choice, and it will be the heart-centered choice she desires.

Card 10: King of Wands. The King of Wands reminds Janice to trust her dreams and potential. He will encourage her to think positively about what she wants so she herself can realize her own goals.

Card 11: Queen of Pentacles. Another helper arrives here with the Queen of Pentacles, who assures Janice that the decision she makes will bring her monetary rewards. With all this help at this end of the reading, it's clear that Janice's patience early on will pay off.

Card 12: 9 of Swords R. At the end of the year, hope will return. Janice will not only be ready to move on to her new career, she *will* have moved on.

With the return of hope in the twelfth house, time is on Janice's side. She's hoping to retire in six months, but the cards suggest she wait a little longer, perhaps even keeping her current job part-time rather than leaving it completely while easing into the spiritual work. By the end of this reading, an air-sign lady (Queen of Swords), a fire-sign man (King of Wands), and an earth-sign lady (Queen of Pentacles) will have arrived to help Janice achieve her goals. "I can't wait!" said Janice, but as the cards indicate, the answer seems to lie in the timing, and patience will pay off here.

Your Tarot Journal Worksheet: Do a Reading

If, like Janice, you're curious about the future but just want an overview, a Horoscope Spread is the reading for you. And it works! If you're ready to try such a spread of your own, get out your cards and start shuffling.

When you're ready, divide the cards into three stacks, and then select whichever stack feels right. Place the top 12 cards from that stack in the pattern shown here.

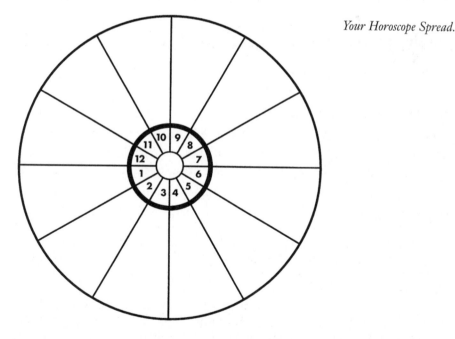

Your Horoscope Spread.

In the spaces that follow, write the names of the Tarot cards you've dealt in the appropriate slice of the Horoscope form, along with your interpretations of the cards.

"How will your year be? What can you expect?"

Card 1: _____

Card 2: _____

Card 3: _____

Card 4: _____

Card 5: _____

Card 6: _____

Card 7: _____

Card 8: _____

Card 9: _____

Card 10: _____

Card 11: _____

Card 12: _____

Past/Present/Future: Taking Stock

This spread relates our past experiences to the present and it then shows a future outcome. It's used to show the interrelationship between lessons you have learned and those you will learn in the future.

This is quite an interesting spread. Arlene has used it many times when clients really wanted to know why something happened in their past, how they're affected presently, and what will come of that past experience in the future.

A Sample Spread

Brad had been working for others for many years and felt the time was right to begin his own e-commerce business. He wanted to know if this was the right time, so he asked the cards "How will my e-commerce business go in 2003?"

For the Past/Present/Future Spread, seven cards are put out on the table after the deck has been shuffled and divided by three. The Querent again chooses the stack from which the cards are dealt.

Brad's Past/Present/Future Spread: "How will my e-commerce business go in 2003?"

What the Cards Mean

The first two cards of this spread represent past conditions.

Card 1: 4 of Swords. In the recent past, Brad has contemplated the best time to pursue this business. Because the 4 of Swords is in the first position, it would seem his rest and relaxation is coming to an end!

Card 2: King of Pentacles. Brad did a lot of research about the best type of Internet business to pursue. It seems that the research portion of his effort is coming to an end as well.

The next three cards represent Brad's present conditions:

Card 3: Queen of Swords. A wise partner is helping Brad steer through some rocky waters. Good advice is always welcome, and Brad has been listening closely to this person.

Card 4: 5 of Wands. Brad's struggles aren't over. It could be that he has too many Wands in the fire, or that others aren't making themselves clear. It's a good thing he has the Queen of Swords to guide him.

Card 5: 6 of Swords. This last card of the present shows that Brad will ultimately begin to move away from the current difficulties.

The last two cards speak to Brad's future. The sixth card is the future, and the seventh is the future resolution or outcome.

Card 6: 2 of Wands. In this card, we see a man looking hopefully toward the future, waiting for his efforts to bear fruit. This is precisely where Brad hopes to be with his business in the near future.

Card 7: The Star. You go, Brad! The Star reflects Brad's own hopes for his venture and shows that a positive, consistent investment of time and effort will prove to be not only profitable, but rewarding.

Fools Rush In _____

If you don't want to know what the future holds, don't ask! The Tarot is a powerful tool for getting in touch with your subconscious and the energies around you. Sometimes you might want to walk toward your future cheerfully ignorant of what might happen next. We understand the impulse, but don't ask the Tarot or you may find out what you don't want to know.

Your Tarot Journal Worksheet: Do a Reading

Now it's your turn to try a Past/Present/Future reading. First, shuffle the cards. When you're ready, divide the cards into three stacks, pick one stack, and then deal the cards out as shown here.

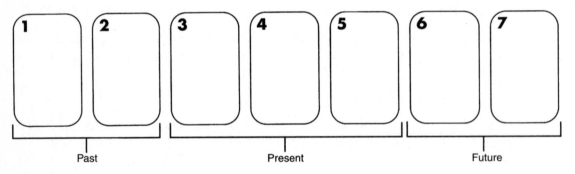

Your Past/Present/Future Spread.

Write your cards in the diagram, and then write your interpretations in the spaces that follow.

Past:

Card 1: _____

Card 2: _____

Present:

Card 3: _____

Card 4: _____

Card 5: _____

Future:

Card 6: _____

Card 7: _____

Cover Your Celtic: Double Your Info

The Celtic Cross, which we last encountered in Chapter 18, is one of the most ancient methods of reading the Tarot. In the old days, the reader would ask the Querent to write his wish or specific question on a piece of paper, then fold the paper, and place it on the table where the reading would take place. The reader would then shuffle the deck and meditate on the Querent—without asking the Querent anything and without reading the paper with the Querent's wish or question! The deck would be divided and dealt in a Celtic Cross, and the cards would be placed over the folded paper with the question on it. This way, both Querent and reader concentrated together on the reading—and the Querent never questioned the reader's psychic powers!

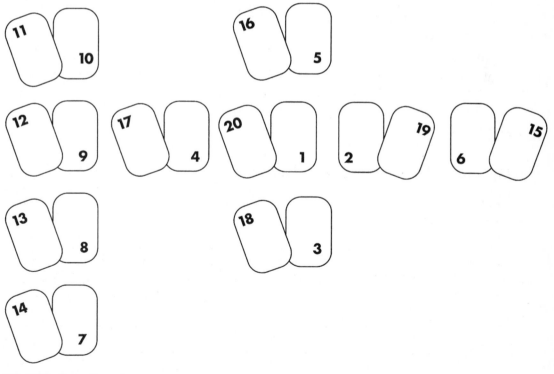

The Celtic Cover Spread.

Adding a second 10 cards to the Celtic Cross enhances the meaning of the original spread. Let's review the meanings of the first 10 cards, showing you how the second 10 cards connect to them. (Cards from the first and second spreads are separated here with a slash.)

◆ **Cards 1/20.** The Querent (what surrounds the question)

◆ **Cards 2/19.** Favorable or unfavorable conditions

◆ **Cards 3/18.** Foundation of the matter

◆ **Cards 4/17.** Conditions passing away

◆ **Cards 5/16.** What might materialize

◆ **Cards 6/15.** What will occur

◆ **Cards 7/14.** Negative feelings/fears

◆ **Cards 8/13.** Others and the question

◆ **Cards 9/12.** What you have to go through

◆ **Cards 10/11.** Final outcome

As you've probably guessed, each of the second 10 cards amplifies the card it covers. The eleventh card reveals more about the outcome; the fourteenth, more about your fears; the seventeenth, more about the past; and the twentieth, more about you! But rather than try to explain it any further, we've got a sample Celtic Cover Spread to show you.

A Sample Celtic Cover Spread

Suzanne wanted to know if a new relationship would be coming into her life, and if so, when. Because this is really a two-part question, Arlene selected a Celtic Cover Spread.

Suzanne concentrated and shuffled as she asked, "When will my new relationship come into my life?" Difficult twofold questions like this can be challenging, but we like to take such challenges on: We know as readers that the more you challenge yourself, the better you become.

Suzanne's Celtic Cover Spread: "Will a new relationship come into my life, and if so, when?"

What the Cards Mean

Card 1 and its cover (card 20): The Sun R/8 of Swords. Not only does Suzanne have a fear that no one will come into her life, her present conditions are not optimistic about a new relationship. It's almost as if, even though she wants a relationship, she is skeptical. Thus, right now, the future feels uncertain.

Card 2 and its cover (card 19): 9 of Wands/10 of Cups. On the other hand, Suzanne is well prepared to handle a good, solid commitment. She has been through a lot of emotional lessons and is now willing to take another chance at love. These cards indicate that she can handle anything that comes her way and that she now knows what she needs to give and receive love.

Card 3 and its cover (card 18): Knight of Wands/6 of Pentacles. The foundation of the question has a Knight bringing love, passion, and change into Suzanne's life.

The cover card suggests that the conditions in relation to the when and where of Suzanne's question are possibly through work or the sharing of resources or information, such as in a class. No matter when or where, however, good energy abounds, and the way is clear for her success.

Card 4 and its cover (card 17): Knight of Cups/8 of Wands R. Although Suzanne's past relationships were good, they ended in ways that caused hurt and pain or jealousy. In the recent past, Suzanne's relationships simply fizzled out—but she did enjoy them while they lasted! Remember that the energy of these cards is passing away, though.

Card 5 and its cover (card 16): 9 of Swords/6 of Cups. Suzanne could go through some of her old patterns or old feelings of loneliness or depression. She could return to her old thinking that no one is coming or that she will have to wait for a new relationship for a long time. Although her feelings are right on the surface here, because these are Free Will cards, whether or not she indulges in their energy is up to her.

Card 6 and its cover (card 15): 5 of Cups R/Ace of Cups. Ah yes! Here we find the beginning of a new romance, and with it the return of hope into Suzanne's life! Cups represent emotions, so there will be a return to a good, solid, romantic relationship. But note this is the Ace of Cups—Suzanne hasn't met this new love yet!

Card 7 and its cover (card 14): 2 of Wands/10 of Swords R. Suzanne might fear that she has to wait again, or over and over, but she needs to break the pattern that she fears the most: that a new relationship will take too long and might not end well. It's as if Suzanne's own fears are the only thing standing between her and a new relationship!

Card 8 and its cover (card 13): 7 of Pentacles/The World. Suzanne's new relationship will be accepted by all her friends and family, as well as by the community at large! Everyone will see this as a beautiful and successful relationship for her. In addition, these cards once again focus on where her new romance will be found: at her place of work, career, or creative focus.

Card 9 and its cover (card 12): King of Cups R/Page of Pentacles. Here comes the King of Suzanne's heart—slowly, slowly (he's reversed), but ultimately arriving through communications via work, school, or career (the Page of Pentacles). The fact that the King is upside down could mean he has been delayed because he's been working on some old emotional baggage, too. Or maybe he hasn't yet become open to getting involved again. Still, when he meets Suzanne—*ta da!*

Card 10 and its cover (card 11): The Star/The Hierophant. Good luck, good fortune, hope, plus inspiration from above—what better cards can Suzanne have for her reading's outcome? A commitment is arriving, and marriage is sure to be the focus of this new relationship! A great outcome is assured when this person arrives. This will be a union blessed from above, with both people appreciating its beauty and harmony.

Card 6 and Card 10 of the Celtic Cross readings indicate the timing and direction surrounding the Querent's question.

And now for the second part of the reading. Remember, Suzanne also asked when this new relationship would come into her life. The sixth and tenth positions of any Celtic Cross Spread give us a sense of timing and possible direction.

Card 6 and its cover (card 15): 5 of Cups R/Ace of Cups.

Card 10 and its cover (card 11): The Star/The Hierophant. The new meeting could occur as early as summer (Cups rule summer) or from one to five months after the reading. Major Arcana cards don't reveal timing, but Minor Arcana can. Here are the suits and the timing they represent.

Suit	Period of Time
Wands	Days to weeks
Cups	Weeks to months
Swords	Days (fast!)
Pentacles	Months to years

So Suzanne can likely look for the love of her life soon according to these cards! *Bravo!*

Your Tarot Journal Worksheet: Do a Reading

Now that you've seen a Celtic Cover Spread in action, it's time to try one of your own. Shuffle the cards as many times as you like and then lay them out as shown here. Record each card in its space on the diagram.

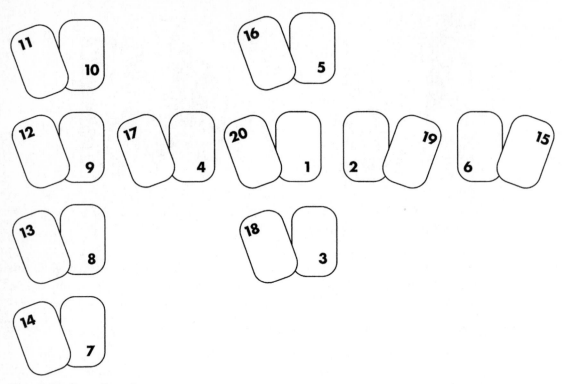

Your Celtic Cover Spread.

Now that you've done your spread, the key to reading it is to synthesize the messages of the two cards. What do you feel the two cards mean together?

The Least You Need to Know

◆ You can look ahead to your next year using a Horoscope Spread.

◆ The connection between the past, present, and future of a question can be explored with a Past/Present/Future Spread.

◆ You can double your information from a reading by covering your Celtic Cross with 10 more cards.

20

Decisions, Dreams, Karma: Searching for Answers

In This Chapter

◆ A spread to help you make a decision

◆ A spread to help your dreams come true

◆ A spread to find your karmic lessons

◆ Getting to the answers you want

It's natural to want to have some control over your future, and the three spreads in this chapter help you do just that. The first spread is called the Decision Spread, which allows you to examine at your options regarding a question. The second, the Gypsy Wish Spread, is the one to use if you really want to know if you're going to win the lottery or get a date with that cutie in the next cubicle.

The last spread is a bit different. Its four cards show your karmic lessons, which in turn can help you understand why you're going through what you're going through at the moment.

What Should You Do? The Decision Spread

The Decision Spread can help you make a decision by showing both past information and present conditions about the subject, as well as the possible future direction(s) your decision may engender.

To begin your Decision Spread, lay out three cards in a row. Then go back over the original three cards with three more cards, and then place one more layer over the first two sets of three cards, as shown in the following figure.

The Decision Spread.

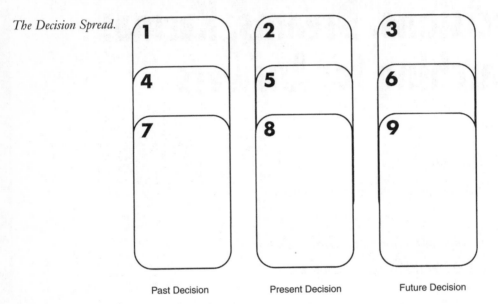

Past Decision   Present Decision   Future Decision

A Sample Spread

For our sample spread, Bob asked a question about choosing between his freelance graphic work and going to work for a global software company.

Fools Rush In _____

It's important to remember that the reader wants to give as much information as possible to the Querent. But it's the *Querent* who makes the ultimate decision on any question. It's the reader's duty and responsibility to help empower and support the Querent to his or her highest good—and let the Querent do the rest.

Here are Bob's cards after the deck was shuffled and divided into three stacks:

Bob's Decision Spread: "Should I go to work full-time for a global software company, or should I stick with my freelance business?"

What the Cards Mean

The Past: 9 of Wands R, Ace of Wands, Temperance. The first three cards represent Bob's anxiety about leaving what he has already created: his full-time, freelance job as a graphic artist/designer. He's finally gotten to a point of self-sufficiency and is now looking at how he could make more money. The Ace of Wands and Temperance say that he could go and work for a large company, but to wait and be patient for an offer that might come in.

The Present: The High Priestess R, Page of Cups, Queen of Cups R. The second three cards show that an offer will come from a woman at a software company, but because both the Queen of Cups and the High Priestess are reversed, they indicate that the offer is not what it appears to be and Bob might have to give up what he believes in. It could mean that the offer might have some hidden problems or deceptive agendas. It's nice to get an offer (Page of Cups), but what is the real motive behind it? These cards suggest that Bob should think about what he truly wants from a corporate position.

The Future: 10 of Swords, 2 of Wands R, Magician R. The third set of cards indicates that it might be best for Bob to wait for another offer from the company rather than take the first one. After all, Bob is doing pretty well on his own. The 10 of Swords indicates that he needs to realize that he has done well as a freelancer up to this point. Any offer he receives will require a review to see if he wants to sacrifice (2 of Wands reversed) some of his creativity (and independence) or not. The Magician reversed also says that he might have to give up not only creating the way he would like, but also that time and energy might be forsaken for money. Bob has to decide what he is willing to give up to go to work for someone else and move toward a corporate life.

It seems that Bob's decision is more Free Will than fated, because only three of the nine cards are Major Arcana. In other words, if Bob said no to this offer, he wouldn't be missing a calling or his life's work. It would be just another job at stake, not his future career.

We do know that the Queen of Cups reversed has light brown hair and light eyes and would make this offer to Bob. Because she's reversed, it's likely that either she will not tell the whole truth about the position or that she might not be aware of changes that could come attached to the offer.

When this Queen is reversed, either the Querent can't see the whole picture, or the Queen is not forthcoming with enough information for him to make a decision. For Bob, this suggests that he should use his own intuition if he is offered this job. Arlene told Bob to follow his innermost thoughts and heart and he wouldn't miss out on anything. Because Bob already has his career set as an entrepreneur, he would be fine to stay where he is for now.

When you read a Decision Spread, always keep in mind that the Querent wants to make a decision. Make him aware of the choices the cards present—and don't forget the timing. But remember: The decision is still up to the Querent!

Your Tarot Journal Worksheet: Do a Reading

It's your turn to try a Decision Spread. First, shuffle the cards. When you're ready, divide the deck into three stacks and select one stack. Then deal out nine cards in the configuration shown here. Use the space under each card to write down what it is and its interpretation. Happy deciding!

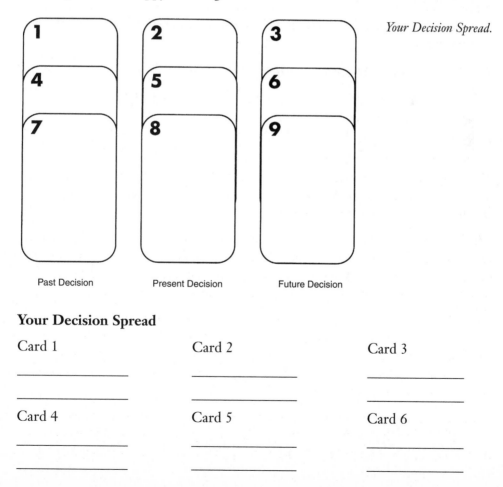

Your Decision Spread.

| Past Decision | Present Decision | Future Decision |

Your Decision Spread

Card 1   Card 2   Card 3

_____   _____   _____

_____   _____   _____

Card 4   Card 5   Card 6

_____   _____   _____

_____   _____   _____

Card 7   Card 8   Card 9

_____   _____   _____

_____   _____   _____

Past decision   **Present decision**   **Future decision**

When You Wish Upon a Card: The Gypsy Wish Spread

This spread is a fun one. At one time, it was used for predicting the outcome of a personal wish, and the Gypsy's fortune-telling ability was strongly evident when this spread was read. A question with a wish or desire attached to it works best with this spread. Some possible questions for this spread include the following:

- "Will I win the lottery?"
- "I wish to make have a strong retirement portfolio started before I'm 35. Will I?"
- "Will I become pregnant or adopt a child soon—real soon?"
- "I wish I could go to Europe this summer. Will I get to go?"

The key to this reading is the 9 of Cups, also known as the wish card. This spread is simple: If the 9 of Cups comes up in the reading, the Querent's wish will be granted!

To do a Gypsy Wish Spread, the Querent should first select a card to represent herself. This card goes at the W in the following figure. Next, have the seeker shuffle the deck while making a wish.

Then, instead of dividing the deck, have the seeker fan the cards on the table so all the remaining 77 cards are face down; you don't want the face sides to show. From the fanned-out deck, pick one card at a time until 15 cards are set aside.

These are the cards you'll use for the spread. Have the Querent shuffle the 15 cards until she feels they're ready to be placed in the Gypsy Wish Spread.

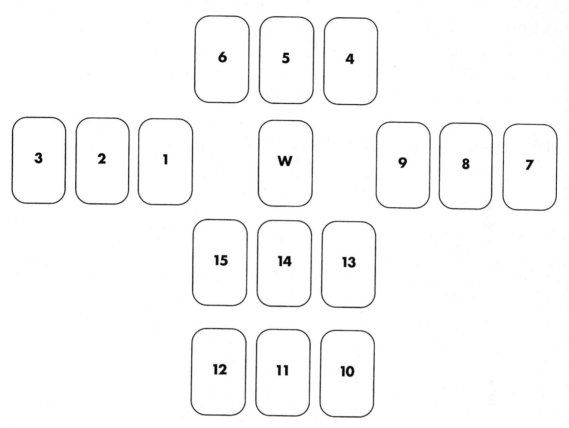

The Gypsy Wish Spread.

In the Cards

The key card in any Gypsy Wish Spread is the 9 of Cups. If it appears upright, you'll get your wish. If it appears reversed, the wish you're asking for won't occur the way you expect or want it to. It might be delayed, or it's possible you're not really sure you want what you're asking for in the first place. If the 9 of Cups doesn't come up in the spread at all, you can look at any other favorable cards to see if what you asked for will come about. You don't need the 9 of Cups to get an ultimate yes; other positive cards can do the same.

A Sample Gypsy Wish Spread

Mike recently put down earnest money on a house. He wanted to know if he'd be able to buy the house and take advantage of historically low interest rates now that he'd made that first big step.

Mike's Gypsy Wish Spread: "I wish to be able to buy the house I've put down earnest money on. Will I?"

What the Cards Mean

>   **Card 1: Knight of Cups**

>   **Card 2: 2 of Swords**

>   **Card 3: Page of Swords**

The first three cards concern the conditions around the wish. The offer was made (the Knight of Cups is here because Mike was already emotionally attached to the house), but the 2 of Swords indicates a hesitation or slowdown.

Mike said that when the mortgage company first began reviewing his file, they noticed a few small glitches—that would be the negative message from the Page of Swords. (Who applies for a mortgage without a glitch arising?) Let's see what else is going on surrounding Mike's wish.

Card 4: The Moon

Card 5: Death

Card 6: The Lovers

The next three cards represent Mike's wish or the goal of his wish. The Moon indicates that a change is going on in Mike's life—perhaps a change of residence! Death, in the fifth position, is also a card about change, but change was what Mike wanted; he wanted to move out of his parents' house and into his own. The sixth card, the Lovers, is a good omen, indicating that Mike made the right choice about the house.

Card 7: The Chariot

Card 8: 9 of Wands

Card 9: The Hanged Man

These three cards represent opposition to Mike's wish, but if they're all positive, then no opposition takes place. Here we find the Chariot, the 9 of Wands, and the Hanged Man—all upright. These cards indicate that Mike could follow this through and get his wish of homeownership, even if it means he'd have to make a sacrifice.

Mike needed to be strong, be stable, and have perseverance. He said he was really focused on this wish, and Arlene could really feel that he was. Mike was focused like the man on the 9 of Wands. He was well prepared to deal with any opposing conditions.

Card 10: 9 of Cups

Card 11: Ace of Cups

Card 12: The Emperor

The 9 of Cups! Yes! The Ace of Cups! Yes again! And the Emperor! Triple play! These three cards show what Mike would realize. It clearly looked like he would get his wish, with the Emperor, or the decision makers, approving his loan so he could buy his home! Remember, any time the 9 of Cups shows up in a Gypsy Wish Spread, the Querent's wish will come true.

Card 13: The World

Card 14: Ace of Wands

Card 15: 9 of Pentacles

These last three cards show what will come into your life, and for Mike, the pretty amazing conclusion to this reading was that he himself was clearly the 9 of Pentacles: self-reliant, doing this on his own, and focused on his intended wish. The outcome cards gave his wish a resounding "Yes!" A few more slowdowns might be encountered, but it looked like Mike's wish was going to come true just as he wanted.

Your Tarot Journal Worksheet: Do a Reading

Do you have a wish you'd like to see granted? Find out if it's possible by doing a Gypsy Wish Spread of your own. Be sure to pick out a card to represent you, the Querent, before you begin.

> **Wheel of Fortune**
>
> Remember, pick the 15 cards by fanning the whole deck face down and then picking the cards one at time. Keep them face down, put aside the rest of the deck, and then shuffle the 15 you have until you're ready to put them down in their positions.

Shuffle the deck and concentrate on your wish until you're ready to fan out the cards face down. Then pick out 15 cards, leaving them face down as well. Put the rest of the deck aside and shuffle the 15 cards you've selected until you feel you're ready to place them in the Gypsy Wish Spread.

Is the 9 of Cups there? Lucky you! If not, you still can find out how your wish will turn out by noting which cards you have and writing your interpretations of them in the spaces that follow.

What surrounds you

Card 1:

_____

Card 2:

_____

Card 3:

_____

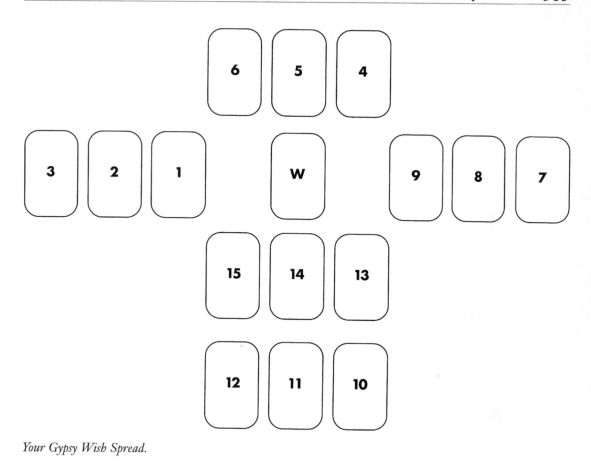

Your Gypsy Wish Spread.

Your wish

Card 4:

_____

Card 5:

_____

Card 6:

_____

What opposes you

Card 7:

_____

Card 8:

_____

Card 9:

_____

What you will realize

Card 10:

_____

Card 11:

_____

Card 12:

_____

What will come into your life

Card 13:

_____

Card 14:

_____

Card 15:

_____

Your Lesson Is in the Cards: The Karmic Spread

The Karmic Spread is a deceptively simple four-card spread. It can help you understand why you seem to go through the same sorts of situations again and again. Often, these are karmic lessons (refer to Chapter 7) that you're fated to practice over and over until you get them right. A Karmic Spread always answers the same question: "What are the karmic lessons I'm learning now?"

Focus on your question as you're shuffling the deck. When you're ready, divide the deck while continuing to concentrate on the question. Then pick the four cards any way you want and place them in the form of the Karmic Spread shown here.

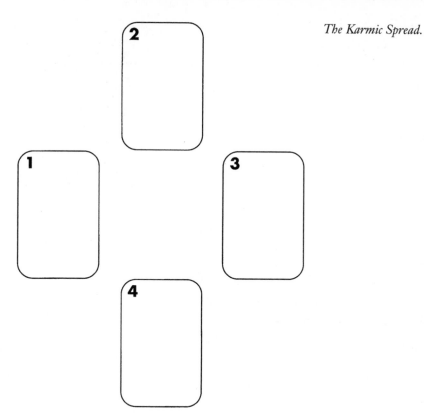

The Karmic Spread.

A Sample Karmic Spread

It seemed to Arlene that she'd been learning the same lessons waaaay too long, so she asked to be the subject of this reading. Here are the four cards she came up with:

Arlene's reading can help her decide which way she needs to go in her present conditions. Her cards indicate what she's learning presently and what's important *now* that she should pay attention to.

Arlene's Karmic Spread: "What are the karmic lessons I'm learning now?"

What the Cards Mean

Card 1: Judgement R. Arlene might be learning to deal with delays and misjudging what is going on around her. She will have to look beneath the surface of events now and evaluate them closely. Arlene might have some old fears resurface, and she might have to look at them again. She might have a sudden fear of losing what she has accomplished, or she might fear that she will not find happiness with what her goals are.

Sometimes a paralyzed feeling can come over you when you get Judgement reversed. When that happens, breathe deeply and ask for guidance. Take a timeout to evaluate where you really want to go.

Card 2: Page of Pentacles. Arlene's karmic lesson—and duty perhaps—is to pay attention to studying the issues at hand. This card suggests that if she feels inadequate about an issue, ideal, or subject, she should study and learn more about it before she makes any permanent decisions. With her inborn curiosity, Arlene loves to study anything, and she knows this would be a great way for her to learn how to apply practical applications to situations she encounters in her work as an astrologer and intuitive counselor.

Arlene did well in high school and college, but there will be some things that she, like us all, is in constant training for. In Arlene's case, the Page of Pentacles is advising her to study things she doesn't presently understand. If she doesn't understand the stock market, for example, she should study that. If it's cyberspace, she should take classes on computer science. Sometimes this card represents going back to school to learn something new.

Card 3: The Magician. This card shows that Arlene knows how to manifest both ideas and dreams into reality! Her karmic lessons might have her call upon these talents now so she can move out of the indecisiveness indicated from the two previous cards.

Remember, Judgement reversed means fear. If Arlene can learn to use the Magician to her benefit and recall that she has always been able to get out of negative situations in the past, she can gain some confidence about getting "unstuck" again.

The Magician always indicates that something great is developing, because something is being *created*. "Ask and you shall receive," says the Magician. Arlene's karmic lesson is to use what she already has within her power: her unique ability to think things through and create new ideas that will help her move out of her old fears and back into the creative territory where she thrives.

Card 4: Queen of Pentacles. This Queen can either be Arlene herself or a woman who can help Arlene. A Queen upright always represents assistance, good advice, and support. This Queen knows how to take care of the financial issues in life and can manifest all kinds of abundance. In addition, she is patient when it comes to finding the right time to move in new directions.

The Queen of Pentacles is good at business careers and at taking care of children and gardens; she is also not afraid of hard work. She enjoys seeing things grow, be it a family, a garden, or a career. So if these are not virtues Arlene has in abundance herself, then they likely belong to someone who will be of assistance to her. The Queen of Pentacles has a quiet personality, is responsive to others, has an easygoing nature, and will always fulfill her duties.

All these cards show that Arlene is now learning to release any present fears or danger she sees in her life. Arlene will be at a crossroads during this next year. Any time we have to make some major changes, it is truly nerve wracking, but these cards indicate that Arlene will learn to accept these new challenges and get through any doubts she has about herself. Plus, help is on the way to encourage her to stay on track: That good ol' Queen of Pentacles will help—if it isn't Arlene herself!

In the Cards

The four-card Karmic Spread shows what you need to work on presently —the "now"—and it can help you make decisions about how to respond to present conditions (both good and bad). This spread can help you remember that the cycle you're in has a beginning as well as an end.

Although Arlene's reading starts out showing difficulties that she has to deal with now (Judgement reversed), the other cards—the Page of Pentacles, the Magician, and the Queen of Pentacles—are all upright (good news!). In addition, both the Magician and the Pentacle suit indicate timing: The Magician is the time of year of Aries (spring), and Pentacles are the time of winter, so from the beginning of winter (December 21) through the end of spring (June 21) Arlene will have grown and learned her present karmic lessons well.

Your Tarot Journal Worksheet: Do a Reading

One of the great things about a four-card Karmic reading is that it helps you acknowledge feelings, ideas, or concerns that you have and might never have shared with anyone before. The spread is not only good for showing you how you're feeling, but it's also useful for helping you decide if you should act on those feelings or just accept the lessons as they come. The answer to that question is entirely up to you, the seeker.

Are you ready to find your karmic lessons?

Shuffle the deck until you feel you're ready to deal the four cards into the Karmic Spread shown here. After you have, you're ready to interpret the cards and see which karmic lessons you're learning now.

Your Karmic Spread

Card 1: _____

Card 2: _____

Card 3: _____

Card 4: _____

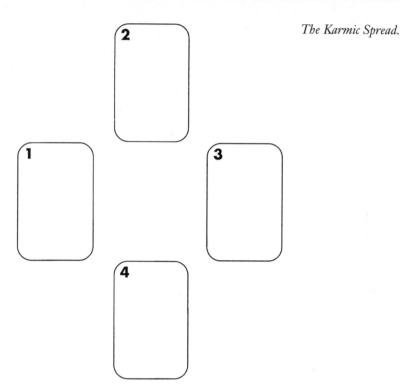

The Karmic Spread.

Are You Satisfied with the Cards' Message?

When you're not satisfied with what the cards tell you, you always have the option of reshuffling the deck and asking for your lessons to come through again. Ask the question "What is essential for me to know right now in my life? "

This question can help you focus as you reshuffle and replace the cards in the spread. Interestingly, though, when you do this, the reshuffled cards' message will be quite close to the original one.

You might not always be satisfied with what the cards tell you, but the cards don't lie. Then again, you know that by now!

The Least You Need to Know

◆ Use a Decision Spread when you need to know your options and to evaluate past, present, and future influences surrounding the decision you are asking about.

◆ A Gypsy Wish Spread can let you know if your dreams will come true.

◆ A Karmic Spread can help you find out which karmic lessons you're learning now.

◆ You can always reshuffle the cards if you don't like the way they came up the first time.

Part 6

More Ways to Interpret the Tarot

Coupled with the Tarot, you'll find a spiritual tradition reaching back thousands of years. Discover the hundreds of Tarot decks and learn how you can create a deck of your own.

Numbers are connected to Tarot symbolism as well, and Tarot shares basic principles with numerology. So join us for a tour along other fascinating paths to self-discovery through the Tarot.

Chapter 21

Tarot, Humankind, and the Future of the World

In This Chapter

◆ A spread to find your life's purpose and challenge

◆ Our Tarot reading for the year 2005

◆ What Oprah might ask the cards

◆ The world is at your fingertips

Every life has a purpose, and yours is no exception. Finding your life's purpose and challenge is what's behind the Mission Spread—a 21-card spread that enables you to look at your past, present, and future life mission and purpose.

Our curious minds wanted to know what Oprah, a woman who to our minds embodies precisely what the World card represents, would ask, if she'd only return our calls, so we asked a question for her.

What's Your Life's Purpose and Challenge? The Mission Spread

The Mission Spread begins with three rows of seven cards. The first row of seven represents what you've accomplished so far as part of your mission; the second row represents what you're presently doing about your mission; and the third row represents what you'll accomplish and contribute to this world, the mark you might make on the world, or how you'll touch the world and how it will touch you.

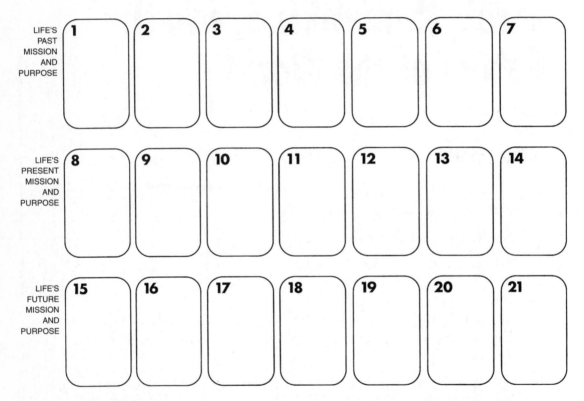

LIFE'S PAST MISSION AND PURPOSE
1 2 3 4 5 6 7

LIFE'S PRESENT MISSION AND PURPOSE
8 9 10 11 12 13 14

LIFE'S FUTURE MISSION AND PURPOSE
15 16 17 18 19 20 21

The Mission Spread.

Wheel of Fortune

When you read a Mission Spread, do it as if you were telling a story. The story will include what you've done regarding your mission in life, what you're working on now (the present), the outcome of what you are, and how the world sees your mission and accomplishment. It may also include how you will accomplish your mission, or as Arlene's students would say, how you left your mark on the world!

A Sample Mission Spread

We know you're curious about the United States and the future conditions in our country, so we thought we would do a Mission Spread for the United States, post–September 11. Because so many big changes are taking place in our country these days, we wanted to use the Tarot's infinite wisdom to get a glimpse of the United States' future possibilities and potentials, as well as an assessment of our future security.

The Tarot can reveal the potentials in a condition, person, or country. Destiny is at work, and Free Will of the collective consciousness can steer destiny's opportunities to a positive outcome. Let's see what the United States' Mission Spread looks like from today to the year 2005!

A Mission Spread for the United States, December 2002: "What is the United States' mission from now through 2005?"

1st Row: Death, 8 of Pentacles, 3 of Swords, The Chariot, Knight of Cups, Knight of Swords, The Moon

2nd Row: 9 of Cups, Queen of Swords, The Fool, Page of Cups, The Magician, 2 of Swords, 10 of Swords R

3rd Row: Devil R, Temperance R, 7 of Wands, Queen of Cups, Ace of Swords R, Judgement, 10 of Pentacles

The United States' Past Mission and Purpose

The first seven cards look at our country's past mission and purpose. We can see the Death card beginning this spread, which covers the time leading up to this cycle. During this time, our country has been going through a major transformation—Death—as we release our old ideals and goals. We have always been a prosperous country, and American citizens have always had a strong work ethic—8 of Pentacles. But as we move out of the past, we will feel hurt and sad—3 of Swords—as we alter our old way of life and learn to adjust to restrictions and new ways of looking of things.

It's important to note that Americans are innovative, and thus far we've been moving through the difficulties of our changed world. The Chariot, the two Knights (of Cups and of Swords), and the Moon indicate our continued desire to act, rather than sit by passively as our world changes. After all, we are a country of "doers" and don't want to be stopped from moving in new directions. The Moon here likely represents all Americans, who have been emotionally drained by all that our country has been through recently. Just like the phases of the Moon, the last several years have been up and down, in constant flux, with no permanent stabilization.

The final card of the first row, the Moon, reminds us that things aren't always as they seem. The Moon challenges us to tell the difference between what is an illusion and what is real in our world. We must try to avoid the tendency to become paranoid or overwhelmed by worries about what might or might not happen. Instead, we must learn to collect our thoughts and not get so overwhelmed that we can't see the forest for the trees. The message of the Moon card is to use our intuition rather than fear when making decisions.

The Moon also represents our collective development of the intuitive powers we all possess. As one of Arlene's teachers asked—and she always answered a question with a question—"When all other answers fail, where do you go?" Arlene's answer was to turn to her own intuition. Her teacher then asked, "And when you are desperate to make a decision?" Arlene answered, "We must slow down, take a breath, and ground ourselves in the reality of the moment." "Good," her teacher said. "Your intuition will be the best advisor you have at the moment of a crisis."

The Moon card tells you that sometimes your own intuition is best, and observing the crisis rather than reacting to it will help you make the right decision. The Moon reminds us to have no illusions, no deception, and, most important, no fear when we work with practical applications.

The United States' Present Mission and Purpose

The second row of seven cards shows what our country is dealing with in the present. We start with the 9 of Cups, or the wish card, which assures us that the United States will get its wish and turn things around by using the energy of creative and inventive people, such as those represented by the Queen of Swords, the Fool, and the Page of Cups. There could be a renaissance in healthcare, medicine, technology, or environmental awareness. We could read these cards as a focus back toward basics, using our native logic and good sense to get our country back on track. Our health, our land, our jobs, and our children will become a strong focus for the United States by 2005.

War could come and go in this next cycle, but the focus will hopefully turn instead to our country's security, the economy, and our self-preservation. The Magician shows us that we have the power to create new frontiers in order to restructure our society. Rather than go forth blindly or "Fool"-ishly, we should consider the mistakes we've made in the past as learning experiences. With our talented and diverse population, we can learn to create rather destroy.

In the Cards

The Magician, the 2 of Swords, and the 10 of Swords reversed indicate the possibility for both new inventions and ideas because of our crisis. Remember the old saying, "Crisis is the best counselor"? That's what applies here. In order to create, you have to be able to re-create.

Note that this row for the present aspects of our mission contains both the first Major Arcana card, the Fool, and the second, the Magician—numbers 0 and 1. These two cards indicate we are starting over and that we as a country will discover our ability to dig deep within our collective talents to achieve the goals we desire. We will get a chance to reinvent the wheel, so to speak—or ourselves at any rate.

Remember the Chinese saying, "May you live in interesting times"? This row tells us that rather than give up, we should start anew. The last card in this row, the 10 of Swords reversed, indicates that we will create a steady improvement in both our economy and our overall health, and that any losses we have incurred will be overcome using a whole new approach to societal reform. Every established institution will go through a major overhaul or reorganization, and that will be better for us, not worse.

Any traumas we suffer in the present will truly become our past in the next year or so. We will come out with a fresh approach, start clean, and renew our lives. These cards assure us that a healing will take place in our country. A karmic cycle will conclude, releasing us from a long and difficult struggle. Remember, we asked this question for today through 2005, so we are in the middle of the past-present-future cycle right now, just like the middle row of these cards. We are halfway to getting back on top of the mountain!

The Future Mission and Purpose of the United States

The third row of cards shows what our country will realize by the end of the time period asked about, 2005. This last and final row of cards, with both the Devil and Temperance reversed, shows the United States being able to release its preoccupations with both economic and material global issues. Instead, we will begin to focus on what's happening here in the United States, as indicated by the Queen of Cups, which represents the astrological sign Cancer, our country's birth sign. We will start taking care of our own basic needs, including our homes, roots, finances, and children. We will learn to nurture ourselves and let go of our fears, while at the same time recognizing that we have all had addictive behaviors that we need to learn to let go of. Temperance reversed represents learning not to go to extremes, but instead to attain a balance again.

Hindsight suggests that we've been heading toward this crisis over the last decade. It's time to reevaluate our consumer society. Is mindless consumption really the best way for us to go? We have the power to release ourselves from the bondage we have created as a society. We just have to decide and accept what this bondage is.

The final four cards in this row are the 7 of Wands, the Ace of Wands reversed, Judgement, and the 10 of Pentacles, so the future definitely looks better by 2005. We will go through some rough times with both others and the economy, and at times we will feel threatened by the ups and downs of this cycle. But we should be cautious about using anger or force to resolve things—Ace of Swords reversed. We need to keep a level head and try to recognize that everything happens for a reason.

Yes, it is sometimes hard to accept that what appears to be going backward has a reason for happening. But Judgement shows us that the collective awakening we will go through as our country renews its optimism, despite all the challenges we now face, can only make us stronger. The desire for an improvement in our country's overall health, the health of the economy, and both national and personal healing is what's important for us. These cards indicate that we have the power to use our resources more wisely and utilize good solid common sense as well.

In the twenty-first century, we will find the need to look more deeply within our collective consciousness and seek ways to come to terms with how we need to lead our country and deal with our economy. Even though the phrase "You can't go home again" seems to hit home these days, we will create new ideals for "home and country."

The three rows of a Mission Spread are read like a story, and no one row of cards is more dominant than another. Rather, they thread together like the notes of a song, with the last card of each row meshing with the first card of the next row. In this case, the Moon finishes up row one and therefore becomes the beginning theme of row two, reminding us that a major lesson for the United States at present is that "things aren't always what they seem."

We will make it through these times and emerge as a far different and more evolved country. New jobs, new work, and new hope will be created by 2005. With the 10 of Pentacles as the last card, we will bring prosperity back, perhaps in different forms than we expect today. But nonetheless the desire for equilibrium and fairness in trade and economics will be the main focus of our efforts by then. In fact, this reading assures us that life will be breathed back into our country in a manner we have never seen before.

Your Tarot Journal Worksheet: Do a Reading

Do you want to know your life's mission and purpose? Of course you do! Begin by shuffling the deck and asking the question, "What is my life's mission and purpose *now?*"

When you're ready, deal the cards into the spread shown here.

Your Mission Spread.

Write your interpretations of the cards in the space provided. Take your time—this is *your* story!

Your Mission Spread

Row 1

Card 1	Card 2	Card 3	Card 4	Card 5	Card 6	Card 7
___	___	___	___	___	___	___

Row 2

Card 1	Card 2	Card 3	Card 4	Card 5	Card 6	Card 7
___	___	___	___	___	___	___

Row 3

Card 1	Card 2	Card 3	Card 4	Card 5	Card 6	Card 7
___	___	___	___	___	___	___

We Imagine What Oprah Would Ask Us

There's something about Oprah that makes some of us feel as if we know her person-ally, like a good friend. And Oprah *is* a good friend, not just on a personal level, but on a universal one as well. As all her various efforts have made clear, Oprah really cares about the general public knowing more in order to better understand and improve society. With that in mind, we imagine that Oprah would ask a question like this of the Tarot: "What can the Tarot tell me about the role of women in the United States in the twenty-first century?" We don't know whether Oprah has used the Tarot in her life or how she feels about the Tarot, but we *do* know that Oprah is passion-ately interested in helping people improve their lives. We'll ask the question on her, and our own, behalf.

As we began in this section of readings, so shall we end—with a Celtic Cross, the basic 10-card spread that's been tried and true over the centuries. After all, as the Tarot illustrates, every journey eventually returns to its beginning.

Oprah's Celtic Cross Spread: "What can the Tarot tell me about the role of women in the United States in the twenty-first century?"

What the Cards Tell Us

Arlene shuffled the cards while contemplating Oprah and thinking about our question. We think you'll find that what the cards have to tell Oprah applies to all of us, which should come as no surprise.

Card 1: The Star. This card represents the conditions surrounding women in the twenty-first century. The Star here indicates that women will bring hope, inspiration, and guidance toward optimism in the years to come.

Card 2: The Emperor. The second card is the opposition or conditions that could prove to be difficult for women in the twenty-first century. The Emperor here clearly represents male authority. It might indicate that power through men could be a struggle or a point of contention, but as it's upright, we think it indicates that women and men will work together far better in the twenty-first century as they learn to understand and appreciate each other's differences.

Card 3: 4 of Swords R. Here we find the foundation—why we asked the question to begin with. The 4 of Swords reversed indicates renewed activity as women become more involved in society, politics, and government and labor issues. This card might be saying that women will connect to society in a more intellectual or logical way. By working in labor, politics, communications, and literature, women will make more real progress than in the past.

Card 4: The Moon R. Here we find the past—in this case, the years preceding the twenty-first century. This is where women collectively have been or what past experiences women have collectively learned up to this point. The Moon reversed here shows that women have already learned about using their intuition, feelings, sensitivities, and nurturing energy for the good of society. Women have enjoyed taking care of people, attuning themselves to family, personal issues, and emotions. But as we know, that's their past role!

Card 5: 3 of Pentacles. The fifth card represents a condition that might occur or be avoided, and the 3 of Pentacles here is a good card. We think this card could inspire women to take the opportunity it suggests: The 3 of Pentacles upright is the recognition of women's skills and abilities, an understanding that everyone has gifts, abilities, and talents. The role of women in the twenty-first century could well be one of equal partnership with men, for being widely appreciated for having skills other than those of homemaking. Look at this card: On it you can see a man *and* a woman looking approvingly at a young artist's work. In the future, men and women may very well work better together than they have in the past!

Card 6: Ace of Pentacles. This card represents what will happen or conditions that will manifest themselves. The Ace of Pentacles is all about new beginnings connected to money, resources, or investments. This indicates new work for women on the horizon, perhaps more job opportunities or new types of employment women weren't usually considered for in the past. Clearly, this card illustrates new work to do, new soil to till, and new seeds to plant.

Card 7: 4 of Pentacles. In the seventh position, we find fears or negative thoughts about the role of women in the future, and the 4 of Pentacles upright represents the fear that women might keep the status quo, remaining where they've been in the past. Holding on to old ideas, concepts, or values associated with women's roles would certainly inhibit forward movement.

Card 8: 10 of Wands. The card in this position shows how others might see women in the twenty-first century. The 10 of Wands indicates that women will still have to struggle and carry extra burdens or responsibilities in the future, or that women's roles of handling the added responsibilities of family or community might still be a big issue in our society. This could indicate that things might not change that dramatically for women.

Card 9: 2 of Pentacles R. The ninth card represents what women will have to accomplish before reaching the outcome. The 2 of Pentacles reversed represents a need to handle many situations at once, juggling so many balls that personal plans can be interrupted. It looks like women will have their work cut out for them—not only bringing home the bread, but baking it, too. Sound familiar?

Card 10: The Lovers! Here's the final outcome as we look ahead to women's roles in the twenty-first century, what all our present work is leading to. The Lovers card here shows women becoming conduits for all relationships, with their roles possibly including both unconditional love and helping others choose the direction of their lives.

This card could represent that women will become the connection between the material and spiritual worlds. Of course, women have always had this role, but because this card is upright, in the twenty-first century women might be strongly supported in their efforts to help others who need material and spiritual help.

As you look at the Lovers card, you can see that the woman looks up to the angel directly while the man looks toward the woman to make that connection with the above. We could say that the message of the card is that the male self—in both men and women—looks toward the female self in order to connect to the higher, spiritual self. Women's roles in the twenty-first century, then, will be one of love, says this card, with the heart and understanding, but also teaching others to connect to their spiritual natures.

In the twenty-first century, women will be put in positions that help open up the spirit of humankind, making it easier for us all to look at what's truly important. Women's roles will be ones of individual spiritual awakening and of enabling society to look at the heart and soul of our collective lives, helping all to discover what really makes us work as human beings.

The World at Your Fingertips

If we could, we'd have a full rhythm section playing here. You know—drums, cymbals, maybe even some fireworks. That's because we really believe that the Tarot can bring the world to your fingertips.

The more you use Tarot cards to explore yourself and the world around you, the more attuned you become to the world's—and your own—rhythms. The Tarot is more than a metaphor for a journey; it's a tool to take on the journey that is your own life.

May all your readings be Stars!

The Least You Need to Know

- You can find your life's mission and purpose by doing a Mission Spread.

- Our Mission Spread for the United States through 2005 shows transformation and change leading to better times.

- We imagine what Oprah would ask about the role of women in the twenty-first century.

- With the Tarot, the world is at your fingertips.

Choose the Deck That Suits *You*

In This Chapter

- So many decks, so little time
- Discovering the deck that's right for you
- One card, many decks
- Care and storage of your Tarot deck

In Chapter 4, we told you how many Tarot decks are available to choose from and discussed the cards' symbolic systems and possible meanings. Now that you've spent some time with each card and experimented with some Tarot spreads, it's time to think about a deck of your own.

You might choose to be traditional and choose a deck like the Universal Waite Deck we use throughout this book. You might find that the round cards of the Motherpeace deck or the ancient imagery of the Marseilles deck make you most comfortable. Or you might decide to put your own artistic talents to the test and create a Tarot deck of your own. No matter which you choose, this chapter will equip you with some of the things to consider as you discover the Tarot deck that is uniquely your own.

So Many Decks, So Little Time

U.S. Games Inc., publisher of the *Universal Waite Deck* we've used in this book, also publishes hundreds of other Tarot decks. Among the decks they sell are the *Angel* Deck, the *Aquarian* Deck, the *Cat People* Deck, the *Marseilles* Deck, the *Morgan-Greer* Deck, the *Native American* Deck, the *Witches* Deck, the *Egyptian Black and White* Deck, and *Zolar's Astrological* Deck, to name just a few. Their terrific catalog of Tarot decks and books is available by calling them at 1-800-544-2637 or by logging on to www.usgamesinc.com. The site includes links to other Tarot websites, a number of them interactive.

Card Catalog

The Universal Waite Deck, the Angel Deck, the Aquarian Deck, the Cat People Deck, the Marseilles Deck, the Morgan-Greer Deck, the Native American Deck, the Witches Deck, the Egyptian Black and White Deck, and Zolar's Astrological Deck are some of the most popular Tarot decks in use today. Tarot connoisseurs refer to the decks as the Universal Waite or the Marseilles—and so should you!

As you work with the Tarot, you'll want to try different decks. You'll also prefer different decks at different times and for different moods. This is all quite natural, so go with whatever feels right to you!

Which decks you ultimately choose to own and work with is a highly personal matter. We've included a few of the many possibilities here to whet your appetite. Ultimately, you'll find a variety of decks to suit each one of your moods. Happy shuffling!

Traditional Decks

The Universal Waite Deck we use is complemented by other versions of the Waite Deck, including the Rider-Waite, the Albano-Waite, and a Tiny Universal Waite Tarot, which is great for carrying in your purse or backpack.

We like the deck we've used, the Universal Waite, for its colors and accessibility, but any of these decks would be good basic ones:

♦ **Symbolic decks.** Among the many choices in this category are the Morgan-Greer, the Unicorn, the Witches Tarot, the Gendron Tarot, the Goddess Tarot, the Fairy Tarot, the Dragon, the Haindl Rune Oracle, and many, many more. There's a symbol for everyone among these decks!

♦ **Native American decks.** Quite a few decks in recent years have applied Native American symbolism to the Tarot. Among the decks that use this motif are the Santa Fe Tarot, the Native American, the Tarot of the Southwest Sacred Tribes, and the Medicine Woman Tarot.

Unusual and Collector Decks

So many decks fall into this category that the few we've selected only begin to give you a taste. The Motherpeace Round Tarot deck "celebrates women's culture throughout the world," and, with its lack of squared edges, reminds us that all the world's a circle.

The Tarot of Baseball deck is divided into the suits of Balls, Bats, Gloves, and Caps and is illustrated with players such as "The Rookie" and "The Pitcher of Balls." It's very clever and definitely worth a look if you're a baseball fan.

The Dali Universal Tarot deck was designed by the great surrealist Salvador Dali himself. Each card has a copy of the artist's signature (not an original one!), and the deck comes in special packaging. If you're interested in what a master artist made of Tarot's symbolism, this is a deck worth exploring.

The Chinese Tarot deck, with its lovely brush paintings, is a fine deck for meditation, as is the Ukiyoe Tarot, which uses Japanese imagery. The Tarot of the Cloisters uses stained-glass windows from the thirteenth century. The Kazanlar Tarot explores the connection between the Tarot and Christianity, Judaism, and Islam—in living color.

The Halloween Tarot translates Halloween images into Tarot symbolism. The Experimental Tarot features astrological and cosmological symbols. The Ibis deck uses Egyptian figures and symbols. The Art Nouveau deck is, well, Art Nouveau; it's lovely.

Do You See What I See?

To help you understand the differences between decks, we're going to discuss how the High Priestess (key 2) varies from deck to deck. We'll look at symbolism, imagery, and colors, and tell you what we personally like and why. Remember that this is a very subjective account. How *you* feel about the High Priestess can—and should—be very different.

The High Priestess in the Universal Waite Deck is sometimes called the Papess. She's sitting on her throne, a waxing crescent moon at her feet, a cross on her breast, the Hebrew Torah in her lap, and a pillar on each side of her. The letter on the black pillar to her right is B, and the letter on the white pillar to her left is J.

According to Tarot authority Leo Louis Martello, the black pillar is Boaz, the negative life principle, and the white pillar is Jakin, the positive life principle (the names come from the pillars of Solomon's Temple in Jerusalem). The Torah symbolizes hidden knowledge; the moon, ancient witchcraft-based religions; and the cross, the Church.

The High Priestess from the Universal Waite Deck and the Aquarian Deck look quite different.

When *we* look at this card, we're drawn first by the colors: the pure blue and white of the High Priestess's gown and the rich red pomegranate seeds bursting from their bright yellow pods. We're struck by the flow of the High Priestess's skirt, the way it seems almost liquid as it approaches the moon. We don't worry about what any of this symbolizes; we just feel a strong feminine current of intuition, the immortality of the life force, and the emotional knowledge that exists just beneath the surface.

But different decks depict this card in different ways. Sometimes you'll find the High Priestess shown as a young woman all in white. Maybe she stands at the base of a long black stairway, carrying five-pointed, star-shaped flowers in her left hand and a pomegranate in her right. Or she might be depicted in a decidedly modern way or in some variation of the huntress archetype. She might be more witchlike in some decks, or the two pillars might appear as trees or some kind of poles.

What's most important to consider about the High Priestess is that she represents our intuition or Third Eye—our all-knowing, all-seeing ability. Yes, we all need both our male and female sides (the black and white pillars) to function, but the High Priestess sits *between* the two pillars. She *is* intuition—or Third Eye, those "gut feelings" that come when we need more than just emotion and/or logic. When the High Priestess appears in your reading, she's asking that you go within and listen to your intuitive inner voice.

So what does this mean to you? If you're artistically inclined, you might want to draw your own image of what the High Priestess represents to you. Or you can examine how she appears in various Tarot decks and find the one that feels right to you.

Discovering the Deck That's Right for You

Most bookstores, including the big chains, have good selections of Tarot decks. Many keep the decks behind their counters, and, if you ask, some will let you take out the individual cards and look at them before you buy a deck.

We like to explore the used decks at our local New Age bookshops. It's fun to feel the previous owner's energy coming from a deck, and because these decks have already been opened, it's much more likely you'll be allowed to look at every single card before you decide to buy a deck. And they're cheaper, too!

You don't have to have a deck of your own to read this book, but we bet you'll want one by the time you've finished. May all your readings be adventures.

Designing and Making Your Own Tarot Deck

Are you starting to dream of a Tarot deck of your own? If so, you may want to create that deck for your own personal use. The act of creating your own Tarot deck can serve to help you refine, explore, and investigate the meanings of the cards both in a universal context and in a more personal one.

Create your own Tarot cards, such as this individualized vision of the High Priestess, on your computer using a graphic program.

If there is a store in your area that specializes in papers, such as Papers in Albuquerque or The Art Store in San Francisco, you may want to begin there. The material you choose to create your Tarot deck from is limited only by your imagination. You'll likely want to use a heavier stock, so that your cards may be shuffled easily, but if something lighter appeals to you, go with your instincts.

Your card images don't have to be drawn or painted. You may want to experiment with collage, whether using more paper, or creating your images from found objects.

In the Cards

You don't have to have a Bachelor of Fine Arts degree to design your own Tarot deck. What you will need are the inclination, the time, and an understanding of Tarot basics. If you think you've got a new idea for a Tarot deck, go for it! Who knows—your deck design could become the hottest item next Christmas!

You might choose to cut images from magazines: Perhaps a photo of a nursing mother in a maternity magazine struck you as the perfect image for the Empress, or a shot of the night sky reminded you of the Moon.

You can also design your Tarot deck using a computer graphic program. More sophisticated programs, such as Adobe Photoshop, will help you create professional quality decks, but you're your computer's reliable old Paint program can help you create the deck of your dreams.

Your dreams, in fact, can be an important source as you consider the images for your Tarot deck.

Care and Storage of Your Tarot Deck

Although you might initially keep your cards in the box your deck came in, the more comfortable you become with your deck, the more you'll want to give it a special home. Special boxes, some designed for Tarot decks and some simply well suited to them, are a popular choice. You might even want to make your own box, an option that's become quite popular in recent years.

Most people like to wrap their cards in a piece of lovely fabric where they can rest between readings. Velvet and satin in dark, soothing colors are common choices, but the fabric you choose for your own deck will ultimately be a very personal choice. Wrap the cards loosely in this cloth each time.

When you unwrap the deck, you might want to say a special affirmation. Here's one Arlene likes: As she unwraps and admires a new deck, she says, "With the receiving of this new deck, may it focus and help me focus on revealing wisdom to myself and my client."

As we discussed in Chapter 6, you'll want to "season" your Tarot cards at least once a week—more often if you use them more frequently, less often if you use them less. Seasoning your deck can be as simple as dividing out the suits and Major Arcana, one card at a time, contemplating each card as you come to it. Then shuffle the cards together, one pile at a time, until all the cards are once more well shuffled.

Dealing the Deck: Turning Cards and Shuffling

"How do you shuffle?" is one of the most commonly asked questions. The answer is that, like everything about the Tarot, how you shuffle is really up to you. Most people come to their own particular method of shuffling and cutting the deck. Here are some examples from people we know:

- Alice shuffles five times, reversing her right hand stack each time. She cuts after the fourth shuffle, then shuffles one more time.

- Mike does his shuffling on the floor of his condo. He pushes the deck all over the floor, in a sort of "Go Fish" free-form shuffle, thinking about his question until he feels the cards are ready.

- Judy likes to season her deck before every use, so before she shuffles, she goes through her cards one at a time, dividing them into five stacks, one for the Major Arcana and one for each of the Minor Arcana suits. She doesn't put the cards in order within their stacks, however. Once she's separated the cards, she shuffles the stacks together, one at a time, flipping the right hand stack as Alice does.

Most people deal from the top of their shuffled deck, but even this is up to you. You might decide to cut the deck into three stacks and then deal from the middle stack. Or you might decide to cut one last time, and then deal after that cut.

Another question we are often asked is whether you deal the cards in the position they are in from the deck or use a flip-of-the-wrist to turn them one more time. We'll bet you know our answer to this one: It's up to you! Like the cards themselves and the readings they provide, everything about dealing Tarot cards is intuitive. In other words, there are no wrong ways to shuffle and deal the cards.

What do you do when your deck gets dog-eared? Well, Arlene's cat is famous for chewing on the ends of the cards—or sometimes right through them! Arlene has decided that if you enjoy your deck and don't mind it being dog-eared (or in this case, cat-eared), you should use it. However, the problem she had with that cat-eared deck was that she knew which card was which! No fair! If that's the case, you can save your dog-eared (or cat-eared) deck and use a new one for readings. (Of course, Arlene wished her cat would have chewed up the 3 of Swords, but he never touched that one!)

Whether you find the deck of your dreams in a store or decide to create one of your own, the images on the deck you choose will have a personal resonance for you that will strengthen every time you use your deck. If, like us, you choose to have a separate deck for your own use, it will become a trusted friend on whom you can depend for advice and reassurance.

The Least You Need to Know

◆ A variety of Tarot decks are available to suit every personality—including your own.

◆ The imagery of the deck you choose will have personal resonance for you.

◆ Some decks are more pictorial and some more symbolic, making them easier or harder to read, depending on what comes naturally to you.

◆ Designing your own Tarot deck is a powerful way to commune more closely with the meanings the cards have for you.

◆ How you shuffle and deal your Tarot cards is a matter of preference and intuition.

◆ Store your Tarot deck with care and season it regularly.

Chapter 23

Tarot and Numerology

In This Chapter

- ◆ Numbers in the Tarot
- ◆ The numbers of the Major Arcana show you the steps toward enlightenment
- ◆ The numbers of the Minor Arcana show you your path in daily life
- ◆ Find the timing in the numbers
- ◆ Your personal year number

What's with the numbers on the Tarot cards anyway? Are these numbers important? Do the numbers influence the cards? Yes and yes. The numbers on the cards add meaning to your interpretation of the cards; they tell more of the story. In metaphysics, no accidents exist, so the card you draw and the number on that card have a message for you.

To look more closely at what numbers mean, let's investigate a science devoted to just that: numerology.

Numerology Is the Language of Numbers

Numerology is the ancient science of names and numbers. One of the oldest sciences, it's a companion to both astrology and the Tarot. Numerology gives meaning to the numbers. Understanding the meaning of the numbers allows us to do many things, including:

- Understanding relationships
- Analyzing human qualities
- Awakening spiritual awareness
- Predicting the timing of events
- Having universal understanding

Numerology is used in the Tarot deck in a number of ways (pun intended, of course). How? Here's the scoop.

Card Catalog

Simply stated, **numerology** is the language of numbers. Numerologists study the meanings of numbers and their connection to everything in the universe.

The Numbers and the Tarot Deck

As you already know, the Tarot deck is divided into two sections: the Major Arcana and the Minor Arcana. (Note that the "2" is for balance.) Each card bears a number, but precisely applying the meaning of a particular number to the corresponding meaning of a particular card doesn't always hold consistently throughout the 78-card deck.

Although numerology and the Tarot are unquestionably connected, exactly what the numbers on the cards mean is open to debate. In fact, the first recorded Tarot decks from the sixteenth century didn't contain any numbers at all. The numbers came later. Still, two significant facts exist about the Tarot deck and its numbers: the Major Arcana consist of 22 cards and the Minor Arcana, 56. The numerological significance of this is that 56 adds up to 11 (5 + 6), a *master number*, and 22 is also a master number. This can't be a coincidence, so we begin our discussion of the cards and numbers from this premise. The numbers on the cards are important symbols to be used for understanding your destiny.

Card Catalog

The **master numbers**, which include 11 and 22 (along with 33, 44, 55, and so on), are numbers with special properties. Master numbers teach self-mastery. They indicate great power but carry great responsibility.

The master number 11 is the number of self-illumination through spiritual inspiration appropriate for the Minor Arcana. The number 22 is the number that brings cosmic law into the material and physical world to build a new world of highest principles (the essence of the Major Arcana).

The 22 Major Arcana (22 Is a Master Number)

The Major Arcana have 22 cards—0 through 21 to be exact—and as we've already explained, the number 22 is a master number. In fact, 22 is considered the most powerful of all the numbers. It's called the master builder number because it symbolizes the potential for bringing spiritual understanding into physical form. The 22 symbolizes mastery and inspiration, and it utilizes intuitive insights, coupled with practical methodology. The 22 is meant to serve the world in its mastery.

In *Choice Centered Tarot* (Ramp Creek Publishing, 1984), Gail Fairfield calls the Major Arcana "the twenty-two steps of the spiritual path from the material world … back to oneness with 'God.'" So we might say that the Major Arcana cards serve to bring spiritual knowledge to our earthly life—not bad for a pack of cards, eh?

The Minor Arcana Add Up to 11 (The Way to Heaven!)

The Minor Arcana have 56 cards. If we add 5 + 6 (this is called reducing the number), we get the master number 11. The 11 is the most intuitive of all the numbers. It symbolizes illumination and intuitive understanding, especially of spiritual truths or principles. The 11 focuses energy on "otherworld" consciousness, but we can use that same energy to turn inward to create fears and intense conflict in our lives. The 11 symbolizes truth found in faith, not in logic, and the Minor Arcana are all about how to live life.

Because the Minor Arcana are ruled by the 11, these cards hold an intuitive understanding on how to live in the everyday world. Where illuminated truth is lacking in the events of our lives, we can either meet the challenge with fear or with faith: The cards will point the way.

> **Wheel of Fortune**
>
> Numerology Rule #1: Reduce numbers by adding digits together until only one digit remains. Numerology Rule #2: Don't reduce master numbers like 11 and 22.

> **Wheel of Fortune**
>
> We want to remind you that, like every meaning of the Tarot, its numerological representations are a starting point rather than an end point. As we've said all along, what the cards mean is up to you!

What's Behind Those Numbers?

Now that we know the Major Arcana will show us the steps and the Minor Arcana will point the way, let's see about the numbers themselves. We'll start at the very beginning with the basic meaning of numbers.

Number	Meaning
0	Unformed, empty and full, free will, no karmic debt
1	New beginnings, courage, originality, the self
2	Balancing, relationship, duality, psychic knowing, intuition
3	Creative and emotional expression, synthesis, celebration (party time!), joy, happiness
4	Stability, foundation, form, order
5	Change, instability, adaptation, rebellion, the maverick
6	Idealism, assistance, advice, problem solving, matters of the heart, committed responsibility
7	Perception, insight, inner work, reflection, wisdom
8	Power, control, organization, mastery, materialism
9	Endings, loss, grief, completion, fulfillment, vision, wisdom, intuition
10	Renewal, karmic completion, mastery

The Meanings of the Numbers in the Major Arcana

Because single-digit numbers have straightforward meanings but double-digit numbers are a little more complicated, we'd like to look at the numbers in groups before we go into them individually.

- ◆ **Cards 0 through 9.** These numbers' meanings are fairly straightforward, with the exception of the Hierophant card, which we'll discuss shortly.

- ◆ **Cards 11 through 21.** These numbers are double digits and, therefore, have double meanings: one for the double-digit number (that is, 12), and one for the reduced number (for 12, 1 + 2 = 3). For the Major Arcana, although it's important to consider both numbers, the double-digit one is the most significant.

- ◆ **Cards 11 through 19.** In addition to being double-digit numbers, the karmic numbers are found here as well. As you'll recall, "karmic" refers to a law or universal principle of individual responsibility and signifies some kind of past lesson or debt that hasn't yet been resolved. The karmic numbers are 13, 14, 16, and 19; the karmic cards are 11 (Justice), 12 (Hanged Man), 13 (Death), 14 (Temperance), 15 (Devil), and 16 (Tower).

- ◆ **Cards 20 and 21.** The number 20 is the beginning of another cycle. This number trumpets a new time, only now it's with even greater awareness and a higher vibration. The number 21 belongs to this third cycle as well, so it signifies a newness, one of greater importance than in the first and second cycles of 10 cards.

The Beginning of the Journey: Numbers 0 Through 9

0 The Fool. The 0 is the number of the unformed or unmanifest. Zero is empty and full at the same time, an open channel to the spirit world. It stands for Free Will (that's to say, no karmic debt!).

1 The Magician. The 1 is the symbol of individuality and originality. It stands for the inventive, courageous, independent, and strong-willed—all in keeping with the qualities of the Magician.

2 The High Priestess. The 2 deals with sensitivity, intuition, and psychic awareness. The number 2 signifies the balancing of opposites (good/evil, honesty/deceit, male/female, and so on) as well as relating to all subtle forces. This is the essence of the High Priestess card.

3 The Empress. The 3 symbolizes a trinity—the union of the 1 and the 2 to make a 3. The 3 is about synthesis and can also be spontaneity and enthusiasm. But in its negative form, it is about luxury and extravagance. At its best, 3 is the number of creativity—creative expression, and the ultimate creative force—motherhood.

4 The Emperor. The number 4 rules establishments and foundations, creating order, management, and stability. The Emperor is an appropriate card for the 4, which is about establishing a foundation for the self by setting boundaries, rules, and order.

5 The Hierophant. The number 5 is the number of the unconventional, the rebel, and the search for freedom. The 5 wants to break up tradition. Here the number doesn't seem to fit the card, except in situations where one opposes convention, seeking freedom from the rigidity of the Emperor or rebelling against the status quo. The 5 is about adaptation and change, while the Hierophant is decidedly the status quo.

6 The Lovers. The 6 rules love, commitment, and responsibility, and the Lovers card is about making choices in these matters.

7 The Chariot. Here the number 7 relates to perfection, the sacred, and inner wisdom that must be sought. The Chariot card is a victory over imbalances in the human soul and life, and it's the inner strength of the Charioteer that allows him (or her) to conquer the foe.

8 Strength. The 8 is the number of achieved power and success. The number here seems to suggest that your power comes from the strength to control the beast within (your "lower passion" or lust). Success is possible here.

9 The Hermit. The 9 is the number of the cosmic teacher, one with wisdom and healing power. It's the number of the visionary, too. The number 9 is about completion, closure, and endings, and it seeks wisdom through spiritual insight and inspiration. The Hermit card, bearing the number 9, speaks to an inner journey, a time of silence where wisdom might be revealed. It also indicates that a wise teacher is present to help you in your search. The 9 completes the first circuit of your journey.

The Middle of the Journey: Numbers 10 Through 19

10 Wheel of Fortune. The 10 is the number of completion and rebirth. It's a karmic number (but good karma). The 1 stands beside the 0 of unmanifested energy, and the 1 has moved through an entire cycle of 9. Now, at the 10, the 1 energy is ready to begin anew. Some experts believe the Wheel of Fortune itself is represented by the 0 of the 10 and that the post holding the wheel is the 1. So for the Wheel to be balanced, the circle must be completed, a full revolution. Only then is the Wheel ready to spin a new cycle.

11 Justice. Two 1's side by side stand ready to begin a new cycle, but a warning must be made that this cycle must be a new beginning in a balanced manner using the mastery gained in the first cycle of 10 cards. The number 11 is a master number and therefore carries the energy of spiritual force. As a result, careful thought must be given to individual thoughts, words, and deeds. Like the justice scales, each thought and deed must be weighed carefully. After all, we're dealing with karmic justice and fairness here. An individual (the 1) can no longer hold out for personal gain; it's time to move into a higher awareness. The union of the 10 (rebirth) + the 1 (self) becomes the master number 11.

12 The Hanged Man. This card's numbers are 10 and 2, which added together (12) bring in the force of the 3 (1 + 2 = 3). Here's a card that can signify a need to surrender, being trapped, and a guy who's definitely "hung up." He has to maintain balance even though he's hanging upside down (his bent knee provides the balance). Let's face it, though, this guy needs help. Note, however, that his halo is still on straight (that's his spiritual aura, remember). Because this is the second part of the journey and the card is grouped in with the karmic cards, maybe the number reflects the struggle between his inner and outer selves: He has to find the balance between them. His spiritual power is available to him.

The conflict between the 1 (independence) and the 2 (joining forces with others, in this case with a higher power) keeps him hanging until he realizes a balance is necessary. Enlightenment is possible by accepting appropriate limitations between self (1) and others (2). Then he moves to a happier state (3), as indicated by the glow on his face, and his karmic debt is lifted.

13 **Death/Rebirth.** The numbers on this card are 1 + 3, which add up to 4. The 3 in this karmic number suggests the creation of something new. A rebirth is at hand, for a death has occurred at this part of the journey. An individual (1) will engage in the hard work (the reduced number 4) of death and rebirth. As a karmic number, the 13 reveals that the past contained frivolity (God forbid), excess, and disregard for the creation of life. Superficiality dies at this point, and it's now time to cut yourself free so the new can be born. It's not easy (4); it takes transformation of your energy from one form to another to give birth to the joy of the new.

14 **Temperance.** In Temperance, we have the number 14 (10 + 4), with the 4 demanding self-control, discipline, organization, and planning. Its reduced number 5 (1 + 4 = 5) suggests adaptation, change, speaking out, communication, and resourcefulness—all qualities of the number 5. This makes a successful combination, which is the essence of the Temperance card. The 14 is a karmic number and implies that past abuses existed around a lack of discipline, hard work, frugality, and practicality. It's time to temper this karma with moderation, adaptability, and change. This card also suggests that it's time for an integration of self-control (4) and change (5). Because this card belongs to the 10 cards in the "middle of the journey," the type of change indicated is to move to a higher plane of consciousness where the aspiration is to reach a spiritual vision.

15 **The Devil.** In the Devil card, the 5 reflects the negative aspects of its number: addictions, abuse of sensual pleasures, or failure to make changes. Because 15 is also in the second part of the journey, where the 10 is joined with the 5, it's a time to complete these "devilish" habits and rise up into the energy of the 6 (1 + 5). The 6 leads you back to making the choice again, with the reward of getting to live with love—in other words, back to the Garden of Eden and the Lovers (card number 6).

16 **The Tower.** This nasty little karmic number is about housecleaning. The 6 here demands balance at the domestic level and is the number of duty, responsibility, family, and love. The 6 is about commitment and the truth that lives in the heart. The karmic number 16 tells of abuses of commitment and responsibility from the past, usually involving poor choices (echoes of the Lovers card). The reduced number 7 (1 + 6) symbolizes purification and a time for reflection

and a search for wisdom; the number 7 brings an insight into murky things hidden from view. It's important to remember, though, that this card is part of the middle journey, so you have the force of the 10 with the 6—a time of renewal. This is all part of your climb upward in the evolutionary awakening of yourself.

Card Catalog

According to Hindu tradition, the body has seven **chakras,** or energy centers. Each corresponds to places in our body or emotions. The seventh chakra is the center of spirituality.

17 **The Star.** The number 7 is the key number in the Star. The seven stars represent the seven *chakras,* or energy centers, of the body, and the number 7 symbolizes purification, inner reflection, and spiritual awareness. The reduced number 8 (1 + 7) is about the power you have achieved to make your wishes manifest. The combined influence of the numbers on this card brings inspiration, leadership, and confidence. An inner power has awakened, and self-confidence has returned!

18 **The Moon.** The number 18 of the Moon card implies an exploration of the secret realms, the inner path of wisdom. The Moon card numbers are 10 + 8, which suggest a degree of mastery is present to examine the illusive (as in illusions) forces of one's psyche: the unconscious, dreams, illusions, and deceit. This karmic card means you have the power (the 8) now available to travel the inner chambers of the psyche. The reduced number 9 (10 + 8 = 18 = 1 + 8 = 9) is strongly present in this Moon card, too. It's reminiscent of the first 9 of the Major Arcana, the Hermit. The number 9 tells us this is a card of intuition, an unfolding of psychic abilities, and a time to look within for truth and wisdom.

19 **The Sun.** The number 9 in this card is paired with the 10 and brings us to the completion of the second part of the journey. The 9 here represents all the positive aspects of the number: rewards, completion, and fulfillment. The karmic number 19 symbolizes the past abuse of spiritual and psychic wisdom, but the 19 of the Sun card, the last card of this karmic cycle, means that these past transgressions are completed. Spiritual and material success are now yours. Joy and happiness shine on you. The cycle of karma is over!

The Completion of the Journey: Numbers 20 and 21

20 **Judgement.** The Judgement card belongs to a new cycle. It's a rite of passage and, therefore, calls for a paradigm shift. The number 2 stands for cooperation and sensitivity to others—connecting the dots, so to speak. The 2 coupled with the 0 brings all the power of the spirit world to bear upon the union of people, things, attitudes, and your psychological process. An awakening takes place here,

and the power belongs to he or she who knows. You've journeyed through the evolution of the 2 energy from the High Priestess (2) to the Hanged Man (12) to Judgement (20).

The 20 here suggests that the highest qualities of the 2 and the 0 are present and potent at this juncture: psychic awareness, intuitive knowing, a balance of opposites, the resolution of duality, and sensitivity to the forces of nature and man, as well as of heaven and earth. The number 20 on the Judgement card signals that you are now on the verge of blending it all together: The Fool has successfully completed his journey and has found what he needed along the way. Now he's ready to merge with the universal.

21 **The World.** It's been said that the number 21 is the most joyful of all the numbers. It blends the 2 and the 1 into a third energy, the 3. With 21, the second cycle in the numbers is complete and you stand at the threshold of a new cycle, which has been called the "cycle of angelhood." The issues of duality (2) are no longer separating you from yourself (1), and your higher consciousness has merged with your independent earthly self. The number 3 (2 + 1) is strongly present with this card as well, bringing a profound feeling of being glad to be alive and a sense of "dancing with joy." As numerologist Eden Gray says, "It is a life well lived and a job well done." The power of spirit-inspired creativity (3) fuels your next cycle.

The Numbers and the Minor Arcana

The Minor Arcana are made up of four suits; each suit has four court cards, and the rest of the cards are numbered Ace (1) through 10. The significance of these numbers is that 4 represents order and 1 through 10 represent a cycle completed. That's a lot of cards to remember—56 to be exact—so a quick way to learn the cards is to pay attention to the numbers. A basic understanding of the numbers helps, too.

Do the Numbers Really Matter?

With no historic evidence to say what the meanings of the cards' numbers are, we'd nonetheless like to offer a few ideas as to why they're there.

First, the numbers give order to the deck. It's a neat system for knowing which cards belong where.

Second, the numbers on the cards usually symbolize the time span for the question asked. The number on the card will indicate how many days, weeks, or months are involved until the Querent's wish is granted or her question answered. This applies only to the Minor Arcana, which are about the daily life events over which we have direct control. For example, if you draw the 4 of Swords, it would indicate that your need for recuperation from stress or illness will take four weeks or four months. The numbers relate a time span. For more information, see the later section "Timing and Numbers."

> **Wheel of Fortune**
>
> On any specific card, count the number of Pentacles, Swords, Cups, or Wands for a clue as to how many people might be involved, how much time a situation might take to be resolved, or how much money is involved. The numbers do count!

Third, what we can trust about these numbers is that they provide a method of sequencing the cards, hence the journey one is making through the cards. For example, if our life finds us working our way through the journey of the Cups (emotions), we can see our progress from the 7 of Cups (where we're fantasizing and deluding ourselves) to the 8 of Cups (a time to withdraw oneself or leave a situation), to the 9 of Cups (the perfect dream come true). Without the numbers to indicate the sequence, we might fail to note that progress is in fact being made and that we're at some specific point in this process.

Here the Numbers Count

Right side up or upside down, the numbers' meanings don't change. Regardless of the suit, the numbers reveal a theme for each card.

Numbers—No Matter What Suit They Wear

Aces. Aces are the number 1, and all Aces deal with the potential for beginnings, a new time, initiating a new start, or a birthing.

Twos. The number 2 deals with duality, balance, and relationships. In the Tarot, the 2 deals with choosing or comparing two people, options, viewpoints, or situations.

Threes. The 3 symbolizes fun, joy, playfulness, celebration, creative expression, and emotional expression. The number 3 is also about triangles or threesomes. Hmmm …

Fours. The number 4 represents foundations, stability, and the status quo. It also deals with health and hard work.

Fives. The 5 is the number of change and adaptation, and in the Tarot it usually means conflict and strife. The change that's required is what causes the conflict, and the Minor Arcana fives tell us that a need exists to adapt to unpleasant changes.

Sixes. The number 6 represents the benefit of giving to others, problem-solving, and assistance. The 6 is the number of service and responsibility.

Sevens. The number 7 deals with awareness and wisdom. It's the number of inner work, research or study, reflection, and rejuvenation. In the Tarot, it signals changes brought about by wisdom and insight into a situation.

Eights. The 8 is the number of money, power, success, control, authority, and expansion. In the Tarot, the 8 shows control or mastery over a situation (or lack of it), where self-reliance and autonomy might be required (your power!).

Nines. The number 9 is about endings, loss, completion, and fulfillment, as well as the wisdom and understanding that come from the completion of the cycle. It's an intense number, filled with the energy of all the numbers (and all the cards in each suit—Ace through 9).

Tens. The number 10 means rebirth and renewal at the end of the cycle of Ace through 10. The 10 is a karmic number and means renewal is earned through work from the past. In the Tarot, the 10 indicates that lessons have been learned and mastery has been achieved, so a rebirth is at hand or is necessary. When one sword will do the job, who needs 10?

Timing and Numbers

The numbers on the cards in the Minor Arcana (but *not* the Major Arcana) can indicate the time interval covered for a question. As you discovered in Chapter 19, the suit tells whether it will be a matter of days, weeks, or months, and the number tells how many!

The Cards	The Timing
Ace through 10	1 to 10 days, weeks, or months (depending on the card, of course)
Page	11 days, weeks, or months
Knight	12 days, weeks, or months
Queen and King	Unknown time—it's up to you!

The Suit	Period of Time
Wands	Days to weeks
Cups	Weeks to months
Swords	Days (fast!)
Pentacles	Months to years

Combining the numbers and the suits tells the story. For example, the 8 of Wands means it will be eight weeks until the new project will start. The 2 of Pentacles indicates two months until the money comes in. The 4 of Cups shows it will take four days until you get his letter. And the 9 of Swords indicates an undetermined amount of time until your mind is made up.

In cases where the timing can't be determined, it's because too many factors are present to indicate accurate timing. The message when this happens: It will take more time for the angels to get things lined up.

The Personal Year and the Tarot

Although the Major Arcana numbers aren't used to find the timing of an event, they *can* be used to tell the theme for a given year. In numerology, we have a way of discovering what a current calendar year's theme is for each individual. Called your "personal year," this method was pioneered by Angeles Arrien in *The Tarot Handbook* (Arcus Publishing Co., 1987). If you want to know what a specific year means for you personally, here's how to do it.

First, to find your personal year number, add your birthday numbers together—in a very specific way. Use the month and day of your birthday only, and then add them to the current calendar year.

Fools Rush In

Don't use the numbers of the Major Arcana to tell time! The Major Arcana are about the here and now because they're governed by forces outside you and indicate the ongoing process you're involved in psychologically and spiritually.

To see how a personal year resonates for an individual, let's look at former U.S. president Jimmy Carter's acceptance of the Nobel Peace Prize in 2002. Jimmy Carter's birthday is October 1, 1924, so we'll be using his birth month and day for our calculations.

Month	10
Day	1
Calendar year	2002
Total	2013

Now reduce this number for the total: 2 + 0 + 1 + 3 = 6.

So in 2002, Carter had a 6 personal year, corresponding to the Lovers Major Arcana card. The Lovers has a broader meaning than just for lovers. It makes sense that the Nobel Peace Prize should be awarded to Carter for a lifetime commitment to furthering global health, harmony, and happiness for all the world family during a

6 personal year for him. After all, like Carter's Libra astrological sign, the 6—and the Lovers card—are all about balance and harmony. It is probably also no accident that the announcement of Carter's prize came on October 11, 2002—11 is a master number of high spiritual energy signifying the uplifting of humanity, and is the number of the peacemaker.

Important note: If the final total is a double-digit number, don't reduce it if it's between 10 and 21. Your personal year equivalent is a Major Arcana card.

Now that you know your personal year number, the next step is to find the Major Arcana card that matches your number. Note that you can't have a 0 year (even if it feels like it!), so the Fool doesn't figure in to the personal year system. Sorry, Fools.

Personal Year	Major Arcana Card
1	The Magician
2	The High Priestess (once in a lifetime)
3	The Empress
4	The Emperor
5	The Hierophant
6	The Lovers
7	The Chariot
8	Strength
9	The Hermit
10	Wheel of Fortune
11	Justice
12	The Hanged Man
13	Death
14	Temperance
15	The Devil
16	The Tower
17	The Star
18	The Moon
19	The Sun
20	Judgement
21	The World

Another note: Your personal year begins in January of each year.

In the Cards _____

Here's a look ahead at what the personal year looks like for the United States on its birthday, July 4, 2006:

7 + 4 + 2006 = 2017 = 2 + 0 + 1 + 7= 10

The 10 is the Wheel of Fortune card, so 2006 will be a Wheel of Fortune personal year for the United States. This is a year for self-realizations, a time of major breakthroughs. The Wheel of Life has turned and new opportunities are possible at this time. It can be a lucky time and a change for the better. The number 10 means rebirth, yet karma and fate play a role with this card. It is said that whatever was started in the Emperor year (2002 = 4) or the Chariot year (2005 = 7) will come to fruition. We'll no doubt be ready for better times by then.

So You Say You're Having a Devil of a Year?

If you've got an attitude this year, maybe it's in the cards. Here are the meanings for each personal year number and its corresponding Major Arcana card. All the Major Arcana cards (1 through 21) are used for this part except the Fool (0). Once you've located the number and card for your personal year, read the corresponding description for an insight into the theme and direction for your year.

1 **The Magician.** A year of independence, strong will, enterprise, and new beginnings.

2 **The High Priestess.** A year to develop intuition, with an emphasis on the need for harmony and balance. Not recommended for marriage, although relationships might be prominent this year.

3 **The Empress.** A year for emotional clarity or a time for creative expression—even the creation of new life.

4 **The Emperor.** A year to establish foundations and build something. This year finds you having to set boundaries, claim your own authority, and order your world. Stability is the goal.

In the Cards _____

Interestingly, we only have one High Priestess year in a lifetime. Maybe that's why we haven't developed much intuition—we only get one chance to learn!

5 **The Hierophant.** A desire to be free and unrestricted runs through this year, even though you'll be dealing with conventional laws. Rebellion and restlessness could be present if you got into a rut in your Emperor year. Change is predominant this year, as well as an intense need to "get out there" to explore beyond your own world.

6 **The Lovers.** A year of making a choice, usually about love or relationships. It's a time of commitment, responsibility, and family obligations. Some kind of choice must be made between risk and security. It's a time of combining the head with the heart, a time of integration.

7 **The Chariot.** A year of purification in health or a time of gaining wisdom through change, even possible transformation. Spiritual questing and rejuvenation through nature are hallmarks of this 7 year.

8 **Strength.** A personal year where you'll find the strength to endure and to come into your own power. A time to wrestle with control issues and the right use of power, this 8 year is about manifesting and learning the laws of abundance.

9 **The Hermit.** A year of major completions, endings, and closure, the 9 year brings wisdom and connection to higher forces. It's also a time of great reward and mastery. You might be called upon to hold the lantern for others on the path.

10 **Wheel of Fortune.** A karmic year of rewards from past efforts. This is a time of breakthroughs and self-realization. This can be a time of initiation and rebirth. You're moving in a positive direction!

11 **Justice.** The 11 year's theme is about fairness and balance, as well as karmic justice and the resolution of legal issues. The search for truth about yourself and finding balance both demand your attention now, and cooperation and negotiation are major components of this year.

12 **The Hanged Man.** A year to listen to your inner self. It's a time of waiting and patience—suspended action, in other words—and you'll find the emphasis to be on receptivity. You might find yourself feeling a bit like a victim this year—definitely an old pattern to break. This is another karmic year in which patterns from the past are dissolved.

13 **Death (Rebirth).** A year where new growth is possible (the 3) through elimination and severance. Because the karmic number 13 reduces to 4, this year can be hard work. It's a time to transform the old and to release old karmic situations.

14 **Temperance.** A time to be open-minded, free, expansive, adapting, and resourceful (all reduced number 5 qualities). It's also a time to adopt a conservative attitude, use moderation, and to be self-disciplined (the 4). This karmic number 14 year suggests a past influence of irresponsible ways that needs to be tempered.

15 **The Devil.** A personal year where you deal with things you're attached to or that are addictions in your life (like the opposite sex, work, substances, sugar,

the Internet …). Negative 5 energy is present in this karmic card. It's a time to look at possible co-dependency (the reduced influence of the 6) and all those things that "bedevil" you.

16 **The Tower.** This is a year for spiritual awakening—a bolt of insight, a time for self-analysis and purification—all influences of the reduced number 7. You might have unexpected karmic awareness this year because some kind of a wake-up call is being made. The path changes. This karmic number suggests a past abuse of commitment and love (the karmic quality of the 6 in the 16), and now's the time to wake up.

17 **The Star.** This is not a karmic year! It's the emergence from the karmic influences of the past, a personal year for meditation, inspiration, and spiritual regeneration. Inner wisdom brings power this year (the essence of the 7). This 17 personal year is one for manifesting your wishes and analyzing your hopes for the future. Using systems of insight such as astrology, the Tarot, and numerology will be helpful this year. You face an opportunity to be a leader, a "Star."

18 **The Moon.** This year brings psychic power or illumination to areas where you might be living in denial. This is a time for manifestation (the 8 influence), but it's not about money. It's a potent time for psychic manifestation, a time to get something from the "other side."

19 **The Sun.** The 9 heavily influences your Sun year. It's a time of clarity and wisdom. The self comes full circle in this year of creativity, recognition, and high hopes. You have the potential to be intensely happy this year. You draw to you what you need, because you're energized, vital, and magnetic this year. This is the last of the karmic numbers, as it suggests that past abuses of power and wisdom have resolved as the Sun shines on you this year.

20 **Judgement.** In this rite-of-passage year, you'll have a strong desire to merge (2). This year is a call to the spiritual (0) and a time of breaking through old self-judgments and moving toward cooperation with others. The emphasis is on integration of the past and present. Integration is good—it sure beats isolation or endings!

21 **The World.** A year of joy and rapture, creativity, and vision. The energy of the 3 is fully present this year, but you might be called to expand to higher ground (it's the world, after all!). It's a time of living from a spiritual knowing, a time of universal service, and seeing with global awareness. You've arrived!

Your personal year is a 52-week journey of learning the lessons and evolving in an upward spiral of self-mastery. Knowing your personal year number and personal year card will help you target these lessons and chart a course through the murky waters of life.

It's clear that the combining of numerology and Tarot is very powerful. Use and master these tools to wend your way through the mystery of life. May all your karmic lessons be in the cards!

In the Cards

To find out more about numerology, check out *The Complete Idiot's Guide to Numerology* (Alpha Books, 1999), also by Kay Lagerquist and Lisa Lenard.

The Least You Need to Know

- The numbers on the Tarot cards have specific meanings.

- The Major Arcana numbers represent your life's journey in 22 steps.

- The Minor Arcana numbers show the timing of an event.

- The Major Arcana numbers tell the theme for each personal year.

- Your personal year can help you understand the theme for each year as well as your karmic lessons.

Glossary

air signs   People with these signs are great thinkers, always applying their mental capacities to any problem they encounter. The air signs of the zodiac are Gemini, Libra, and Aquarius.

allegory   A symbolic system in which words or images represent a much larger story than is told or shown. The allegory of the Prodigal Son, for example, represents a parent's love for his child.

ankh   The Egyptian ankh is an ancient symbol of the cross of life.

archetypes   The various types common to all our stories. Jung called archetypes "mythological motifs."

astrological chart   Also called a birth chart, this is a representation of the position of each of the planets at the time you were born.

astrology   A discipline that uses the cycles of the universe and the position of the planets at the time you were born to draw a unique picture of who you are and who you can be.

birth sign   Also called a sun sign, this is the astrological sign the sun was in when you were born. Twelve of these signs make up the zodiac, the pattern the earth follows on its elliptical journey around the sun every year.

Celtic Cross Spread   Also called the Keltic Cross Spread, this Tarot spread represents everything there is to know about a question. Although it uses the Christian symbol of the cross as its basis, it uses this form to show how a question (and Querent) move through time.

chakra   According to Hindu tradition, the body has seven chakras, or energy centers.

creative visualization   The process of using mental pictures to achieve one's goals. One example of this is a long-distance runner picturing herself breaking through the winner's tape.

Cups   The cards of emotion and sensitivity.

day residue   Any dream image that derives from the day's events. You might, for example, repeat a conversation you had, only in a dreamlike way, or you might dream you're sitting at a traffic light as you did that day.

earth signs   As their name implies, people with these signs are down to earth and content with the status quo. They're not, as a rule, big adventurers. The earth signs of the zodiac are Taurus, Virgo, and Capricorn.

elements   Fire, earth, air, and water represent the basic qualities of the zodiac signs and of life. The four elements are the four basic materials that make up everything. In the Tarot and in astrology, these are also used as types by which to classify the nature of things.

extrasensory perception (ESP)   The experience of knowing that something's going to happen before it does. It also includes the ability to see auras and other subtle energy fields, as well as past lives.

fire signs   People with these signs are always the first in line, ready to try everything from bungee jumping to signing on for the next space shuttle. The fire signs of the zodiac are Aries, Leo, and Sagittarius.

Gabriel   *See* Raphael.

graphology   The study and analysis of handwriting to find clues to a person's character and personality.

hieroglyphs   A form of ancient carving on stone. Hieroglyphs are a symbolic system, while another form of carving, petroglyphs, use representative pictures to tell their stories.

horoscope   Also called a birth or astrological chart, this is an astrological map for the moment of your birth. It's divided into 12 pie sections called houses, each representing a specific area of your life.

Horoscope Spread   A 12-card spread that looks at your year in cards.

hypnotherapy   A therapy that begins with information uncovered during hypnosis.

karmic lessons   Also called life lessons, these are lessons that are necessary for you to learn in this life because of past errors. You might have resisted them, but karma will always find a way to make certain you learn what you need so you can proceed to the next level of awareness.

key numbers   These numbers of the Major Arcana cards can be thought of literally as keys to opening up a card's meanings and possibilities.

life lessons   *See* karmic lessons.

Major Arcana   Also called the fate cards, these 22 cards represent your life's journey toward enlightenment. These cards depict situations of major, archetypal significance in your life. You could think of these cards as the many forks along your own particular road.

master numbers   The master numbers 11, 22, 33, 44, and so on are numbers with special properties. They indicate giftedness and leadership qualities for people and master qualities for the numbers themselves. For example, the number 11 is the number of inspiration, and the number 22 is the number of the master builder.

meditation exercises   Ways of helping us to use more than our logical, analytical left brains to look at things. Looking at Tarot cards in this way, without preconceived ideas and allowing the images to "tell" us what they mean, is one such exercise.

metaphors   Tarot readers consider Tarot cards to be metaphors, rich images that hold meanings that can be transferred or carried over to the Querent's particular situation or question.

Michael   *See* Raphael.

Minor Arcana   Also called the Free Will cards, these 56 cards concern your daily life, including everyday events, your beliefs and behavior, and how you relate to others.

Mission Spread   A 21-card spread that enables you to look at your past, present, and future life's mission and purpose.

myths   The stories we tell ourselves to explain the unexplainable.

nimbus   Represented by a halo or bright disk around someone's head (this is often seen around the heads of saints in religious paintings from the Middle Ages), a nimbus stands for someone's spiritual aura. People who have such an aura are blessed and protected by a higher power.

numerology   The language of numbers. Numerologists study the meanings of numbers and their connection to everything in the universe.

oracles   Sacred objects or altars used by many cultures throughout history for the reception of divine guiding messages and holy truths. The site of the oracle is considered a holy place, and traditionally often only priests or shamans could visit it.

past life regression   This technique employs hypnotherapy to learn about the lives one lived before the present one.

Pentacles   The cards of the material world, money, and possessions.

petroglyphs   *See* hieroglyphs.

progressions   These movements show how you and your birth chart evolve throughout your life.

psychic experiences   Also called postconscious cognitive experiences in psychological jargon, these are experiences that we perceive in ways other than our usual waking consciousness. They can include everything from ESP to UFOs—anything, in fact, that modern science is at a loss to explain.

Querent   From the Latin word *quaero*, meaning "to inquire or seek" or to embark on a quest, the Querent is a person who asks questions of the Tarot.

Raphael   The angel of air and one of three archangels who appear in Tarot imagery. The others are Michael, the angel of fire and the sun, and Gabriel, the angel of water.

reincarnation   The belief that the spirit or soul moves from one physical body to another after the death of the first one.

REM (rapid eye movement) sleep   Discovered in 1953, this is the time during sleep when our most vivid dreams occur. This dreaming is accompanied by rapid eye movement beneath the lid, hence its name.

reversed cards These occur when the lessons of a particular card are challenging for a Querent, or when a Querent is fighting him- or herself on an issue.

royal Minor Arcana cards Also called court cards, these cards can stand for various aspects of your self or for those around you. Sometimes they stand for certain times or seasons as well.

shadow side Our archetypal hidden self, our secret nature.

sun sign *See* birth sign.

Swords The cards of mental activity and action.

synchronicity The principle of meaningful coincidence, studied in depth by psychoanalysis pioneer Carl Jung. Jung also postulated that human experience could be categorized into common archetypes, typical patterns, situations, images, or metaphors that recur among all humankind.

Tarot The word *Tarot* has several meanings, each based on several different possible sources of the words. In Egyptian, *tar* + *ro* means "a path royal"; in Hungarian Gypsy, *tar* means "a pack of cards"; in Hindustani, *taru* also means "a pack of cards."

Tarot readings These occur when the cards are laid out to reveal a particular story. A Tarot reading brings together a Tarot reader and a Querent with a question. The reader uses a Tarot spread, or card layout, to explore the Querent's question.

Tarot spreads Different methods of laying out the cards during a Tarot reading.

transits The current movement of the planets through your birth chart.

Wands The cards of enterprise, growth, and development.

water signs People with this sign are the intuitive among us, ruled by their emotions, changing with the tides. The water signs of the zodiac are Cancer, Scorpio, and Pisces.

yods Representations of the Hebrew letter *yod*. Not only is this letter used to represent the name of God, it is also symbolic of the life force, or the light from heaven that protects us all.

Index

CHECK OUT THESE BEST-SELLERS

More than 450 titles available at booksellers and online retailers everywhere!

978-1-59257-115-4

978-1-59257-900-6

978-1-59257-855-9

978-1-59257-222-9

978-1-59257-957-0

978-1-59257-785-9

978-1-59257-471-1

978-1-59257-483-4

978-1-59257-883-2

978-1-59257-966-2

978-1-59257-908-2

978-1-59257-786-6

978-1-59257-954-9

978-1-59257-437-7

978-1-59257-888-7